EVALUATING EDUCATIONAL TECHNOLOGY

Effective Research Designs
for Improving Learning

EVALUATING EDUCATIONAL TECHNOLOGY

Effective Research Designs for Improving Learning

Geneva D. Haertel
Barbara Means

Editors

Foreword by Linda G. Roberts

Teachers College
Columbia University
New York and London

Published by Teachers College Press, 1234 Amsterdam Avenue, New York, NY 10027

Library of Congress Cataloging-in-Publication Data

Evaluating educational technology : effective research designs for improving learning / Geneva Haertel, Barbara Means, editors.
   p. cm.
  Includes bibliographical references and index.
  ISBN 0-8077-4330-5 (cloth: alk. paper)
    1. Educational technology—United States—Evaluation. 2. Educational innovations—United States. I. Haertel, Geneva D. II. Means, Barbara, 1949–

LB1028.3.E962 2003
371.33—dc21   2003044046

ISBN 0-8077-4330-5 (cloth)

Printed on acid-free paper

Manufactured in the United States of America

10 09   08 07   8 7 6 5 4 3 2

Contents

Foreword

Linda G. Roberts

Dramatic advances in computer and telecommunications technology have occurred over the past decade. These advances have lowered the cost of technology while increasing capabilities for applications that cut across society, including education. If we were to draw a map of the "technology horizon," we would see tremendous forces shaping the future of teaching and learning (Grove Consultants International and the Institute for the Future, 2000), including massive amounts of information accessible via the Internet; smarter appliances and devices that are becoming increasingly interconnected; miles of fiber-optic cables that are bringing high-speed access to more and more schools, homes, and communities; and users who are inventing applications never dreamed of by the designers.

Since 1995, local communities, states, and the federal government have invested heavily in technology for the nation's schools and classrooms. This first national technology plan challenged America's schools to reach four goals: training for teachers, computers for students, classrooms connected to the Internet, and development of effective software and online learning resources (U.S. Department of Education, 1996). Today virtually all our public K–12 schools and almost three-fourths of classrooms connect to the Internet. The student-to-computer ratio has improved, to a national average of five students per computer. In a small number of schools, every student has a computer. Increasing numbers of new teachers are coming to the classroom with preparation to use these 21st-century tools, and they join colleagues who are also gaining skill and confidence in using technology across the curriculum (U.S. Department of Education, Office of Educational Technology, 2001). But what is missing?

The prevailing view that schools are slow to embrace change notwithstanding, much of the investment in technology has been driven by schools' willingness to experiment and innovate. Parents believe that their children should know how to use modern technology and should become technologically literate, and schools have responded to this demand. Increasingly, however, educators and government officials (from Congress to local school boards) believe that it's time for schools to demonstrate the value of the technology infrastructure. They want to see evidence of effectiveness before they invest further in more computers, more teacher training, and expanded telecommunications capacity.

As director of the Office of Educational Technology, I listened as the calls for research intensified. In March 1997, the report of the President's Committee of Advisors on Science and Technology, Panel on Educational Technology (PCAST) (1997) called for a large-scale program of rigorous, systematic research. Many other reports and policymakers echoed these recommendations. In response, the U.S. Department of Education required Technology Innovation Challenge Grant projects to build evaluation into their 5-year programs and partnerships. Similarly, states and districts began to conduct their own studies of educational technology, including some that encompassed a large number of students and classrooms. A number of these studies have helped identify applications and strategies that work. The Interagency Educational Research Initiative was established with the goal of building on prior work, identifying technology-supported innovations that had some evidence of effectiveness and funding investigations of their effectiveness on a broader scale. (This initiative is supported by the National Science Foundation, U.S. Department of Education, and the National Institutes of Health.)

Nevertheless, I was still convinced that we could do better. Most studies of technology's impact on students looked only at short-term effects and were either small in scale (e.g., a few selected classrooms or schools) or lacking in detailed information about just what technology-supported learning experiences students had had. I believed that researchers could improve the design and collection of data. Just as new technology created new opportunities for learning, it created ways to invent new tools for research and evaluation, particularly ways to track and monitor what, how, and when learning occurred. The question for me was, How to move forward in a practical way? A compelling strategy emerged at a high-level seminar on Technology and Education held by the U.S. Department of Education and the Brazil Ministry of Education, hosted at SRI headquarters on December 2–3, 1998. This meeting in Menlo Park, California, was the Second U.S.–Brazil Binational Education Dialogue, an activity of the U.S.–Brazil Partnership for Education launched in Brasilia on October 14, 1997, with support of President Clinton and President Cardozo.

Participants heard again that many studies pointed to the promising impacts of technology but also learned that, in all too many cases, there were more questions than answers. Classroom access to technology was expanding. All across the country, there were districts that could be rich sources of data and schools that could be laboratories for the development of the next generation of interactive learning resources. Certainly, this was the time to invest in research and evaluation: What would it take to conduct a set of rigorous studies? Was there a base of theory to build on? Were the tools for analysis adequate? Was it possible to conduct serious evaluation in classroom settings where change and revision were continuous? Where to begin?

The researchers around the table suggested a compelling strategy for getting started: Invite experts in research and evaluation from diverse fields to share their knowledge and experience and design new studies that could be undertaken. Soon after the U.S.–Brazil Dialogue, SRI submitted a field-initiated proposal to the Office of Educational Technology; the result is the collection of chapters, dialogues, and analyses presented in these two volumes.

The chapters in this volume and the analysis and discussion of the chapters in the companion volume, *Using Technology Evaluation*, provide both theoretical constructs and pragmatic designs that address different uses of technology within different settings for different purposes. A reading of the papers from the experts makes clear that no one study will answer all the critical questions. Furthermore, the process won't be easy, given the many different purposes for which various technologies are used and the complexity of fully integrating technology into teaching and learning. The research and evaluation designs also make clear that it will be essential to develop new assessment tools to tap into the kinds of deep understanding and complex skills that technology-based innovations are trying to foster.

These volumes will be an invaluable resource for the academic community and those who are engaged in evaluation of projects and initiatives in the United States and other countries. Examples of better assessment will help state and local educational decision makers plan new evaluation efforts using measures that are more sensitive than standardized tests at detecting technology's effects. These new assessments can not only provide evidence of technology's effects on knowledge and skills in subject areas but also reveal the degree to which students have acquired technology skills that can be used to support their schoolwork and other activities. The volumes also present examples of more rigorous research and evaluation designs that can guide the collection of evidence in order to confirm or refute causal claims about the efficacy of technology in educational settings. Such multivariate designs illustrate the need for studies that attend to the many influences that can moderate technology's effects.

I am hopeful that the challenges to be faced, along with the chance to shape the development of the next generation of technology for learning, will capture the interest and imagination of a new cadre of researchers, those not yet immersed in educational technology but already involved in the study of cognition and learning, and those who have gained their expertise in other related fields.

These volumes are timely. The Elementary and Secondary Education Act of 2002 calls for rigorous evaluations of programs, particularly those funded under Title II, Part D, Technology. Congressional leaders want to see evidence of the impact of the technology programs on student academic achievement, including the technological literacy of all students. The legislation also calls on states and districts to evaluate the effectiveness of their technology efforts, particularly with regard to integrating technology into curricula and instruction, increasing the ability of teachers to teach, and enabling students to meet challenging state academic content standards. Finally, the new education bill requires the secretary of education to conduct an independent, long-term study of educational technology.

There is much to be accomplished. I am confident that this collection of chapters and new thinking on the design of rigorous evaluations of technology and learning and the assessments that can best document their effects will make important contributions to the field in these areas: (1) gaining the attention of researchers as well as bringing experts from other disciplines into the field; (2) improving the evaluations of technology-supported innovations; (3) stimulating the development of technology-based data-collection tools and analysis; (4) shaping the federal education research agenda; and, most importantly, (5) expanding our theory and knowledge.

The work in this book and the companion volume also lends support to policies and practice that focus on the integration of technology into teaching and learning. In the process of asking better questions and improving the tools for analysis, we can enhance our ability to get the most solid contributions to students' learning from our investment in technology.

REFERENCES

Grove Consultants International and the Institute for the Future. (2000). *The educational technology horizon map and user guidebook*. San Francisco: Author.

President's Committee of Advisors on Science and Technology, Panel on Educational Technology. (1997). *Report to the president on the use of technology to strengthen K–12 education in the U.S.* Washington, DC: Author.

U.S. Department of Education, Office of Educational Technology. (2001). *E-learning: Putting world-class education at the fingertips of all children*. Washington, DC: Author.

U.S. Department of Education, Office of Educational Technology. (1996). *Getting America's students ready for the 21st century: Meeting the technology literacy challenge*. Washington, DC: Author.

EVALUATING THE EFFECTS OF LEARNING TECHNOLOGIES

Barbara Means
Geneva D. Haertel
Lincoln Moses

At a time when educational research in general is often characterized as weak and inconclusive, both in national policy forums (Brookings Institution, 1999) and in congressional testimony (Bennett et al., 2000), few research areas have been more controversial than studies of the impact of technology on student learning (Oppenheimer, 1997; Stoll, 1995). With the dramatic increase in computer and network technology in U.S. schools (National Center for Education Statistics [NCES], 2000), many are looking for the fruits of the investment in technology infrastructures. While technology proponents hold forth a vision of students and teachers participating in technology-supported learning environments featuring individualized instruction, interactive simulations, and tools for knowledge representation and organization, policy makers look for positive effects on large-scale assessments linked to content standards. Some argue that traditional approaches to schooling have resisted any significant reshaping in response to the availability of technology, just as they proved impervious to the influence of television, teaching machines, and radio (Cuban, 2000). Other critics argue that technology does indeed affect schools but that its impacts are largely negative—diverting resources from more worthy pursuits (such as art, music, or basic skills) and wasting students' and teachers' time with the intellectually trivial mechanisms of technology use (Healy, 1999).

The President's Committee of Advisors on Science and Technology (PCAST), in its 1997 *Report to the President on the Use of Technology to Strengthen K–12 Education in the United States*, pointed out that given the stress on current educational reform efforts, policymakers are looking to the research base on the effectiveness of, and critical implementation factors for, applying technology to the improvement of student learning. Unfortunately, PCAST found that policymakers had little convincing evidence to turn to regarding technology's effects: "We are not yet able to answer this question . . . with the degree of certainty that would be desirable from a public policy viewpoint" (p. 87). PCAST called for a program of "rigorous, well-controlled, peer reviewed, large-scale empirical studies to determine which [technology-supported] educational approaches are in fact most effective in practice" (p. 10).

In the 5 years since the PCAST report was published, the research base on technology has grown, but it is still without large-scale experimental studies or even very many studies with carefully matched comparison groups (Mislevy et al., 2002).

Premise of Multiple Studies and Approaches

No single study, or even set of studies, could investigate all the ways in which educational technology affects student learning and technological literacy, let alone the conditions under which such effects occur and the practices and conditions that enable teachers to successfully integrate technology with academic instruction. The breadth of computer technology applications now being applied to education is staggering—and continues to grow. We have electronic analogs to virtually every educational resource traditionally employed for teaching and learning—not only books, encyclopedias, chalkboards, pencils, and typewriters but also drafting boards, three-dimensional models, slide rules, and dissecting tables. In addition, computers expand the range of skills and understandings that schools even *attempt* to impart. The high school curriculum in particular now contains topics and competencies made relevant and teachable by the availability of technology supports for working in areas such as chemistry, statistics, and design.

This volume is based on the premise that a serious investigation of the impacts of educational technology on student learning will require multiple studies and more than one methodological approach. The nationally recognized experts in research methodology who were invited to contribute chapters viewed the issues in evaluating technology's effects through the lenses of their particular experience and methodological expertise. We have grouped the chapter according to theme. The chapters in a given thematic section do not necessarily propound the same design approach, but they do touch on the same issues and challenges to doing rigorous, usable research on learning technologies.

Debate over Experimental Designs

This first section deals with what has emerged as the great methodological debate over whether experiments in which students, classrooms, schools, or districts are assigned at random to either experimental (technology use) or control (no technology use) conditions should be the method of choice in evaluating technology's effects. This debate is particularly pertinent in light of the recent passage of the No Child Left Behind Act, with its call for the secretary of education to "conduct a rigorous, independent, long-term evaluation of the impact of educational technology on student achievement using scientifically based research methods and control conditions." (See Section 2421(a), Part D, of Title II of the enabling legislation.)

The essential features of a random-assignment experiment have been set forth by Moses (2000):

- The treatments being compared are actively imposed on the experimental units, in contrast to the observation of treatments or innovations where they happen to occur.
- All treatments (or the experimental treatment and the control, or no-treatment, condition) are applied within the same time period.
- After a group of eligible study subjects is defined, each receives one of the treatments or is assigned to the control condition by random choice.
- The whole enterprise is organized and conducted in accordance with a written experimental protocol.
- After random assignment, all measures and processes other than the treatment being tested that may affect the data are symmetrically applied to all study subjects.
- The unit of treatment application and randomization (whether students, classes, schools, or districts) is the unit of a statistical analysis and defines the sample size.

Proponents of the use of random-assignment experiments within education argue that no other approach can tell us what would have happened to the treatment group if they had not received the particular treatment (innovation) under study. Drawing on experimental research traditions in other fields—including medicine and agriculture—these methodologists argue that the experiment provides the most definitive, efficient test of a hypothesis of the form *A causes B*.

Moses illustrates this power of random-assignment experiments with examples from medicine. He recalls that in the 1950s, there was a decades-old controversy about the proper surgical treatment of breast cancer. Stage

I and stage II disease were treated preferentially with the Halsted radical mastectomy in the United States, but less mutilating procedures were preferred in Europe. Each school of thought was "known" by adherents to be better. Ambiguities about how to assess the initial severity of disease and patient selection clouded the interpretation of historical data. In the 1970s, thousands of women annually were receiving surgical treatment that others were being denied—or protected from. The inability of observational data to convince allowed this dispute over treatment to persist for decades. Then, in 1977 McPherson and Fox presented the results of eight random-assignment experiments (generally called randomized clinical trials in medicine), each pointing toward the equivalence of survival with the more and less radical surgical procedures for breast cancer, and toward greater surgical trauma with the more radical surgery. Now, another quarter-century later, the proper place of less radical procedures for treating breast cancer is well established.

Other medical examples illustrate the efficiency of random-assignment experiments compared to other research methods. Early papers concerning lung cancer and smoking appeared around 1950, but it was much later, in 1964, that the Surgeon General's Report on Smoking and Health (Office of the Surgeon General, 1964) summarized many scores of studies and asserted that cigarette smoking was a major cause of lung cancer. Truth by experience (in the form of correlational data) won out eventually. But contrast that hard-won, slow success with another study. In the summer of 1954, the Salk vaccine trial (Meier, 1989) compared polio rates in a carefully designed randomized comparison of 201,000 vaccinated children with 201,000 placebo controls in the same schools. In the vaccinated group there were 57 cases of polio, and in the placebo group 142 cases; the corresponding rates, 28 per 100,000 and 71 per 100,000, differed importantly and with high statistical significance ($p < .000001$). The experiment established the effectiveness of the vaccine *in that summer*. The firm conclusion about lung cancer and cigarettes—a much larger effect—took more than 10 years to become established. The relative efficiency of the experimental approach is clear.

While examples of large-scale random-assignment experiments in education are few and far between, they are not totally absent. The most influential current example may well be the experimental test of the effects of class size conducted in Tennessee. The state of Tennessee decided to carry out a substantial experiment dealing with the class size question for 4 years starting in 1985, beginning with kindergarten and continuing through the early grades. The classes were to be of three types: small (13–17 pupils), regular (22–25 pupils), and regular with a teacher aide. Within a school grade, pupils and teachers were assigned to classes at random. The state funded the extra teachers and aides required for the experiment.

The first graders took two standardized tests in reading, the Stanford Achievement Test (SAT) for word study skills and reading, and the Tennessee Basic Skills First (BSF) tests for reading, a curriculum-based test. In mathematics first graders took one SAT (standardized) and one BSF (curriculum based) test.

The difference in performance between groups is often given as an "effect size," here defined as the difference between the group means divided by the standard deviation for individuals in the regular classes. For the standardized test (SAT), both reading and math showed a benefit of about one-quarter of a standard deviation. For the curriculum-based tests (BSF), smaller classes produced an advantage in reading of about one-fifth of a standard deviation and in math of one-eighth of a standard deviation. The addition of an aide also produced better achievement, but the advantages were smaller, averaging about one-twelfth of a standard deviation.

Special interest attaches to the effect of class size on the minorities as compared with Whites. In small classes compared to regular-sized or regular-sized with aide, the effect size for the minority students was just about double that for Whites, averaging over the four tests.

Thus, in a very large study (Finn & Achilles, 1990), at least in the first grade, class size matters and teaching support does also, though not as much. This experiment was carried out in kindergarten, first, second, and third grade. Then all children reverted to regular-sized classes. Over the years the improvement for the smaller classes held up well through the grades. In a follow-up survey for grades 4, 5, and 6, after students returned to regular-sized classes, the students who were in the smaller classes during kindergarten and grades 1, 2, and 3 continued to perform better in reading and mathematics than the students who started out in regular-sized classes.

Because this experiment was so large and so well controlled (randomized teachers; randomized students; scores of schools; thousands of students, including those from urban, inner-city, rural, and suburban areas), the results were compelling. The state of Tennessee introduced the smaller classes in the 17 districts in which students are most at risk of falling behind in their school progress. Other states, including California, have since moved to reduce class size in the early grades (albeit not always with the same positive results).

Alternatives to Random-Assignment Experiments

This part contains four chapters. In the first, Thomas D. Cook of Northwestern University, writing with collaborators from SRI's Center for Technology in Learning, makes a case for the use of random-assignment experiments in education and illustrates how this design could be applied to testing the effectiveness of a use of educational technology. The next three chapters advocate a greater emphasis on understanding the contexts within which innovations unfold and use of nonexperimental approaches to evaluating learning technology. These chapters are written by authors who have been actively engaged in working with schools and school districts implementing technology: Alan Lesgold of the University of Pittsburgh; Katie McMillan Culp, Margaret Honey, and Robert Spielvogel from the Center for Children and Technology; and Eva Baker and Joan L. Herman from the University of California, Los Angeles.

For both Baker and Herman and Culp, Honey, and Spielvogel, the role of local engagement, collaboration, and feedback is paramount. Both point out that local school communities need support to think about evaluative questions and evidence. Teachers and administrators at the local site should be participants in, rather than recipients of, the evaluation. In such cases, information generated by the evaluation is particularly valuable for users of the innovation and for program managers, who gain information to support reflection on their experiences and identification of promising paths toward successful change. These authors conclude that evaluation research that is responsive to local concerns, constraints, and priorities can be structured and synthesized to produce knowledge about effective uses of educational technology that has high face validity within local communities and still informs wider research as well as practitioner and policy audiences.

Both Lesgold and Culp, Honey, and Spielvogel assert that large-scale and summative evaluations have not traditionally been expected to answer questions about why an outcome occurred. From their perspective, knowing "why" something happened entails knowing about the processes through which an intervention had its effects, in contrast to the experimentalists' emphasis on knowing whether the intervention caused the effects. In the view of these authors, only designs that are highly contextualized—that include the "why" question from the start—will be able to inform decision making about the effectiveness of technology in educational settings. In addition, the approaches taken by Lesgold and Culp, Honey, and Spielvogel will provide specific information on the conditions in which effects are produced. Thus, their emphasis on specifying contexts contributes to stakeholders' understanding of what features of the educational setting are associated with what outcomes and for which groups of students and teachers.

For many policymakers, the decision to be made is not whether to invest in technology or not, but rather how best to integrate technology with local educational goals. Highly contextualized evaluations are designed to serve this purpose. They can be responsive to local needs because they typically produce descriptive, complex models of the role that an intervention or program plays in the existing system and how effectively it matches the system's needs and resources. These models can help practitioners make informed decisions about technology implementations.

The question is whether such studies can lead to the accumulation of knowledge in ways that can inform practice. Moses's review of the history of various issues in medicine suggests that individual nonexperimental studies are likely to produce conflicting results and to be hard to aggregate. Lesgold, Baker and Herman, and Culp and colleagues all maintain that such aggregation of results from quasi- and nonexperiments can be done, provided that there is careful documentation of context and implementation variables and that a system for standardizing measures and aggregating data is put in place. Lesgold provides a detailed description of how jointly conducted studies, each with its own emphasis but all using an agreed-upon set of context measures or "maturity scales," might do so.

ISSUES COMMON TO BOTH METHODOLOGICAL APPROACHES

The great many different technology tools used in classrooms, and the nonfeasibility of evaluating all of them, was mentioned above. Beyond their sheer numbers, however, is a deeper layer of complexity in defining what it is that we wish to evaluate.

Defining the Innovation

No one believes that merely pulling up to a school building with a truckload of computers is going to improve student learning. Clearly, it is the teaching and learning experiences supported or mediated by technology that will or will not have the desired effects. In reviewing studies of the effectiveness of computer-assisted instruction, Clark (1985) argued that to measure technology's impact, we need to compare two sets of teachers (or, ideally, the same teachers with two sets of classes) using the same method with the same material, in one case with the material and pedagogy presented by computer and in the other, by more conventional media. Today, most developers and researchers working in the learning technology field reject this design guideline (cf. Means, Blando, Olson, Middleton, Morocco, Remz, & Zorfass, 1993). The point of using technology, developers and proponents argue, is not to do what we have always done electronically but rather to provide kinds of learning experiences that are impossible to provide by any other means. When students interact with computer-generated dynamic three-dimensional representations of molecules in equilibrium, for example, they are having experiences that cannot be reproduced with static textbook diagrams or toothpicks and Styrofoam balls. To limit technology-based experiences to interactions that can be provided offline would be self-defeating. In practice, then, pedagogy and content are usually confounded with the use of technology, and when we do comparative studies we are testing the differential effects of the package, rather than of technology by itself.

Lesgold (Chapter 2) takes this idea one step further, "[T]echnology is generally not a direct cause of change but rather a facilitator or amplifier of various educational practices." Thus Lesgold is explicit in denying that technology is the primary independent variable under investigation. Misunderstandings arise because the computers or software are often the most novel or striking feature of the intervention, and it is easy for everyone to slip into talking about the impact of *technology* rather than the impact of a specific *technology-supported* intervention.

Regardless of whether or not technology is involved, defining the program or intervention being evaluated has always been a challenge with instructional innovations. Teachers, who generally regard themselves as professionals with independent authority over instructional practice, essentially determine the fidelity of treatment implementation through the countless decisions they make every day (Cohen & Ball, 1999). Their personal views about how to make learning occur and what priority to give different curriculum objectives compete with external theories of how teachers should use educational resources. This competition typically produces variability in the way an intervention is delivered, particularly in the case of more open-ended or "concept-based" instructional strategies.

Early developers of technology envisioned that it would create greater uniformity in practice; some even predicted replacing teachers altogether. Clearly this has not come to pass, and many qualitative studies document the variability in teacher practice with the same technology (Means, Penuel, & Padilla, 2001; Shear & Penuel, 2002). Even given an order to have students spend a specified number of minutes per week with a specific piece of software, different teachers might provide their students with very different experiences. The way that a given teacher embeds the software or Internet use within classroom time, the subtle cues he or she gives to students, and the students' responses to both explicit direction and implicit cues all become variables that influence the enactment of any externally designed instructional practice, including uses of educational technology.

The extent of variation in teacher practices is likely to differ, depending on the category of technology use. The most common technology uses in schools (word processing and Internet research) involve application of general-purpose software tools that leave the instructional activity wide open for teacher decision making.

SPECIFYING THE RANGE OF IMPLEMENTING CONDITIONS TO BE STUDIED

School environmental factors—most notably, technology infrastructure and teacher technology expertise—and the school's student population are all likely to affect study findings concerning technology's effects on student learning. Minimum conditions enabling implementation must be specified with respect to (1) computer hardware, software, and networking infrastructure, and (2) teacher competency in using the technology under study. Inadequate access to technology and inadequate time to learn how to use it lead to teacher misgivings about using computers for instruction (Adelman et al., 2002; Cuban, 2001; Sheingold & Hadley, 1990). Evaluators need to avoid judging the value of a technology based on student outcomes in settings where the necessary resources are absent.

On the other hand, evaluators must recognize that demonstration or pilot programs are often implemented in schools with atypical infrastructures and technical support. When scale-up occurs, the initial findings may not be replicated with new and more representative classrooms. An analogous situation exists in medical research and is explicitly recognized by that research community. When investigating the effectiveness of a new treatment or drug, researchers first conduct what they call "efficacy" trials, in which every effort is made to provide conditions that support an "ideal" implementation of the treatment (for example, hospital personnel might administer the drug to ensure that dosages are correct and none are missed). After such experiments have established evidence for the positive impact of a treatment or drug under such controlled conditions, researchers then undertake additional experimentation to test the effectiveness in a wider range of contexts and under representative, rather than ideal, conditions (e.g., patients are responsible for administering their own medications). Where practice varies between biomedical and educational research is not the conduct of studies under carefully controlled versus naturalistic conditions, but rather the rarer use of experimental designs in education research in either type of setting.

Beyond setting minimum conditions for infrastructure and teacher training in sites to be studied, there is the question of how to deal with variation in these conditions. If the number of teachers and schools participating in a study were large enough, implementation factors hypothesized to affect the impact of technology on student learning could simply be incorporated into the design as independent variables, or covariates and interaction effects tested through statistical analysis. But because many research studies involve only a small number of implementation sites, they cannot incorporate all potentially important implementation variables into their designs, and it is usually preferable to specify a restricted range of study contexts that will provide the most policy-relevant findings for the available research investment.

Regardless of sample sizes and the range of implementation contexts included in the study, features of the context need to be documented carefully. To the extent that contextual factors are not documented, or are measured differently in every study, it is hard to accumulate findings across research studies or to know whether it is reasonable to generalize from any of the studies to the specific context for which one wishes to make a decision about policy or practice.

Prior research (Becker, 2000a, 2000b; Becker & Riel, 2000; Ronnkvist, Dexter, & Anderson, 2000) documents some of the specific contextual features that influence the extent to which teachers use technology for instruction. These include the availability and quality of support for computer and network use (not just technical support but also advice on subject-specific instructional uses of technology and support for supervising students as they use the technology); the location of the computers in the teacher's own classroom as opposed to a shared lab; and the amount of time allocated for the technology-supported intervention and the way it is scheduled into the schoolday.

Maintaining Fidelity of the Treatment

One of the requirements for either random-assignment experiments or quasi-experimental studies (designs which employ all of the features of experiments except the random assignments of individuals or groups of individuals to treatment conditions) is the maintenance of a clear distinction between the experimental and control conditions. Depending on the technology use under consideration and the student population and time frame selected for the study, instituting and maintaining this distinction can be problematic. Many students, particularly the more affluent ones, have extensive access to technology at home and at friends' houses; others access technology at libraries or community technology centers (Becker, 2000a, 2000b). With certain types of technology applications, particularly the widely used ones such as word processing and Internet search engines, it would be unrealistic to expect that the control-group members would not experience some variation of the technology experiences provided in the experimental group's classrooms. Moreover, students' prior experience with, expertise in, and home access to technology may be significant factors, as may technology use in classes other than those participating in the experiment if middle or secondary school students are the subjects for the experiment.

Obtaining Site Cooperation

A related potential problem is obtaining and maintaining site cooperation. Although a school or district may be comfortable with providing some
portion but not all of its students with a particular technology-based algebra program, it is hard to imagine that many would agree to give word processing or Internet access to only a subset of their students for any significant
period of time. The infrastructure and technical support costs for some technology interventions, particularly those that are web based, are high, and
typically are borne largely at the district level (Blumenfeld, Fishman, Krajcik,
Marx, & Soloway, 2000). This circumstance creates pressure to gain the
maximum perceived benefit from the technology investment by making it
available to as many students as possible. Although educational technology
is not an entitlement in a legal sense, many parents regard it as important
for their children (Peter D. Hart Research Associates, 1997), and its prolonged
or complete absence in control schools or classrooms may not be a politically viable option.

Measuring Student Learning

Finally, the definition and measurement of student learning outcomes is
often problematic. In many cases, technology-based interventions seek to
foster analytic, problem-solving, or design skills that are not covered by
conventional achievement tests. Using an outcome measure that has nothing to do with the intervention under study can easily mask real impacts on
learning. The issue of how to measure desired learning outcomes pertains
equally to studies using experimental and nonexperimental designs and is,
in fact, of such importance that it is the focus of Part II of this volume.

REFERENCES

Adelman, N., Donnelly, M. B., Dove, T., Tiffany-Morales, J., Wayne, A., & Zucker,
A. (2002, March). *Professional development and teachers' uses of technology.
Subtask 5: Evaluation of key factors impacting the effective use of technology
in schools.* Report to the U.S. Department of Education. SRI Project P10474.
Arlington, VA: SRI International.
Becker, H. J. (2000a, November 15). Findings from the Teaching, Learning, and
Computing Survey: Is Larry Cuban right? *Education Policy Analysis and Ar-
chives,* 8(51) [Online serial]. (Retrieved January 12, 2003: http://epaa.asu.edu/
epaa/v8n51/)

Becker, H. J. (2000b). Who's wired and who's not: Children's access to and use of computer technology. *The Future of Children, 10*(2), 44–75.

Becker, H. J., & Riel, M. M. (2000, April). *The beliefs, practices, and computer use of teacher leaders.* Paper presented at the American Educational Research Association, New Orleans. (Retrieved January 13, 2003: http://www.crito.uci.edu/tlc/findings/aera)

Bennett, W., Finn, C., Hansen, W., Loveless, T., Manno, B., Ravitch, D., Rees, N. S., & Vinovskis, M. (2000). *Principles for reauthorizing OERI, NAEP and NAGB.* (Retrieved January 8, 2003: http://www.edexcellence.net/education_2001.html)

Blumenfeld, P., Fishman, B. J., Krajcik, J., Marx, R. W., & Soloway, E. (2000) Creating useable innovations in systemic reform: Scaling-up technology-embedded project-based science in urban schools. *Educational Psychologist, 35*(3), 149–164.

Brookings Institution. (1999). *Forum: Can we make education policy on the basis of evidence? What constitutes high quality education research and how can it be incorporated into policymaking?* Washington, DC: Author.

Clark, R. E. (1985). Evidence for confounding in computer-based instruction studies: Analyzing the meta-analyses. *Educational Communication and Technology Journal, 33*(4), 249–262.

Cohen, D. K., & Ball, D. L. (1999). *Instruction, capacity, and improvement.* University of Pennsylvania, CPRE Report (CPRE RR-43). Philadelphia, PA: Consortium for Policy Research in Education.

Cuban, L. (2000). *So much high-tech money invested, so little use and change in practice: How come?* Report to the CCSSO State Educational Technology Leadership Conference—2000: Preparing teachers to meet the challenge of new standards with new technologies. Washington, DC: Council of Chief State School Officers. (Available: http://www.sri.com/policy/designkt/found.html)

Cuban, L. (2001). *Oversold and underused: Computers in the classroom.* Cambridge, MA: Harvard University Press.

Finn, J. D., & Achilles, C. M. (1990). Answers about questions about class size: A statewide experiment. *American Educational Research Journal, 27,* 557–577.

Healy, J. (1999). *Failure to connect: How computers affect our children's minds— and what we can do about it.* New York: Simon & Schuster.

McPherson, K., & Fox, M. (1977). Treatment of breast cancer. In J. P. Bunker, B. A. Barnes, & F. Mosteller (Eds.), *Costs, risks, and benefits of surgery.* New York: Oxford University Press.

Mcans, B., Blando, J., Olson, K., Middleton, T., Morocco, C. C., Remz, A., & Zorfass, J. (1993). *Using technology to support education reform.* Washington, D.C.: U.S. Department of Education, Office of Educational Research and Improvement.

Means, B., Penuel, B., & Padilla, C. (2001). *The connected school: Technology and learning in urban schools.* San Francisco: Jossey-Bass.

Meier, P. (1989). The biggest public health experiment ever: The 1954 field trial of the Salk poliomyelitis vaccine. In J. M. Taurnur & F. Mosteller (Eds.), *Statistics: A guide to the unknown* (3rd ed.) (pp. 3–14). Belmont, CA: Duxbury Press.

Mislevy, R., Penuel, W., Means, B., Korbak, C., Whaley, A., & Allen, J. E. (2002). *Design patterns for assessing science inquiry*. Technical Report 1. Menlo Park, CA: SRI International.

Moses, L. (2000, February). *A larger role for randomized experiments*. Paper presented at the invitational meeting: Building a Foundation for a Decade of Rigorous Systematic Educational Technology Research, SRI International, Menlo Park, CA.

National Center for Education Statistics (NCES). (2000). *Internet access in U.S. public schools and classrooms, 1994–99* (Statistics in Brief #NCES 2000-086). Washington, DC: Author.

Office of the Surgeon General. (1964). *Smoking and health (Report of the Advisory Committee of the Surgeon General of the Public Health Service)*. Washington, DC: U.S. Department of Health, Education and Welfare. (Public Health Service Publication No. 1103).

Oppenheimer, T. (1997, July). The computer delusion. *The Atlantic Monthly*, pp. 45–62.

Peter D. Hart Research Associates, Inc. (1997). *Milken exchange on education technology: Public opinion survey*. Washington, DC: Author.

President's Committee of Advisors on Science and Technology, Panel on Educational Technology (PCAST). (1997). *Report to the president on the use of technology to strengthen K–12 education in the United States*. Washington, DC: U.S. Government Printing Office.

Ronnkvist, A., Dexter, S. L., & Anderson, R. E. (2000). *Technology support: Its depth, breadth and impact in America's schools*. Irvine, CA: Center for Research on Information Technology and Organizations, University of California, Irvine, and University of Minnesota.

Shear, L., & Penuel, W. R. (2002). Putting the "learning" in adventure learning: Design principles for technology-supported classroom inquiry. *Journal of Curriculum and Supervision, 17*(4), 315–335.

Sheingold, K., & Hadley, M. (1990). *Accomplished teachers: Integrating computers into classroom practice*. New York: Center for Technology in Education, Bank Street College of Education.

Stoll, C. (1995). *Silicon snake oil: Second thoughts on the information highway*. New York: Doubleday.

Chapter 1

The Case for Randomized Experiments

Thomas D. Cook
Barbara Means
Geneva D. Haertel
Vera Michalchik

This chapter seeks to show how randomized experiments can be productively used to learn about the effects of important aspects of educational technology and even about technology writ large. To achieve this, we first work through a hypothetical example and then later present an abstract analysis of the example. The point is to elucidate the conditions under which random assignment is desirable and feasible in studies of educational technology.

PURPOSES

The chapter begins by documenting the ubiquitous concern with causal issues in both academic and policy circles relating to educational technology. It then details why the experiment is usually espoused for answering causal questions that estimate whether some innovation brings about more change in some educational outcome than would have occurred had the innovation not been in place. The chapter then outlines a hypothetical study of the effects of educational technology. Since objections to experiments are widespread within education, we also briefly review these objections and show them to be exaggerated. Since causal analysis is not unique to experiments, the case for experiments also has to show that alternatives to them are generally not as good at providing valid causal estimates and do not warrant being regularly preferred even if they are less burdensome to implement than experiments. Randomized experiments can and should be done more often in education in general as well as in work on educational technology. But many factors complicate the ability to mount experiments cleanly outside the laboratory. The example we discuss illustrates many of these difficulties and some ways of completely or partially solving them. We do not argue that randomized experiments constitute a "gold standard" for unimpeachable causal inference. Rather, we contend that the causal answers they provide are epistemologically better warranted, more efficient, and more respected in policy and social science circles than are the results of other forms of causal inquiry.

Of course, educational research deals with important issues that are not causal. Educators often want to learn whether the theory behind a program's design is well established empirically. They also want to learn how well the program details have been implemented, how implementation quality is related to outcomes, and what unintended side effects might have occurred. They also often want to know why the program has the effects it does, how cost-effective the results are, and how they can be transferred to other kinds of curricula and to other kinds of students and settings. Experiments were not designed to answer such a broad range of questions. So, we need to ask which questions they answer well, which they do not speak to (making supplementary methods required within experiments), and which they answer less well precisely because an experiment was done.

CAUSATION AND EXPERIMENTATION

From time immemorial, humans have wanted to know what will result if they make a change. Curiosity has something to do with this. So does utility. We want to learn what we can manipulate to make good things happen and keep bad things from happening. We want to learn how to keep warm in winter. Does wearing a loincloth help? Wearing a bearskin, lying under a bush, erecting a tent, sitting on a block of ice, or lighting a fire?

Laypeople often gain valid causal knowledge about the consequences of manipulable events. But sometimes they fail. They "learn" that a certain dance brings rain. Like laypeople, scientists, too, sometimes fail to identify causes correctly, as with thalidomide. However, the belief is widespread that scientists err less often than laypeople. This is due to many factors, some shared with multiple other methods and not unique to experimentation—for example, the willingness to be critically minded, the tenacity to surface alternative interpretations to initial causal guesses, and the discipline to consider openly all evidence contrary to these initial guesses.

However, the enhanced accuracy of science is probably in part due to the use of experimentation. In its earliest days, experimentation connoted the identification or creation of situations that allowed humans, in Bacon's famous words, "to twist Nature by the tail," to unconfound what is normally confounded. Observation and control over known disturbances were then the keys, and so many scientists went into the laboratory. There, they used lead-lined walls to keep out extraneous noise and they set up vacua in sterilized test tubes, all designed to keep out extraneous causal agents. But the need to experiment outside the laboratory became apparent, and Fisher (1926) used Mill's canons to create a form of experimentation with some of the same goals as the laboratory experiment but without its physical isolation and apparent artificiality.

The key to Fisher's innovations was the use of random assignment to create groups that are initially equivalent except for whatever treatments are being contrasted. This contrast might entail a difference between two or more ways to solve a particular problem or between one way to do so and a no-treatment control group. So long as the only difference between groups is the treatment being tested, any group differences observed at a later date are a product of this treatment and nothing else.

The utility of causal knowledge has meant that the nature of causation has preoccupied philosophers, practicing scientists, and laypeople struggling to keep warm, attract a mate, or placate the gods. Political actors are also preoccupied with cause, often in order to learn what it takes to get reelected or keep a job, but also sometimes to learn what makes citizens' lives better. So the public sector funds medical research to learn about ways to improve health, and it funds the Food and Drug Administration to make sure that drugs really achieve what is claimed for them and do not have negative side effects. In the private sector, billions are spent each year to learn how to produce goods more cost-effectively and how to increase product sales. Underlying all this is the utility of identifying what can be deliberately varied under human agency in order to bring about a desired end.

Accurate knowledge of the consequences of manipulable agents is useful even if the processes mediating the consequences are incompletely understood. Even if we do not know why aspirin is so broadly effective, it is of great benefit to learn that it reduces headaches and alleviates some cancer and cardiovascular problems. To know that smaller schools and smaller class sizes increase learning is also very useful, even if we do not fully know why these relationships come about. We can often describe a stable (though still probabilistic) causal relationship that we do not understand. Causal description and causal explanation are not identical in the world of practical action—our ancestors did not know why dressing in animal furs felt so good in winter, just as politicians do not know why American economic policy in the 1990s generated surpluses.

It is better to know why a relationship occurs. Causal explanatory knowledge can improve a causal agent by getting rid of all those components that do not contribute to its efficacy. Also, we can sometimes re-create effective processes in settings clearly different from those where the basic causal relationship was first described. Thus, if we know how to generate electricity, we can do this under the polar icecap and in space, places where electricity may never have been created before. And we can use wind, sun, waves, coal, water, uranium, or human feet as the immediate causal agent that sets in motion the process creating electricity. Knowledge of causal mediating processes helps transfer causal knowledge to novel circumstances.

Fortunately, it is usually easy to add explanatory measures to an experiment in order to probe various theories about why a cause–effect relationship comes about. It should therefore be done—and routinely so. But adding explanatory measures does not negate the fact that experiments were originally designed to promote knowledge of descriptive causal connections and not of any processes that mediate between the manipulated cause and the observed effect.

A HYPOTHETICAL STUDY

Selecting Study Questions

The question policymakers and journalists most often pose about educational technology is, "Do computers enhance student learning?" This is not a very helpful formulation, and not just because technology and student learning are so poorly specified.

More important is the high likelihood that computers will be in all schools and most homes within a decade, thus raising the profile of questions about how often and in what ways technology is used rather than questions about its global impacts.

The simplest causal questions about use concern the impact of particular pieces of software. But this focus is so narrow that it fails to address policymaker concerns. Nonetheless, many parents and educators do seem to want independent, up-to-date, and critical appraisals of commercially available software products—a sort of *Consumer Reports*. When technology is actually used in schools, the software does not by itself convey the subject-area content (Becker, Ravitz, & Wong, 1999). It is teachers who assign students work, and this work inevitably involves general applications such as word processing, spreadsheets, web browsers, or help from parents and friends as well as more specific subject-area concerns. To determine *all* the technology-related factors that promote student performance would be daunting. But experiments do not seek to identify all the factors involved in creating some outcome. Rather, they estimate the marginal impact of a clearly specified individual component from within some more global experience, whether this component is a software package, a general application, or anything else.

Schoolwork involving Internet research appears to be the fastest-growing and second most common area of teacher-directed student technology use after word processing (Becker et al., 1999). So our thought experiment involves designing an experiment to answer the question, "What effect does doing Internet research have on student learning?" This question is itself very global. How to make it more specific?

Explicating the Relevant Substantive Theory

The first step in any evaluation is to outline the theory-derived processes that are presumed to mediate from the intervention particulars to the major outcomes. This usually entails drawing a series of boxes and arrows that go from the most distal inputs on the left-hand side of a page (Internet search instructions) to the most proximal on the right (changes in a student's work). Coming between are other intermediate boxes and arrows that specify the causal pathway from left to right.

To be brief about this here, Internet research assignments can be done in many ways that might entail different consequences for students. However, positive effects are likely to depend on the specific content of the Internet assignments and the quality of teacher coaching and feedback. These deserve to be outlined as boxes coming after the most distal causal variable of Internet research. Then come some impacts prior to the crucial one of students' producing a quality research report. Such early impacts might include giving students access to content that is more abundant, of higher quality, and more current, or it might include increasing their intellectual engagement and developing their inquiry and communication skills. While these processes are all supposed to contribute directly to greater knowledge of the topic and better written or oral reports on it, they might also contribute to learning more general skills about technology that will pay off in other domains and in later life.

Although experimentation requires only one outcome, nothing precludes measuring all the outcomes above and thus testing multiple causal relationships rather than a single one. Since collecting outcome data is usually less expensive than adding new schools or classrooms, multi-outcome experiments are common. Perhaps the trickiest single factor in selecting measures is the dearth of knowledge about temporal sequence. Which outcomes should change earlier than others, and what are the exact time lines in which a given change should come about?

In tests of educational technology, content-knowledge measures should cover the topics on which some students have been asked to do Internet research in order to contrast their performance with that of some other students asked to do different forms of research on these very same topics. Both sets of students should also have spent equivalent amounts of classroom time on the topic. Informal time is another matter, for the hope is that students with Internet access will spend more time on self-directed topic-relevant activities, this being one possible motivational consequence of newer technology.

The need for content-knowledge measures suggests the advisability of doing our hypothetical study within a common curriculum area and grade level. Thus, studying American history in eleventh grade allows us to adopt or adapt existing content-knowledge assessments. And since technology adherents often argue that technology-supported activities emphasize depth over breadth of knowledge, we would want to ensure that the chosen knowledge test requires in-depth understanding, not just memory for names and dates (Bransford, Brown, & Cocking, 1999). Ideally, the test would yield at least two scores, representing both depth and breadth. Each can be measured from written reports, though this requires expensive content analysis by teachers who do not know the treatment assignments.

Internet search skills—the ability to use browsers and search engines efficiently and effectively—can be measured "hands on," or through self-report inventories, or both. A number of research organizations and states have already developed such measures, parts of which could be adapted for this purpose. Engagement in learning activities can be measured in any number of ways, including by ratings, self-reports, and behavioral indices such as attendance and observed time-on-task.

Inquiry and communication skills refer to judicious decisions about which information to obtain, the utility and reliability of this information, and how to synthesize it into a coherent product for a given audience. These attributes are the most difficult to assess. Typical standardized tests do not capture them well, and we are likely to have to rely on tests currently in development or else to develop our own measures, probably based on the content analysis of written products.

The Sampling Plan

The sampling plan of districts, schools, classrooms, and children is of great importance. To examine the performance of eleventh graders in American history necessarily entails a study that is restricted to those who have not dropped out of high school, a group probably especially well acquainted with the Internet. Studying second graders would be quite different, for we would then have to struggle more with their inadequacies in reading, writing, attention span, and computer knowledge. Thus, studying eleventh graders features the Internet in a context where it is most likely to succeed. So any replications of the study should strive to make heterogeneous those factors correlated with dropping out—age, class, ethnicity, region, and prior computer use. Only then could we begin to learn about the generalized causal impact of using the Internet for research projects. However, our emphasis here is on implementing random assignment to test causal propositions about computers and learning, and for space reasons we pay less attention to issues surrounding the sampling plan within which such assignment is inevitably embedded.

The Experimental Design

One kind of intervention we want to represent is "best practice" as this is most often defined within the learning technology community. Our protocol for the treatment group should therefore specify a high number of Internet research activities that students are asked to perform within a given time period (say, 10 in a semester). But technology connotes more than how information is gathered. Some researchers want student research to be structured around a "driving question," perhaps a mystery, controversy, or some other topic relevant to students. The assumption here is that student engagement in learning can be captured. Another element of best practice is that learning should take place in a social context, given the benefits that cognitive psychologists attribute to students' expressing and defending their ideas in joint work and conversations. Thus, students should perform their Internet research and prepare their products in pairs or small groups. A final component of best practice includes incorporating a "real" audience for students' reports of their search results. The web makes it much more feasible to find such audiences, either through identifying groups of classrooms that send their products to each other, or by creating a public website, or by linking to a site maintained by an external organization, such as a local historical association. Thus, the Internet treatment should be linked to having a driving question, doing research on the Internet, collaborating with peers, and presenting one's work to a real audience.

This raises the issue of what the control group should experience. It should obviously be asked to perform the same number of searches, although not by Internet. The procedures to introduce and motivate the student work should be similar to what is used in the best practice treatment group. The general operating principle is that comparison groups should be as identical as possible except for how they search for information—one group uses the Internet and the other does not. Even without the Internet, high school history faculty can organize their teaching and student research around a driving research question and collaboration with peers, as well as presentation to live and vicarious audiences. These are trans-situational elements of quality teaching, and so the control-group students should also be exposed to them. This results in a treatment contrast defined only by the presence or absence of the mechanism for seeking research evidence—that is, the Internet.

If we did not equate the other elements of best practice, we would then be contrasting best teaching using the Internet to average teaching without it. Any findings from such a design would be causally ambiguous. Is the causal attribution to factors that include the Internet, or is it instead relevant to the mundane proposition that better teaching (as defined by the elements above) is superior to worse teaching? Of course, equating the two groups with respect to a driving question, peer collaboration, and having an audience does not take these factors completely out of the causal explanatory picture in the best practices group. Technically speaking, any student-learning differences achieved after comparing best practice groups with and without Internet searches are due to a pure Internet exposure effect plus any interactions that occur because Internet availability enhances the contribution of driving questions, shared study, and having an audience.

This suggests another complication. What about no-treatment students who want to use the Internet to do their assignments, either at home or in school? Should they be forbidden to do so just in order to maximize the planned experimental contrast? Forbidding use of the Internet to control-group students maximizes the experimental contrast but at the cost of realism, since some students already use the Internet to do assignments. To forbid them to do so for the experiment would be to enforce a contrast with a world that does not exist for the sake of a purer test of the theoretical hypothesis that Internet search generates superior learning products. In the extreme case, we might find ourselves comparing one group of students whose teachers request and guide Internet searches with another group whose teachers do not request or guide them but where students mostly do them anyway and get guidance from their parents, friends or even other teachers.

Here there is a genuine dilemma between maximizing theoretical purity or practical utility. Since our hypothetical study is about best practice, we are inclined to do everything possible in the treatment group to enhance Internet searches and to let control-group practices vary freely. Control teachers should not suggest Internet searches, but they should not proscribe them either. However, from this decision follows the importance of measuring which students in either treatment group do and do not use the Internet for each of their 10 semester products. Such an implementation measure is vital.

A design based solely on linking Internet searches to best educational practices has a further drawback. While it might evaluate Internet searches at their best, it fails to estimate their effects as teachers and students now use the Internet, however suboptimally. This suggests the need for two other groups. One is asked to do Internet searches without the teacher requiring a driving question, joint work, or presentation to live audiences, though students can add these if they so choose. The final group is of no-treatment controls who do not conduct Internet searches and are not asked to do any of the things that constitute best practice.

Adding these two groups creates a factorial design in which the presence or absence of the request to do Internet searches is linked to whether the teacher does or does not instruct students to use best practices. This more complex design permits testing the effects of both main effects—Internet searches and best practices—and also testing whether the combination of Internet searches and best practices makes a nonadditive difference to student outcomes. These three questions thus become the centerpiece of the design summarized in Table 1.1.

At this juncture, advocates for more computer use in schools might object that the explication of best practice is itself a product of new knowledge about effective teaching that was generated by past studies of computer use in schools. Is it therefore fair to contrast computerized education with a no-treatment control group that, to the extent control teachers spontaneously use such practices even if not explicitly asked to do so, reflects how the Internet

Table 1.1. Summary of Internet Research Experiment Conditions

Condition	Topics	Internet Research?	Collaborative?	Driving Question?	External Audience?
1. "Best practice" with Internet	10 American history topics	Yes	Yes	Yes	Yes
2. "Best practice" without Internet	10 American history topics	No	Yes	Yes	Yes
3. "Typical Internet"	10 American history topics	Yes	No	No	No
4. "Control" for typical practice	10 American history topics	No	No	No	No

has changed educational thinking? Critics might note here that some pre-computer theories already stressed the utility of driving questions, peer collaboration, or presenting research to audiences, suggesting that advocates of these techniques in technology research did not invent them from whole cloth. Even so, the computer has probably increased the saliency of such practices, has given them a specific form, and has pointed to the benefits of combining them. However, we judge it to be neither feasible nor desirable to try to add a second control group. Current computer applications have to improve on current teaching, whatever the origins of such teaching.

In the best of all possible worlds, it would be desirable to deconstruct the best practices by adding treatment conditions based on each separate component of the three and all possible combinations of any two of them. But this makes the design cumbersome and, for a constant budget, will surely lead to unproductive payoffs between the number of conditions to be tested and the number of units per condition. Moreover, the more experimental conditions there are, the more difficult it becomes to implement each of them well in the hurly-burly of school life. Thus, four conditions are more than enough, and finer breakdowns of best practice should be the focus of possible future studies. Single studies are inevitably part of a program of research even if the programmatic aspects are not at first obvious and other relevant studies come to be done by different investigators.

The Measurement Framework

All causal questions require the assessment of outcomes, in this case measures of student learning and written performance. But other kinds of measures also improve experiments. One is measures of the quality of implementation of treatment particulars. After all, not all students asked to do Internet searches will do them, and some in the control conditions will do them even if not specifically asked to do so. Consequently, it is desirable to measure how many of the 10 projects involve an Internet search and to assess how extensive the search was. In all the conditions, students can and should be asked to do this, and as soon after each project as possible. Such measurement has to be done delicately lest the questions prompt control students to begin Internet searches that they might otherwise not have done. Likewise, it is important to measure, in all four groups, the extent to which teachers develop an engrossing research topic, prompt students to work in groups, and obtain an external audience for presentations.

It is also advisable to measure any intervening processes that the program theory indicates might mediate the relationship between the treatments and outcome changes. Some relevant measures might be the operational status of computer infrastructure in school and district, availability of necessary software for the computer platform the district uses, availability and numbers of websites that can be searched, choice of search engines, creation of state standards for technology proficiency, and district participation in mandated assessment of students' technology proficiency.

Finally, a number of variables might moderate the relationship between treatment and outcome. These include demographics such as age, race, gender, and class, as well as more causally proximal variables such as prior experience with Internet searches and access to a computer at home as well as in school.

Some Technical Issues

Unit of Assignment. The experiment could be performed with the student, class, or school as the unit of assignment and analysis. Using the student has several advantages but also disadvantages, including the fact that using students probably entails higher statistical power because there can be many more students than classrooms. However, the reliability of classroom-based observations is higher than the reliability of individual student responses. Also, student observations within classrooms can be correlated, thus violating the assumption of independent errors when individual data are used. Indeed, classrooms are typically created in ways that make the average student more similar to his or her classmates than to the average student in other classrooms, offsetting the advantage of larger sample size. More important, though, is the distinct possibility that children receiving different treatments within the same classroom will lead to treatment contamination—to children in one treatment group knowing about their classmates' treatment and reacting to this knowledge rather than to the treatment itself. For this reason, doing our hypothetical experiment with students as the unit of assignment is not advisable.

One alternative is to assign each treatment to a different intact classroom within the same school. Then each student in the same class gets the same treatment. This strategy assumes that each school offers at least four American history classes at the same level of difficulty in the same semester. This means the study can be conducted only in large schools. It also assumes that students in the same grade but in different classes do not talk to each other about how they are doing their essay assignments. How realistic is this? Although high school students mostly talk to their friends about personal matters, not class work, it is not plausible to assume that peer talk about class work can be totally ignored as a causal contaminant. So studying classrooms within schools is probably not a great option. If this is done, assessment is needed of the nature and amount of conversation about treatment differences that occurs between students in different conditions.

A third alternative uses schools as the unit, assigning one or more class-rooms per school to the same treatment but randomly assigning schools to the various treatments, perhaps within types of schools. This is best for avoid-ing the possibility of treatment contamination and biased representation of the schools studied. But this option is less desirable practically. Permission has to be obtained from more schools, collecting information is now more complicated logistically, and research costs increase correspondingly. Thus, using schools as the unit is technically preferable when it is practical. Other-wise, the recourse is to use classrooms and to do everything possible to re-duce and also to measure treatment contamination.

Moderator Variables. Many variables might moderate a treatment effect—that is, influence the size of a cause–effect relationship without being part of the explanatory sequence that temporally mediates between the cause and effect. Demographic characteristics of the student body are a major poten-tial moderating influence. There are also differences in writing ability, rele-vant content knowledge, and teaching style, especially those associated with socioeconomic class differences. For instance, teachers with large proportions of low-income students tend to be more directive, and this carries over to teaching with technology. Thus, teachers in urban high schools are more inclined to tell students doing Internet research exactly which sources to go to and which facts to transcribe (Means, Penuel, & Padilla, 2001). Provid-ing a protocol for each experimental condition is meant to reduce such in-structional differences that could function as moderator variables, but relatively unstructured work will still be a greater departure for some stu-dents and teachers than for others. No protocol can be totally comprehen-sive, and none is totally adhered to in school practice. But thanks to random assignment, such teacher differences will be equally distributed across treat-ments and thus not be a source of bias, even if some kinds of teachers pro-duce larger effect sizes than others.

In theory, the sampling design should provide for enough statistical power to detect interactions between the treatment and important potential mod-erators such as variations in teacher style or a school's social-class composi-tion. However, for the same degree of power, detecting interactions requires more units (and hence more money) than detecting only treatment main ef-fects. And the more moderators there are, the greater the need for larger samples. In practice, the number of possible teacher and student moderator variables associated with prior experience with technology, and attitudes toward it is infinite, as are the variables related to technology support and infrastructure. Thus, great care has to be taken to use theory and research experience to come up with a circumscribed list of potential moderators to examine in detail. Although the statistical power required for testing treatment-by-context interactions demands a larger sample of classrooms or schools, it is important to remember that the primary function of experiments is to test technology-related treatment main effects achieved across whatever kinds of persons, settings, and times are built into a study's sampling design. It is not to ask how effect sizes vary by these same person, setting, and time factors. This is very important, but not as fundamental as the quality of the causal main effect answer and the appropriateness of the persons, settings, and times achieved as the background to the causal test.

Implementation Variables, Incentives and Supports. To participate in the study, teachers need to be willing (1) to implement any one of the assigned conditions, (2) to follow whatever protocol the treatment requires and to what the coin toss assigns them, and (3) to tolerate the burdens of measurement. School staff may therefore need some incentive for cooperation. After all, to document treatment fidelity entails collecting data on the amount of time allocated to, and actually spent on, the relevant content; the extent of student engagement in instructional processes; student access to technology; and teacher participation in professional development activities devoted to the use of web-based instructional resources.

Teachers must also create a learning environment that exposes students to the relevant subject-matter content and instructional processes. For example, if a teacher is assigned to a condition where collaboration is required, then the students in that classroom must engage in collaborative problem solving. Teacher logs, lesson plans, and observations could provide evidence of the degree to which desired content and pedagogy are implemented.

A critical implementation variable is the degree to which technology resources are available for student use. Students must have access to Internet resources for enough time to complete the assignments, acquire the content, and complete their projects. Researchers may therefore gather information on difficulties in technology usage, the amount of time students were actually online, whether specific web-based activities were completed or not, the number of times particular websites were accessed, and the proportion of students in the class who were engaged when Internet tasks were taking place.

In many lower-income or small-school settings, participation would not be possible because schools cannot provide the needed Internet access. They do not have enough of the necessary hardware, or teachers do not have the necessary skills to use it, or there is no culture of using it constructively (Cuban, 2001). However, nearly all high schools have at least one computer lab, even if it is sometimes oversubscribed and suffers from outdated computers, network access problems, unacceptably slow download times, district firewall problems (making it impossible to get to Internet sites outside the district), and so on. The study will need to provide fallback technology support and quite likely some equipment if low-income and small schools are to be included. (These problems would be even more severe if elementary rather than high schools were used in the study.) Many teachers do not use the Internet resources they have, and obviously the study would have to be restricted to schools with a culture of sophisticated computer use or with widespread willingness to increase and improve such use. This last requirement pushes the study toward an "efficacy study," designed to test a causal hypothesis at its strongest, rather than toward an "effectiveness study," designed to test a hypothesis at its most representative. The latter would presumably include schools with a poorly developed culture of computer use.

Teacher professional development on the use of web-based technology for instruction may be part of the definition of the Internet search treatment. If so, the attendance of teachers at training sessions should be documented, as well as the amount of practice in which they engaged, amount and type of feedback they received on their skills, and whether they actually received materials and resources to successfully implement Internet searches. These data are most relevant to the Internet search condition. But it should not be assumed that teachers in the other conditions will not get training on the Internet as part of their regular professional development as teachers. Hence, it is also important to ask all teachers about the role of computers in their professional development activities. Since it makes most sense to do this by questionnaire, and since the golden rule of experimentation is that all groups should be treated identically except for treatment exposure, this suggests that questionnaires should be used across all the conditions as part of the assessment of implementation quality.

OBJECTIONS TO RANDOM ASSIGNMENT IN EDUCATION

Having sketched out a possible experimental study, it is time to confront the many objections that have been raised in the educational evaluation community to doing experiments. Although most statisticians and social scientists extol the experiment, many theorists of educational evaluation have explicitly rejected the method. Their objections have influenced the thinking and practice of many generations of young educational evaluators.

Experiments seek to learn whether varying A leads to variation in B that cannot be explained by other forces affecting B. Critics contend that this notion of causation is oversimplified and fails to reflect the way that causal forces operate in the real world. Rather, they contend, causation is multivariate in nature: A affects B not by itself but in consort with many other variables—and typically in a complex, nonlinear fashion.

It is true that most randomized experiments test only a small subset of potential causes of an outcome—often only one. And even at their most comprehensive, experiments can responsibly test only a modest number of the possible interactions between treatments. But this is not a trivial goal. We can see this from how educational researchers write about educational reform. All of them postulate some causal connections that are true enough to merit being treated like summaries of practical causal knowledge—for example, that small schools are better than large ones, that time-on-task raises achievement, that summer school raises test scores, and so on. Critics who deny the utility of propositions like these because they are not explanatorily complete still seem willing to believe that they are often enough true to be useful. They also seem willing to accept the validity and relevance of some causal propositions that are bounded by just a few contingencies. Commitment to a multivariate, explanatory theory of causation has not stopped education researchers from acting as though educational reform can be usefully characterized in terms of some dependable main effects (e.g., small schools work better than large ones) and some simple, dependable interactions (e.g., Catholic schools produce higher graduation rates, but only in the inner city). Hence, randomized experiments should not be rejected simply because the theory of causation that undergirds them does not incorporate every single condition affecting an intervention's effectiveness. Still, experimenters could improve the explanatory yield of their work by incorporating more measures of possible intervening processes. Proponents of random assignment need to offer more than "black-box" experiments.

A related objection to experiments is their incompatibility with the complex organizations and highly localized policies in the American educational system. Education policies and practices reflect the actions of politicians, bureaucrats, and professional associations and unions in thousands of school districts, schools, and classrooms. Many argue that the causal knowledge produced by experiments obscures each school's uniqueness and oversimplifies the multivariate and nonlinear ways in which politics and social relationships structure educational reform.

Despite the uniqueness of each district, school, and classroom, commonalties are also evident. All schools teach approximately the same material until high school. They all want to socialize young people, and they all involve essentially the same set of actors—administrators, teachers, children, parents, and other local supporters. Moreover, similarity is not a requirement for experiments. The fact that each unit is unique does not entail rejecting random assignment. Rather, it calls for carefully considering the types of units to which generalization is sought and for ensuring that the sample size is large enough for reliable estimation of the most central treatment effects.

Some critics warn against employing random-assignment designs prematurely in cases where one or more essential ingredients are lacking: (1) an intervention based on strong substantive theory, (2) schools managed well enough to implement a program or innovation, and (3) consistency of implementation across units assigned to the same treatment condition. Given that we cannot assume either standard program implementation or total fidelity to program theory (Berman & McLaughlin, 1978), few educational innovations of significant duration and complexity would meet these criteria for experimental evaluation.

Experiments primarily protect against bias in causal estimates, and only secondarily against imprecision in these estimates due to extraneous sources of variation. So school complexity leads to the need for large-sample randomized experiments to avoid inappropriate no-difference conclusions. Many researchers are reluctant to let negative conclusions stand and seek to complement them by stratifying schools according to the quality of program implementation before relating the variation in implementation to variation in the planned outcome. It should be remembered that such internal analyses make any causal claims the product of nonexperimental analyses—and thus without the advantages of the true experiment with respect to demonstrations of causality.

This situation can be avoided by (1) making initial sample sizes larger to reduce the need for internal analyses; (2) identifying likely sources of variation in implementation in advance and incorporating them into the sampling, measurement, and statistical analysis design; and (3) studying implementation quality as a dependent variable to learn which types of schools and teachers do a better job of implementing the intervention.

Many argue that random assignment is politically unfeasible in education. School district officials are more comfortable with applying districtwide programs to all schools or with letting individual schools choose their own programs than with implementing the treatment disparities that random assignment generates. Principals and other school staff prefer to make their own program choices and also have additional concerns about disrupting ongoing routines. In addition, ethical concerns arise about withholding potentially helpful treatments.

Political will and disciplinary culture are crucial for implementing random assignment. It is common in the health sciences, where it is institutionally supported by funding agencies, editors, graduate training regimes, and the clinical trials tradition. Little will to experiment exists in education because of the belief that opportunities for such studies are rare.

Yet things could be different. Studies that seek to learn what reduces drug use, violence, and premature sexual behavior tap into the same experimental research culture as the health sciences, and such studies are routinely conducted in schools as randomized experiments.

Randomized experiments entail trade-offs that many researchers do not believe are worth making. In particular, they give priority to obtaining unbiased answers to descriptive causal questions (internal validity), assigning this a higher priority than drawing causal conclusions in conditions of likely application (external validity). Cronbach (1982) strongly argues against giving priority to internal validity. He contends that experiments are often limited in time and space and rely on a biased subset of schools that are willing to surrender choice over which treatment they are to receive and to tolerate the burdens involved in measuring implementation, mediating processes, and individual outcomes. He suggests that it would be preferable to sample from a more representative population of schools even if less certain causal inferences would result.

Random assignment has no necessary implications for representativeness. The latter depends on how units were sampled for study, not how they came to be in the different treatment groups. To optimize internal and external validity jointly requires randomly selecting cases from the universe to which generalization is sought followed by randomly assigning these cases to the various treatments. But studies with random selection followed by random assignment are extremely rare. If principals and teachers choose not to cooperate with the experimenter's assignment to treatment condition at some point during the experiment, there is no way to enforce cooperation. This is why experiments are usually restricted to schools willing to tolerate random assignment and some measurement, and why other schools are left out of studies or are examined using nonexperimental designs.

But these external validity concerns do not negate the requirement for internal validity. We should remember that the external validity being sought concerns a causal claim. How generalizable is a causal assertion? Can the boundary conditions be identified under which the assertion that A causes B does and does not hold? Until a causal claim is established, it makes little sense to ask about its generalization.

Of course, steps should be taken in experiments to increase external validity. Units that will not agree to random assignment can be studied some other way, with the best available analyses being used to see whether the results from these "recalcitrant" sites are generally in the same direction as the experimental findings. If the population to which generalization is needed is known, and if there are some measures of this population shared with the sample, then sample weights can be created that allow extrapolation from the experimental results to the wider population.

Some critics argue that randomized experiments involve withholding possibly beneficial treatments from people who need or deserve them. Advocates of randomization retort that we do not know which treatment is more effective: Otherwise, we would not be doing the study. Even when a treatment has an empirical track record, this is often based on small samples, weak designs, and small "effects." Clinical trials are needed to get larger samples, better designs, and more trustworthy results. Gilbert, McPeek, and Mosteller (1977) reviewed the literature on randomized trials with medical innovations and found that the innovation produced better results than the standard treatment only about half the time. It is likely to be the same in education, including the case of various uses of educational technologies—there is no guarantee that students will do better with than without interventions that sound promising.

Ethical arguments in favor of randomized experiments are especially strong in cases where scarce resources make it impossible to provide treatment to everyone or when alternative treatments are compared and so no control group is needed. In the first case, some participants cannot receive the scarce treatment, and so the only question is by what mechanism this should occur. A lottery (essentially random assignment) strikes most people as more fair than first-come first-served, potentially flawed judgments concerning who has the greatest need or service to those with the most powerful friends. Where resources permit, investigators can offer to provide controls with the treatment at a later date, thus reducing some objections and also creating a crossover design (Fleiss, 1986; Pocock, 1983).

"DESIGN EXPERIMENTS" AS AN ALTERNATIVE TO RANDOMIZED EXPERIMENTS

Objections to the use of random-assignment experiments in education research such as those described above have led most educational researchers to embrace alternative approaches. Most researchers who evaluate educational reforms believe that alternatives to the experiment exist that are more acceptable to school personnel, reduce enough uncertainty about causation to be useful, are relevant to more issues than just causation, and are based on more sophisticated epistemological assumptions about causation. Three of these alternatives—qualitative case studies, theory-based evaluation, and quasi-experiments—are compared to the random-assignment experiment in Cook and Payne (2002). Cook and Payne argue essentially that these approaches are less capable than the random-assignment experiment of identifying true causal effects and are more appropriately viewed as adjuncts to experiments rather than as alternatives to them. A fourth alternative that has been particularly prominent in the domain of educational technology is the "design experiment." This last approach, which is not an experiment in the technical sense in which statisticians use the term, is discussed here at greater length.

Educational technology researchers have raised many of the objections noted above about the feasibility and applicability of random-assignment experiments. In reaction, many of them have become advocates of "design experiments," a significant form of research in the National Science Foundation's Education and Human Resources directorate. Roughly 20% of the Research Evaluation and Communication awards between 1996 and 1998 used this approach (Suter, 2000).

Design experimentation takes its root metaphor from disciplines such as architecture, engineering, and software development rather than from sciences such as physics or psychology. Brown (1992) described her own personal evolution in this regard. She began by doing laboratory experiments on children's ability to use strategies to aid their memory and reading comprehension and then switched to using a classroom-based intervention and research approach she termed "design experiments." Like experimentalists who first left the laboratory 75 years ago, she wanted to investigate learning as it occurs in real-world situations. For Brown (1992), this meant classrooms with all their complexities and interdependencies:

> Central to the enterprise is that the classroom must function smoothly as a learning environment before we can study anything other than the myriad possible ways that things can go wrong. Classroom life is synergistic: Aspects of it that are often treated independently, such as teacher training, curriculum selection, testing, and so forth actually form part of a systemic whole. Just as it is impossible to change one aspect of the system without creating perturbations in others, so too is it difficult to study any one aspect independently from the whole operating system. Thus, we are responsible for simultaneous changes in the system, concerning the role of students and teachers, the type of curriculum, the place of technology, and so forth. These are all seen as inputs into the working whole. (pp. 141–142)

Because the kinds of holistic approaches that Brown believed would be effective in classrooms were not then in place, she felt the need to work with classroom teachers to implement them. However, she quickly discovered that her initial ideas had to be modified to fit the school context, moving her toward a more collaborative model of working with students and staff. While most of Brown's own work was not technology based, her argument circulated within the community of researchers on learning technologies, with Hawkins and Collins (1999), Collins (1999), and Greeno and colleagues (1999) explicating why it would be more profitable to consider research in this area as a design rather than as an analytic science. Like Brown, they found that the kinds of instruction whose effects they wanted to investigate (basically, constructivist approaches supported by technology) had to be first fostered and developed in partnership with teachers and schools. Thus, Suter

(2000), Collins (1999), and Brown (1992) have characterized design experiments in terms of a set of methodological "shifts" away from the laboratory to naturalistic and "messy" settings, from well-specified ideas that drive instruction to emergent ones, from content neutrality to strong ties to the specific content domain, from the wish to control situations to the desire to characterize them, from single to multiple dependent variables, from fixed to flexible design, from single to multiple converging methods, from social isolation to social interaction, from testing hypotheses to developing a profile, and from researchers being apart from respondents to being reflective co-participants with them in design and analysis. The major goal of design experiments is to produce deep understanding of how individual or group outcomes relate to the learning environment (Brown, 1992; Collins, 1999; Suter, 2000). To this end, such experiments are grounded in an iterative, cyclical interaction among phases of design, implementation, and analysis. When combined with observation, video analysis, and interviews—among other data-collection techniques—the design experiment is supposed to yield a complete and valid picture of how knowledge is constructed and used in social settings.

The design experiment is experimental in the lay sense of undertaking an open-minded, problem-solving approach to identify possible solutions to a given problem. In manipulating things to see what brings about a desired end, the function of a design experiment is the same as the function of a formal experiment. However, the two differ in structure, with the design experiment being less formal in terms of measurement waves, control groups, and other ways of creating a causal counterfactual. It is also more iterative, dependent on a series of hypothesis probes over time. The two types of research also differ in what "design" means. The design experiment gets its name from the final program design that eventually emerges from the interactions between actors and from the changes in practice and procedure that they make and then micro-evaluate. In contrast, experimental design connotes the way control features, treatments, and outcomes are deliberately chosen and structured, both to demonstrate a possible cause–effect link and to rule out all interpretations of this link other than that it is due to variation in the cause generating variation in the effect.

Evaluators have no problem with design experiments when they are conceived as formative studies aimed at improving program design. However, many would have problems with the summative claim that they produce valid information about the value of whatever design is eventually worked out. That value still has to be demonstrated, and the best way to do so is via a formal experiment. Experienced evaluators might also worry lest design experiments be used to postpone summative work because the design experiment results are on hand and can be (mis)interpreted as providing acceptable conclusions about treatment effectiveness. Design experiments can play several important roles *within* a program of research that includes random-assignment experiments. One is to prevent the premature use of experiments. Experiments are often expensive and time consuming and only called for when the program particulars have been thought through well and are likely to be implementable in the real world of schools. Design experiments speak to issues of practical integrity and probable feasibility, and so are important preliminaries to the experimental evaluation of educational technologies. Of what use is it to evaluate a design option that is not well thought through and that teachers are not likely to implement well? Thus, design experiments can be viewed as valuable precursors to randomized experiments but should not be regarded as alternatives to them.

Some reasons why design experiments cannot establish causal effects for policy purposes should be obvious by now. There is no valid counterfactual describing what would have happened to students had they not been in the design experiment. In addition, there is the likelihood of reactivity associated with the relationship between the teachers and researchers. Do we want to generalize the results to all school settings, including the many where researchers cannot find staff collaborators? Well-implemented design experiments are likely to be instances of exemplary rather than standard practice. Exemplary practice deserves to be studied in order to assess the potential of a technology or methodology. But this should not be confused with studying what is, or could easily become, normal practice. That is why the study we designed earlier in this chapter included groups with and without best practice attached to Internet searches, and it is also why random assignment was used to assign classrooms or schools to conditions, including a no-treatment condition.

CONCLUSION

In some quarters, the randomized experiment is considered the causal gold standard. It is clearly that in theory, but not in school practice. There are just too many difficulties with implementing and maintaining randomly created groups, with the incomplete implementation of treatment details, with control group units borrowing treatment particulars, and with the limitations to external validity that often follow from how random assignment is achieved. A more modest case for random assignment in education is that (1) it provides a logically more valid causal counterfactual than any of its plausible alternatives; (2) it probably provides a more efficient counterfactual in that, when randomized experiments and their alternatives converge on the same answer, the randomized experiments do so more quickly (Lipsey &

Wilson, 1993); and (3) it provides a counterfactual that is more credible in nearly all academic circles and increasingly more so in educational policy ones. These are compelling rationales for using random assignment even if some external validity losses are incurred thereby.

None of the objections to randomization undermine experimentation in education and in technology studies in particular, however. All the objections have complete or partial refutations. And where an objection cannot be totally refuted, a corrective can usually be built into the experiment. We hope, therefore, to see more experimental studies of how new technologies affect school and classroom practices and student performance. We have outlined such an experiment in some detail. There is currently no alternative that provides as much reduction in bias and error.

REFERENCES

Becker, H. J., Ravitz, J. L., & Wong, Y. T. (1999). Teacher and teacher-directed student use of computers and software. *Teaching, learning and computing: 1998 National Survey* (Technical Report no. 3). Center for Research on Information Technology and Organizations, University of California, Irvine.

Berman, P., & McLaughlin, M. W. (1978). *Federal programs supporting educational change: Vol. 8. Factors affecting implementation and continuation.* Santa Monica, CA: RAND.

Bransford, J.D., Brown, A. L., & Cocking, R. R. (Eds.). (1999). *How people learn: Brain, mind, experience, and school.* Washington, DC: National Academy Press.

Brown, A. L. (1992). Design experiments: Theoretical and methodological challenges in creating complex interventions. *Journal of the Learning Sciences, 2,* 137–178.

Collins, A. (1999). The changing infrastructure of education research. In E. C. Langemann & L. S. Shulman (Eds.), *Issues in education research* (pp. 289–298). San Francisco: Jossey-Bass.

Cook, T. D., & Payne, M. R. (2002). Objecting to the objections to using random assignment in educational research. In R. Boruch & F. Mosteller (Eds.), *Evidence matters: Randomized trials in education research* (pp. 158–178). Washington, DC: Brookings Institute Press.

Cronbach, L. J. (1982). *Designing evaluations of educational and social programs.* San Francisco: Jossey-Bass.

Cuban, L. (2001). *Oversold and underused: Computers in the Classroom.* Cambridge, MA: Harvard University Press.

Fisher, R. A. (1926). The arrangement of field experiments. *Journal of the Ministry of Agriculture of Great Britain, 33,* 505–513.

Fleiss, J. L. (1986). *The design and analysis of clinical experiments.* New York: Wiley.

Gilbert, J. P., McPeek, B., & Mosteller, F. (1977). Statistics and ethics in surgery and anesthesia. *Science, 198,* 684–689.

Greeno, J. G., McDermott, R. P., Cole, K. A., Engle, R. A., Goldman, S., Knudsen, J., Lauman, B., & Linde, C. (1999). Research, reform, and aims in education: Modes of action in search of each other. In E. D. Langemann & L. S. Shulman (Eds.), *Issues in education research* (pp. 299–335). San Francisco: Jossey-Bass.

Hawkins, J., & Collins, A. (Eds.) (1999). *Design experiments: Integrating technologies into schools.* New York: Cambridge University Press.

Lipsey, M. W., & Wilson, D. B. (1993). The efficacy of psychological, educational, and behavioral treatment: Confirmation from meta-analysis. *American Psychologist, 48*(12), 1181–1209.

Means, B., Penuel, B., & Padilla, C. (2001). *The connected school: Technology and learning in urban schools.* San Francisco: Jossey-Bass.

Pocock, S. J. (1983). *Clinical trials: A practical approach.* Chichester, UK: Wiley.

Suter, L. E. (2000). *Guiding principles for mathematics and science education research methods: Report of a workshop.* Washington, DC: National Science Foundation, Division of Research, Evaluation, and Communication.

Chapter 2

Detecting Technology's Effects in Complex School Environments

Alan Lesgold

Overall, we have great need for improved evaluation of new ideas in education. Public trust of educational innovation is very low, and there is good reason for this. All sorts of ideas are touted and all kinds of products are sold. Many of these innovations have little or no effect, and the tools touted in the popular media for establishing effects—standardized tests—may not be able to discern certain important changes and may detect effects that are real but superficial.

A fictitious example may help ground this last point. Suppose that a school system decided to adopt a new curriculum in which graphing calculators were used extensively to give students a better sense of the nature of functions. Suppose further that some other school system were to institute a new curriculum aimed at assuring that all children learn some simple rules of thumb for factoring polynomials. Whether either change showed up on teachers' tests and course grades would depend on many factors of testing and grading that might be rather idiosyncratic across teachers. A standardized test that included factoring of polynomials would probably show a small improvement for the second school system and might show no improvement for the first, depending on how long after the innovations it was given. Two years later, children in the first system might be doing better in math than would have been expected, but we seldom look 2 years down the road in

Selected portions of this chapter originally appeared in an unpublished manuscript entitled *On Evaluating Educational Innovation* prepared for the White House Office of Science and Technology Policy in 1998.

our studies. Perhaps some students learn to pass tests without coming to understand mathematics; we don't know if that is what happens. Indeed, we seldom have good information either about how a given innovation provides a context for later learning or what context is required for it to produce any effects in the first place.

Public concern for improving our education system has stimulated many new innovations in content, teaching style, and technology. Some work, and others do not. Many work when used by certain teachers in certain schools with certain children and otherwise fail. A central tenet of this chapter is the need for educational evaluations to attend to—and systematically measure—features of the *contexts* within which innovations are implemented.

OVERVIEW OF THE PROPOSED APPROACH

A new approach to evaluation and R&D is needed that allows innovative ideas to be understood and evaluated in a context-grounded way. The approach I propose has the following core characteristics:

- A common set of core variables and measurement approaches is developed for the formative and small-scale evaluations that should occur in the early stages of developing an innovative approach. This protocol would make it easier to make later decisions about which innovations merit the costlier kinds of evaluation suggested below and would also facilitate decisions about the range of contexts in which an innovation should be evaluated.
- Long-term longitudinal studies should be conducted in which large numbers of schools, teachers, and students are tracked for a number of years. The models for these studies include the public health efforts sponsored by the National Institutes of Health, though some tailoring would be needed. Both centralized and distributed data collection could work, but centralized data storage and standardization of what is measured are important.
- A collection of basic learning context measures should be collected for all schools, teachers, and students who participate in the study. The specific measures used should be chosen through a process to which researchers and policymakers can easily contribute, and it should be possible to add new measures as the research base grows. This contextual baseline would itself be the basis for studies of how growth in one aspect of context might stimulate growth in others. For example, does a move toward more learner-centered instructional styles (a classroom process contextual variable) predict a move toward

more emphasis on understanding and ability to apply math (a content context variable)?
● Some of the context measures would be generated from maturity models. A maturity model contains (1) a set of features on which students, classrooms, or schools can vary; (2) a set of stages of maturity; and (3) for each feature, a scoring rubric for deciding how mature the student, classroom, or school is on that feature.

These core characteristics represent the approach I would take to evaluate innovative ideas.

WHY NOT A RANDOMIZED FIELD STUDY?

It has become popular to call for randomized clinical trials of educational innovations, since this has been a useful approach in medicine. The problem with this is that drug tests involve specific treatments for specific diseases. For example, comparisons might be made between streptokinase and competing drugs to see which is associated with better outcomes when used in treating ongoing heart attacks. We don't have an agreed-upon taxonomy of ignorance diseases, nor are there educational treatments available that are straightforward in their effects. Rather, in education, we have materials that *might* be put to good use by a good teacher, learning tools that *might* work if embedded in an overall instructional program with certain characteristics, software that can do some good *if* the school's technological infrastructure allows it to run quickly and reliably, and forms of instruction that work in the short run *but not necessarily* in the long run. It also should be noted that clinical trials are not a simple solution even in the world of medical research: When drugs "pass" clinical trials, there is often still uncertainty about potential long-term hazards and thus a need for longitudinal follow-up. Further, most drug trials take minimal account of the possibility that drugs may have different effects or require different dosages depending on age, sex, lifestyle, and even genetic factors associated with race and ethnic origin.

I see two major, related problems limiting the applicability of randomized clinical trials to education. First, in education causation is usually multiplicative and complex. In education, it is quite likely that success comes from a cluster of causes. Picking any one potential cause and simply doing a controlled experiment can work if that cause is sufficient to produce the desired outcome. But this is not always the case. Some factors may exert multiplicative or other nonlinear effects on others. To gain a practical understanding of cause, we need to do two things (Pearl, 2000). First, we need to develop—and validate, to the extent that is practical—a relatively rich and relatively complete causal model for how the desired outcome comes about. This includes paying attention to both the full range of factors that might influence the outcome and developing as much understanding as possible of the character of these influences. Then it is appropriate to conduct randomized field trials in which the causal paths that are less relevant to a policy decision are broken so that the causal paths we care about can be assessed without ambiguity.

For example, socioeconomic status may exert a rather direct influence on learning to read, simply because parents who have high literacy skills tend, as a group, both to do better economically and to spend more time reading to their children. Socioeconomic status may also influence the quality of teachers and the choice of curriculum products, since richer districts can "outbid" poorer ones. When testing a new reading program, then, it is important to somehow break the causal link between socioeconomic status and the decision whether or not to deploy the program. A standard way to do this is to assign students and teachers randomly to either the new program or some comparison standard program, thus breaking the causal links between socioeconomic status and program assignment and between socioeconomic status and teacher quality.

Consider, however, what can be lost in such a situation. Suppose that the new program only works when there is a combination of a teacher who knows how to use it and parents who reinforce the program at home. The randomized trials, if done on large enough samples to permit adequate power, will still show an overall effect of the program, which could lead to a policy decision to use it. However, the beneficiaries could end up being primarily the already privileged. Knowing that "at least it works for someone and is more effective on average than the alternative" can inform policy decisions, but only when we know the full range of policy-relevant causal relationships can we be certain that a policy based on randomized trial data achieves its deeper purposes. This is the goal of context-sensitive evaluation studies. By noting the contextual factors that correlate with successful outcomes, we can at least make a start toward knowing all that is needed for an optimal policy decision.

The second limiting factor is the often-found restriction in an educational practice's effectiveness in certain circumstances or contexts. Even the best educational innovations have some limits on the contexts in which they are effective (sometimes referred to as "conditions of applicability"). In medicine, with a reasonably clear sense about what constitutes standard practice and a stronger body of theory behind many innovations, it is possible to perform clinical trials for which the conditions of applicability are well defined. (In point of fact, even in medical studies, great effort is invested in standardization of treatment protocols.) In education, this is substantially less often the case. Part of the evaluation of educational innovations should include specifying *when* they work as well as whether they *ever* work.

While controlled experimentation can play an important role in producing scientific evidence relevant to public policy, it will often be insufficient to settle policy issues. And certain supplementary information—including case studies and detailed descriptive, even ethnographic, studies—will often be helpful in shaping a policymaker's sense of the overall complexity of the issue being confronted. Given this complexity, it seems quite likely that even with a number of randomized field trials, it will be difficult to establish that a given policy about who gets which reading program, computer software, or teaching style is clearly supported by the results of those trials. Multiple forms of data and analysis can be extremely helpful to policymakers if they help convey the overall character of context effects on the success of a given educational treatment. Systematically recording such data in a standardized form will further increase its policy value.

The medical world pursues answers to research questions that cannot be addressed through randomized clinical trials in humans (e.g., the effects of smoking or high salt intake). The approach of choice in such cases is the use of long-term epidemiological studies. In these studies, *large numbers* of people are followed for *long periods* of time. Periodically, *relatively inexpensive* (on a per-subject basis) information is obtained through questionnaires and sometimes through physician reports. *Smaller and more intensive studies* support these large-scale efforts. Very careful *documentation* is kept of any treatment components that might have been involved. In this chapter, I suggest that educational evaluations can borrow much from this kind of medical study, even if the simple clinical trials model won't really serve our needs.

A Contextualized Evaluation Approach

An evaluation must rest on a model of how actions in particular contexts produce observable outcomes. The appropriate model for evaluation of educational innovation is one in which the measurement process provides answers to the key question: What works under what circumstances? The needed scheme is diagrammed below. A statement of evaluation is a claim that a particular *innovation* produces particular *outcomes* under a defined set of *context* conditions, that is,

$$\text{Innovation} \xrightarrow{\text{Context}} \text{Outcomes}$$

In this approach, much of the analytic work involves determining which contexts will allow a given innovation to lead to a given effect.

within that school. Instructional maturity changes flavor in different subject areas. For example, literacy instruction maturity may involve superficial fluency, functional ability to acquire information from text, integration of information from multiple verbal and graphic sources, and ties between reading and writing. While at some very abstract level mathematics has some component to match to each of the components of literacy, it is unlikely that all that is important about teaching and learning math is the same as what is important in teaching and learning communications and language skills. Still, it should be possible to develop rubrics for assessing the maturity of subject areas taught in a given school environment. For example, in the case of mathematics, one could imagine attending to the proportion of the curriculum focused on content relevant to the New Standards exam (or to any other agreed-upon standard for mathematics learning outcomes), perhaps even having a rubric with a set of features of mathematics classes that prepare students for the performances that students must exhibit to meet the New Standards. Or one could imagine a rating scheme that looks at the proportion of classroom time given to various strands of the NCTM standards (National Council of Teachers of Mathematics, 1989) or some other similar gauge. At a more abstract level, one could imagine conceptual (understanding) goals for mathematics education along with computational (procedural) goals and having a scoring rubric that established maturity at both the procedural and conceptual level.

The process I have in mind might work as follows. A working group of researchers, practitioners, and representatives from major educational viewpoints might be asked to suggest examples of classrooms that reflect higher or lower instructional maturity in their view. These examples could be either fictitious—more likely for negative examples—or real. Using a policy-capturing scheme (in which a set of experts first make holistic judgments of quality for a large set of exemplars and then those judgments are analyzed to identify the factors affecting experts' quality judgments), a set of two or more scoring rubrics could be developed. Features and indicators would then be classified according to the extent to which they contribute substantially to scores on one or more of the rubrics. It might then be possible to produce a list of priority indicators that researchers would be encouraged to report in order to permit more meta-analysis across studies. Conceivably, a subset of indicators would be identified that occur in all of the rubrics, and it might be possible eventually to derive a more universal instructional maturity score based on those.

It is possible to incorporate all of the issues of instructional maturity into decisions about what outcome measures to use. In the early 1970s, for example, many psychologists proposed innovative memorization strategies. Clearly, those strategies would have proven effective in a school that set goals of having more

...morized by more students, especially if the style of teaching and ...ported such memorization. On the other hand, if the same "proven" ...ns are introduced into a school with a more constructivist teaching ...hy and a set of curricular objectives that lean more toward demon-...understanding of concepts and the ability to apply knowledge to new ...ons, the memorization innovations would likely be seen as ineffective. ...his might allow us to conclude that memorization innovations improve ...vement of memorization objectives but not of other objectives. How-..., an innovation will have more influence on classroom and study pro-...ses if it is compatible with the general processes of learning seen in the ...assroom and practiced by students and teachers. That is, we would expect a memorization innovation to be less effective even at producing memorization in classrooms that deemphasize memorization. In the end, instructional maturity will dictate both the outcome measures that are most valued and the likely success of the innovation in producing measurable change altogether. Hence, it needs to be considered as a context variable.

One serious problem is that there is probably no single ordinal scale of general instructional maturity. If one's goals are increased memorization, then classrooms in which memorization is emphasized and supported will seem the most mature. If, on the other hand, the ability to apply knowledge to everyday life or productive work is the goal, then perhaps constructivist objectives and methods will seem more mature. While no single scoring rubric could successfully capture the varying perceptions of instructional maturity, perhaps it is possible to develop a set of features and indicators that could be used generally in evaluating innovations. With such an agreed-upon set, it would be possible for proponents of different viewpoints to share access to evaluation data. They might differ on how they map the various indicators onto an overall instructional maturity score, but they could at least build a cumulative base of studies showing the value, from various viewpoints, of technological innovations.

Technology Infrastructure Maturity. Technological infrastructure maturity refers to factors in a school's readiness to use technology, including the character of the available hardware and software but also the extent of network connectivity, the level of maintenance arrangements, and the level of investment in teacher training. Since technological innovation is one of the most common forms of innovation in our schools today, technological infrastructure is critically important to assess. In the extreme, this is obvious. For example, a program that requires more memory than a school's computers have will not have much effect on learning in that school. As with instructional maturity, it should be possible to develop a set of indicators of technological infrastructure maturity and to train assessors to rate the level of maturity based on those indicators. Of course, if a particular innovation requires some very specific capabilities, these may need to be assessed independent of the generic indicators (although matching software to available hardware is indeed one of the indicators of overall maturity!).

Edmin.com, a private company, has developed an elaborate, usable approach to assessing technological infrastructure maturity (Sibley & Kimball, 1997). Their website (*www.edmin.com/tp/toolbox.cfm*) provides a number of specific scoring rubrics and supporting documentation. Some of its features are quite interesting. For example, it notes that a more mature school system will have a policy that assures that the computers accepted as gifts by a school are compatible with the maintenance and teacher-training plans of the school. This kind of detail is important and will only come from contributions by people "in the trenches." Fortunately, the development of maturity models and refinement of scoring rubrics offer natural opportunities for soliciting and receiving such inputs.

Educational Software Product Maturity. While not quite a context variable, there is another kind of maturity model worth including in evaluations of educational technology innovations, namely, the maturity of the innovative product itself. An instructional idea can be very promising but still fail because the software written for its implementation is difficult to use, unreliable, or unusable on some computers. In the case of software for learning, several kinds of product maturity are important. One can imagine the results of an evaluation being a characterization of the contexts in which a system produced major learning outcomes, plus an analysis of the software's maturity that might allow policymakers to decide whether the product will evolve in ways that make it more valuable. Here are a few features of software product maturity:

- *Interoperability*: Mature software is designed to work interactively with other software likely to be found in the same computer environment. For example, modern office software suites include spreadsheets and database programs from which information can be cut and then pasted into a document as a table.
- *Embedded training*: The operability of a mature system should be obvious, with any needed training embedded in the application and available when relevant.
- *Interface quality*: Mature software includes interfaces that are easily mastered, transparent in their meaning, and efficient to use.
- *Modularity*: Mature software is built in a highly modular manner, so that most of it can be reused for related products that might eventually be built.

- *User modifiability and tailorability*: Mature software is designed to permit its users to tailor it to their personal needs.

Note that the instructional content and the effectiveness of the instructional approach—usually the main content of educational software evaluations—are not included in these categories, since they are addressed under instructional maturity. There are standards for some of the software product maturity categories, such as interface quality, though it is not clear that the standards for the general commercial world or for complex equipment such as aircraft systems are applicable to school software. Standards for school software have tended to be focused on the extent to which the software addresses specific curricular needs such as those mandated by emerging state educational standards. While this is one important kind of standard, it does not directly address the maturity issues listed above.

I conclude that it will be necessary to develop a set of software product maturity standards, though it seems quite possible to do so relatively quickly. Interoperability can certainly be assessed by having a test suite of tools often used in schools and a set of specific tests to see whether those tools can be used with a given software product. For example, it seems important to be able to use a variety of forms of mathematics education software with spreadsheets, so one possible test might be to ask whether data can be moved back and forth between the program being evaluated and a spreadsheet program such as Microsoft Excel. Going one step further, it might make sense to have perhaps a few dozen such tests and then to proceed by selecting the five tests of greatest relevance to the domain addressed by the program being tested and to count how many of those tests the program passes.

Embedded training can also be assessed by surveying the software for a collection of features that seem especially likely to be important in learning and then surveying users to see whether they were able to use each feature after taking advantage of embedded training. One could also specify several kinds of embedded training the system should have: annotated screen pictures, procedural checklists, and so on. Again, refinement is needed for this facet of software maturity, but it seems quite achievable.

Interface quality is again best tested by developing a list of important affordances of the software and then watching new users to see how easily they can use the interface to take advantage of these affordances. There are a variety of standards in the military and in industry for interface quality, but, again, these may not apply as is to school software, which is generally not a simple procedural interface but rather a window onto a range of knowledge bases and experiences.

Tailorability has not really been addressed. Largely, this is because until recently most educational software products were closed systems that were not penetrable by the teacher. However, it is becoming clear that at least in the U.S. educational system, software that can be modified to address locally mandated instructional issues would be especially valued and useful. Further, to the extent that even limited constructivist views of learning are held, there will be a need to shape the context in which ideas are advanced or procedures learned and explained so that it is meaningful to students and teachers in particular schools at particular times. It will be necessary to develop simple schemes for assessing the extent to which a given software product permits this.

People Maturity. Another kind of maturity has to do with the way in which schools and districts are organized. Some organizations are more able to make changes because their structure and practices promote organizational learning. In other organizations, change is difficult because each participant needs to be trained separately and there is no organizational memory to scaffold individual learning. In the more mature level of organization, the following characteristics can be noted (Curtis, Hefley, & Miller, 1995):

- Practices can be repeated.
- Best practices can be transferred rapidly across groups.
- Variations in (successfully) performing best practices are reduced.
- Practices are continually improved to enhance capability.

It is possible to score organizations to reflect the level of maturity at which they operate (Curtis et al., 1995). The scores reflect such issues as team building and teamwork, efficient schemes for professional development and filling of skill gaps, mentoring arrangements, planning of workforce recruiting and development, and systematizing local innovation so that lessons learned are passed on to others. Certainly, districts with higher levels of this kind of maturity will be more able to realize the benefits of new innovations, since they will be set up to internalize and incrementally improve new practices that pay off.

Companies have only one basic kind of people—their workforce. Schools, though, have two—the school and district staff and the students. Certainly, we would expect the success of any innovation to depend on both of these. One part of people maturity on the student side is having ways to provide every student with a platform of knowledge and skills that allows effective learning; the other part is organizing the classroom so that the effective learning can then happen.

Stage Transition Models

Once a series of maturity models is developed, there are some research questions that can be addressed just by collecting maturity data as a part of evaluation studies. Specifically, it is possible that maturity on some scales potentiates maturity on others. For example, there might be content goals, such as the ability to revise and improve an essay, that depend on technological maturity (e.g., ubiquity of access to word processors and backed-up storage for student files). Certain process levels might also depend on technological maturity or might only develop once schools see the value of certain learning outcomes (content maturity). An important part of evaluation aimed at establishing the context requirements for an innovation to be effective is the direct exploration of the ways in which different kinds of maturity interact. Just as developmental psychologists look at the relationships among different aspects of human cognitive, social, and ethical maturity, similar approaches might be applied to the different aspects of maturity in schools, classrooms, and individual learners. Doing this well might require new statistical approaches and other supportive research, but if we can develop the right methods, there is great potential for milking large-scale studies for much more useful information than just the effectiveness of particular innovations.

Causal Modeling: Determining the Contexts in Which Innovations Work

When one examines the myriad causal relationships likely to play a role in technology-enhanced education, the complexity of any statistical analysis is boggling. When one is looking at computer-enhanced professional development—as I am these days—the situation is even more complex. Instructional tools and systems are continually evolving, with new versions delivered regularly. In almost every case, each new version improves on previous ones, at least in some respects. Stuff that appears to work gets into immediate use even if it is not fully proven. And each school uses technology in its own ways for its own purposes. In addition, standard statistical treatments require much more data than any one study can amass. As a result, we need to find ways to accumulate relevant information across multiple studies and multiple levels of technology implementation.

In this section, I consider this problem and suggest the following basic approach.

- Define a rough preliminary model for the effects of technology in various school contexts.

- Refine the model to include clear constructs that reflect hypotheses about the sources of effectiveness for particular technologies.
- Use a variety of partial analytic schemes and qualitative, observational work to incrementally flesh out an overall structural model of the effects of a technology and to establish as best as possible the magnitude of specific effects within that model.

With this kind of approach, it should be possible not only to show whether particular technologies are effective but also to establish some reasons for *why* they are effective. The answer to "What works?" can then be stated in terms of learning-producing activities rather than the presence in the building of particular software.

Rough Preliminary Model

The simplest possible model we could build would be one in which introduction of a particular technology or approach directly causes an improvement in student achievement. This kind of model can be tested in a classic split-treatment design where some students are exposed to the new technology and others not. Generally, student achievement would be measured right before and right after the treatment. To assure that the two groups were similar in membership, we would check whether the pre-treatment mean scores for the two groups were about the same. To check whether the treatment had any effect, we could look at post-treatment achievement means. If the treatment group did better afterwards than the control group, we would declare victory and start on the lecture tour.

There are numerous problems with such a simplistic approach. Two key problems are that (1) this scheme does not help us understand why the treatment works and (2) it does not establish the contextual requirements needed for the treatment to work. After all, it is likely that we will try out our new ideas in environments over which we have a lot of control, whereas later adopters may not have as supportive an environment in which to try the new ideas. Unless we can establish what environmental characteristics are important to the success of a piece of technology, we haven't made much progress. The painful truth is that most educational innovations produce good effects in the environment selected for initial (and well-supported) implementation and are often not effective in many other realistic situations.

If we think a bit about what goes into a technology's being effective, we can quickly specify a number of factors, including characteristics the students must have to benefit from the technology (an online text won't help you if you can't read), aspects of the school's technology infrastructure (if there's one machine for 50 students, it might not matter what software is on that machine), and dispositions and behaviors of the teacher (if the teacher says nothing on the computer will be tested, that may influence how well students attend to the computer-based lesson). In addition, one could imagine indexing the extent to which the technology is used and asking whether those who use the technology for more minutes per day get more benefit from it.

In work I am currently doing, the technology is for teachers, principals, and staff developers to use. In this case, the models of cause are even more indirect, since teachers must learn something and then must use what they learn before children show learning achievement. Figure 2.1 shows some of the complexity that can emerge in such a case. Note that it includes only the underlying variables of the causal model, not the specific measures used to estimate those variables. Assuming some multiplicity of measures, the final structural model will contain more than twice as many elements.

Theory-Driven Causal Model

While the preliminary and superficial approach just sketched can be useful, it has a major weakness. That is, it does not look directly at processes of learning and at what causes learning to take place. *Without a hypothesized underlying causal mechanism, it is difficult to be sure what to conclude from tests of a given structural model.* Suppose we consider a piece of technology

Figure 2.1. Diagram of Causal Model

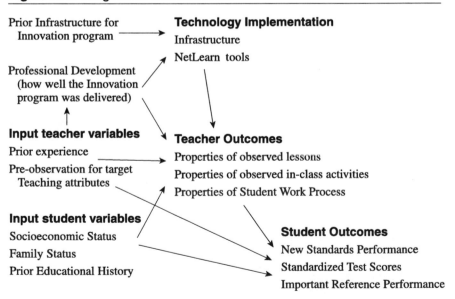

such as an intelligent tutoring system. If we look only at the superficial characteristics we have discussed so far, we don't learn anything about why the tutor works when it does. Consequently, decision makers get no help for deciding whether to use the specific tutoring system or instead to use some other technology that might be cheaper or easier to use. In contrast, if we knew what learning processes were stimulated, scaffolded, or provided by the tutor, we might be in a better position to decide whether the tutor is needed for a given learning goal involving a given student.

With the special case I currently face—of technology to facilitate school restructuring—there are two sets of processes to think about: those that change teacher and classroom behaviors and those that change student-learning processes. Actually, there might even be three sets of processes—in cases where the software prompts teacher thinking that leads to new classroom arrangements that in turn change the thinking that students do in class. If we could assess the extent of each of these processes/activities, we might be in a strong position to advise a decision maker on when to deploy the technology. Again, though, we would be in a much stronger position if we could assume specific mechanisms in the sequence of apparent causes. If we are to accept a model such as

$$\text{Teacher thinks differently} \Rightarrow \text{Teacher acts differently} \Rightarrow$$
$$\text{Student learns more}$$

we need a process account of how these influences occur so that we can come up with the best measures of thought and action to provide a strong test of the model.

Estimating the Coefficients of the Model

The theory-driven structural model discussed above will inevitably be a bit more complicated than the one shown in Figure 2.1, since it includes a more elaborated view of the patterning of causal influences. This makes sense in terms of the questions we want an evaluation to answer, but it does present a problem. Characteristically, the entire investment in an educational technology effort is quite low—perhaps a few million dollars. Yet the research design for the evaluation will be quite complex and hence require very large sample sizes, which may not be economically feasible. In the final section of this chapter, I consider some ways in which important coefficients of rich structural models can be estimated even if the model as a whole requires more data than is yet available.

In the next section, I flesh out the preliminary model, using as an example case the technology my associates and I are currently putting together to support school restructuring activities.

COMPONENTS OF THE PRELIMINARY MODEL:
AN EXAMPLE

Figure 2.1 illustrates a very simple causal model for the effects of teacher professional development efforts. Starting from the right and working backward, it says that student outcomes are produced by some specific things teachers do and that student outcomes also depend on what kinds of students they are and what kinds of teachers they have. The specific good stuff we hope teachers do is dependent, in turn, on who the students are, who the teachers are, how well our professional development effort is structured, and what sorts of technology-enhanced activity is actually available to the teachers as part of the professional development effort. We can work backward even further to see the additional effects of student and teacher characteristics and of the technology infrastructure of the school.

One important thing to note about this sort of causal diagram is that it contains a number of examples of a hypothesized direct effect as well as a mediated effect. For example, we claim that student outcomes depend on what the students are like at the outset, but we also claim that student entering characteristics influence teacher performances, which in turn further influence student outcomes. One reason that we need so much data to confirm a causal model fully is that we want to consider a variety of possible causal paths, both direct and mediated, in order to understand how much a particular innovation added to a web of causal relationships that was already present before the innovation was introduced—and we want to understand which of those preexisting relationships was altered by the innovation. Below, we consider each of the kinds of variables in Figure 2.1.

Input Student Variables

Student achievement depends in part on entering characteristics of the students. Some students will have more learning support at home, and some will have learned more prior to entering school. At the very least, socioeconomic status (SES), family status, and prior achievement measures are needed in any evaluation scheme that is meant to be meaningful over the range of school systems. Far too often, ideas will work when tried out in school systems whose students are easy to teach but not in schools whose children arrive hungry, are without home support for learning, or were deprived of adequate education in previous years.

In the model shown in Figure 2.1, student characteristics are expected to influence both final student achievement and teacher outcomes. Certainly, student achievement outcomes will be related to where they start, but it is also important to note that the range of teaching styles and specific teaching

practices that a teacher exhibits may well be influenced by student characteristics as well. Sometimes this influence is unfortunate, as when a teacher
settles for lots of rote practice in the belief that the students are not capable
of collaborative or self-managed learning. On the other hand, even a teacher
with high expectations may need to alter specific practices in order to boot-
strap the learning of students who start with various special needs.

Input Teacher Variables

Similarly, we need to take account of teacher differences. For example,
the Pittsburgh school system has mostly very experienced teachers, while
many expanding systems in the Southwest have mostly beginners. When trying to understand what technology innovations work where and for whom,
we need to attend to the possibility that the wisdom of experience will help
teachers (at least many of them) teach effectively but may also entrench
methods not necessarily adaptive to technological enhancement. The brand-
new teacher both has less developed teaching capability and is more mal-
leable in the face of new information technologies. Consequently, teacher
characteristics are important control variables in causal modeling of technology effects.

As with the student input variables, Figure 2.1 shows teacher characteristics as influencing final student achievement directly and also via the exhibi-
tion of various capabilities that are the focus of the technology-enhanced training
being evaluated. This helps make it possible to determine whether the training
being evaluated was the source of student achievement or whether teachers
already knew what to do. Also, it captures the reality that various professional
development opportunities will depend for their effectiveness on the capabilities and characteristics of the teachers toward whom they are directed.

Prior Infrastructure for Information-Processing Tool Usage

Another major factor in the success of any technology enhancement for
learning or teacher professional development is the infrastructure already
present in the school system. Because of the many experiences with nonwork-
ing systems that we all have, most of us have a rather short attention span
for technology that is not working well. When a system fails, it is often hence-
forth ignored by teachers, who value their time highly and have little of it to
spare. This tendency to minimize use of the imperfect is enhanced substantially when infrastructural weaknesses make access even more difficult.

Traditionally, we could easily assess school infrastructure by looking at
the nature of networking, the availability of on-site technical support, the
power and memory of computers available in the school, and so on. Today,

this is becoming somewhat more difficult because of the many layers of information sources potentially involved in a system. Here's a simple example. I teach a course that makes heavy use of online content. Students can access many resources for my course via any web browser. However, the rate of access has been depressed for a week or more when certain transient problems have occurred, such as the following:

- A few pages looked fine to me but would not appear when requested by students.
- A few students experienced a period of a few days during which the server on which my pages were located was overloaded and nonresponsive.
- Students off campus experienced a period in which account validation processes added more than a minute to each download.

There were plenty of machines available, lots of tech support, and a rich network infrastructure, yet things happened that influenced student usage rates. No direct measure of technology infrastructure would reveal these sorts of problems, and their effects persist after the problems are repaired, since people remember inconveniences and try to avoid them in the future. The only way these sorts of infrastructural glitches would be detected is via some sort of survey of users that allowed them to provide their personal idiosyncratic ratings of usage difficulties. For that reason, it seems very important to combine objective measures of school information-processing plant facilities and staffing with subjective measures of the perceived usability of the infrastructure. The commercial Internet service providers and e-commerce sites have already learned this lesson the hard way.

A MATURITY MODEL EXTENSION OF THE DEEPER CAUSAL MODEL

I next consider the role that maturity models might play in building a viable approach to causal evaluations of innovations. The hypothesis I wish to advance is that *a collection of maturity models will, as a group, span the range of "input variables" that are essential to a good causal model of educational innovation effects.* That is, if we can find good measures for each of the maturity types discussed above, then those measures, plus outcome measures, should be approximately the right set of data to gather for evaluating an educational innovation. While this hypothesis may be a bit too broad, it seems like a good starting point. Figure 2.2 shows an expansion of the causal model from Figure 2.1 to include the various kinds of maturity.

Figure 2.2. Deeper Analysis with Maturity Models Included

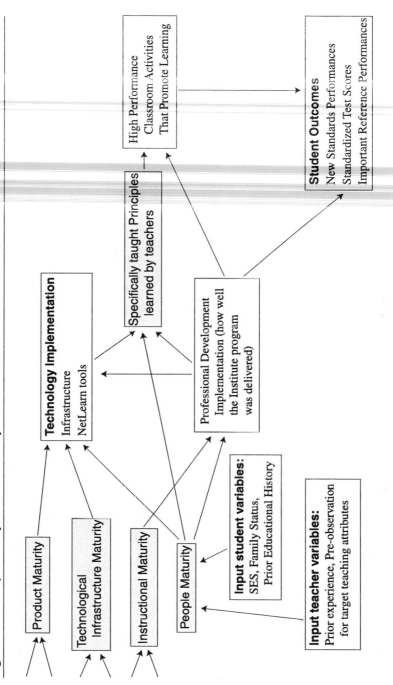

Because of the complexity of the figure, not all the measures associated with each kind of maturity have been included. Unspecified measures that would allow an estimate of the maturities are represented by arrows with no boxes at their tails. In the case of people maturity, we have included two classes of measures—those of teachers and those of students. For the other cases, we have left out any details. This is not entirely accidental. I now offer a second hypothesis: *It is possible to develop relatively global scoring rubrics for each of the maturity types.* I consider this in more detail in the next section.

If one uses a maturity model approach, then the basic causal model becomes simpler: Maturities combined with various interventions lead to an internalization of various principles, which in turn lead to particular classroom behaviors and, through them, to particular student learning outcomes. The model remains complex, and the problem of getting enough data to answer useful questions remains real, but some simplification becomes possible if we can find simple ways to assess the different forms of maturity.

A causal model can be useful for more than the organization of a holistic quantitative evaluation grounded in regression techniques. By clarifying all the categories of influence on an innovation's success—and, indeed, by clarifying the definition of an innovation's goals—a causal model can prompt a variety of qualitative and preliminary and partial studies, and it can provide a framework for organizing those studies' results.

Innovation (Treatment) Variables

After we specify the contexts in which an innovation is being evaluated (using maturity models), we must also specify the nature of the treatment. Pills are integrated and well-specified treatments. Educational innovations are not. Different teachers and students will use different tools and approaches in different ways. Some of this might be related to context. For example, it could turn out that a piece of software is used effectively only in programs that have certain content goals. In that case, an evaluation report could simply relate outcomes to content goals, for example,

> Those schools that had the goal that students will learn how to use mathematics in everyday life experienced a significant improvement in the percentage of students satisfying Standard No. 8 after providing 6 hours of experience using spreadsheet programs to support problem-solving exercises.

On the other hand, the nature and character of implementation might also contribute to the success of an innovation, for example,

When teachers provided at least one modeled example of using a spreadsheet for problem solving and each student used a spreadsheet to solve at least 10 problems, then there was a significant improvement in the percentage of students satisfying Standard No. 8 after providing 6 hours of experience using spreadsheet programs to support problem-solving exercises.

Independent variables will need to be specified in particular ways if these kinds of statements are what we are after. Specific conditions of implementation (e.g., "student solves at least 10 problems with a spreadsheet") will need to be specified in most cases. Especially for innovations of a more diffuse nature (e.g., various forms of self-managed learning), degree-of-implementation scales will be needed.

The basic technology for *degree-of-implementation* measures is simple. A collection of features is specified that the developers of an innovation believe is important to its success. A score is assigned based on which of these features is present in the environment being evaluated. Sometimes, these are global features and can be assessed through periodic observation or even through teacher or student questionnaires. Sometimes, though, implementation is best assessed by fine-grained time-sample studies. For example, an individualized curriculum might be indexed partly by noting the proportion of 10-minute class intervals in which at least one student is given an individually chosen task or individually tailored coaching.

One danger to be avoided with degree-of-implementation measures is the possible confounding of degree of implementation with outcome variables. For example, it would not be interesting to index degree of implementation of a spreadsheet activity by noting the number of occasions on which a student uses a spreadsheet correctly if proportion of correct spreadsheet usages is also used to specify a successful outcome. But it would be sensible to use number of spreadsheet experiences as an independent variable if the outcome measures focused on how the spreadsheet was used or when it was used. Ideally, implementation measures should derive directly from the core design features of the innovation.

Outcome Variables

Evaluation, by definition, is figuring out the value of something, and outcome measures are the variables that index value. There are a number of kinds of outcomes that might be the basis for an evaluation, and there are a number of different ways of expressing them. The fundamental task is to get a clear sense of the goals for an innovation and then to figure out how to represent the results of an evaluation in ways that are understandable.

Normative Versus Standards-based Measures. Incremental normative improvement often is indexed by standardized tests. Virtually every district gives such tests, and they have important properties. Usually, they are highly reliable (i.e., the same capability leads to the same score) and they are also fast and cheap, relative to other assessment approaches. However, some of the speed and low cost comes from a measuring approach that is rather indirect and that sometimes misses deeper levels of enduring competence. Also, the performances that normative tests measure are, of necessity, small and encapsulated ones. Yet we often have educational goals that include the ability to attack and successfully solve rather substantial problems (e.g., to write a really good report, which might take several days). Nonetheless, incremental improvement measures are critical to organizational change, and achievement tests have been our primary incremental measure.

Trials of educational innovations should not focus exclusively on achievement tests. In addition to the problems indicated above, achievement tests can send inadequate messages about educational goals. Even when sophisticated reasoning is required to answer questions, the entire process is brief and does not model the kind of extensive planning, working, and reworking that is part of major cognitive activities. But if we don't focus on standardized test scores, we will surely need some other incremental measures to replace them. It would make sense for outcome measures to support the natural tendency of "teaching to the test" by directly assessing the performance capabilities that are the targets of instruction. This requires, however, that they be based on more substantial performances. And we will need to find ways to index incremental change in the direction of those substantial performances.

The New Standards Project (Resnick, 1999; Simmons & Resnick, 1993) has addressed this concern. Participants have organized their assessment around substantial classroom and home projects that produce major products. Scoring rubrics are then developed that reliably assess these products. In essence, the scoring rubric is a way of systematically checking a performance for characteristics that experts associate with high quality and then cumulating this feature information to arrive at an overall score. This scheme—of using major products and scoring rubrics for their assessment— was based on observation of European approaches to school-leaving exams and also on extensive work with teams of teachers. Through social moderation and the use of clear scoring directions, it is possible to produce scoring rubrics for complex products that can be applied reliably and validly.

Professional Development Implementation. In the present example, where we have both a professional development activity that historically has not depended on technology and a new form of the activity that uses technology, it is possible to look separately at both the core professional development approach and the added impact that might come from technological enhancements. While there may be less uniformity to personally led seminars in school districts than to technology-enhanced presentation of the same ideas, there are still many characteristics of both the goals and the learning models that are independent of how professional development opportunities are delivered. Therefore, it seems appropriate to try to index potentially important characteristics of the professional development agenda and to attempt to measure these indices independent of measures of the technologically enhanced implementation.

Technology Enhancement Implementation. Technology affords some additional opportunities, and it should be possible to measure the extent to which those opportunities result in additional learning-related activity. For example, network technology can easily permit asynchronous participation in continuing discussions, thus extending the professional development experience beyond an in-person workshop. Also, review and follow-up resources can be made available on websites. Often, the extent to which one or another web-based resource is used can be monitored automatically. The proportion of a target group that accesses any given resource can be measured, as can frequency of access.

Teacher Outcomes. Having dealt with the input side of the causal model expressed by Figure 2.2, I next consider the immediate outcomes (changes in teacher behavior) and the desired target outcomes (changes in student achievement), beginning with teacher outcomes. Any professional development activity has the goal of changing how the professional responds to various situations. Teacher professional development, at least when focused on learning, presumably has the goal of changing what the teacher does in the classroom and perhaps what he or she expects students to do. Consequently, it should be possible to measure the success of professional development activities by checking to see whether the desired classroom activities become more common. Some of this can be done with diary measures.

School improvement activities tend to range over various mixtures of coaching, direct instruction of teachers, and incentive schemes. It is not necessarily the case that a leader's sense of which improvements he or she was carrying out matches what teachers perceived. For example, on occasion, efforts to teach principals to do LearningWalks®, a technique of informal observations of teachers designed to provide constructive feedback, have resulted in situations that teachers perceived as punishment for not doing what the principal or trainer hoped for rather than as a source of advice on how to achieve new goals. To understand the ultimate effects of training on student achievement, it is important to know how the training was perceived by teachers as well as what teaching methods, approaches, or skills it taught them. Survey instruments can be devised to measure these perceptions.

Gathering good data on teacher outcomes is relatively expensive and time consuming, but it is important. Without knowing how teaching behaviors change, it is difficult to be sure why various school improvement efforts do or do not work. While some of the needed data can come from surveys that can be automated, much involves observations that must be recorded and scored—usually a very labor-intensive process. Still, some amount of this work is necessary to assure that we understand when various innovations are effective and, especially, why. Because innovations are seldom implemented identically in different locations, it is crucial to determine which aspects of the innovation are important and why. With that information, we can understand which characteristics of an innovation must be preserved for it to work and which are accidental.

Student Outcomes. Many student achievement outcomes are relatively easy to measure. After all, there are broad technologies of standardized tests and a fast-emerging technology of scoring for more substantial pieces of student work. However, certain student outcomes may be more difficult to measure. For example, one goal of a professional development session might be finding ways to stimulate more self-managed learning by students. The appropriate measure of success would then be some kind of indication that students are engaging in more self-managed learning. In principle, it might be possible to measure the products of self-managed learning instead of the process. For example, students could be given self-managed assignments and then the products of those assignments might be analyzed. However, in cases where that more distal measure does not show the expected change, process data can help us discover why an innovation was not successful and how it might be tuned to make it more likely to succeed. For this reason, it might be useful to have some interview measures that at least tap into how students plan a self-managed learning activity and perhaps student diaries describing what they did when.

Some expected student outcomes for some professional development sessions might be even more process centered. For example, a professional development session aimed at improving writing instruction by encouraging more peer critique and essay revision would almost certainly need to be evaluated in part by looking at the critique process and in part by comparing revised products to the critiques that preceded the revisions. Again, this is a relatively expensive kind of outcome measure, and that is a concern to which I return later in this chapter.

PROMISE VERSUS FULLY ESTABLISHED VALUE

One further issue merits discussion as we consider what should be measured in educational evaluation. All major educational innovation efforts go through a preliminary period in which they are very fragile. Because of the stability of the educational system, virtually all such innovations show a strong "hothouse" effect. That is, they work in highly supported, sheltered sites but fail in sites where this high level of support is missing. There are many reasons for this. One major reason is that the different kinds of talent that are needed to produce an educational innovation initially may not overlap with the talents needed to promote its adoption later. One answer to this would be for development teams to include the full range of needed talents from the outset. This would be very expensive, but it is essentially the strategy followed in some of the large demonstration initiatives the federal government has pursued in recent years.

An alternative would be to clearly separate the preliminary evaluation of an educational innovation's potential from later evaluation of its effectiveness as a "shrink-wrapped" package. For this to work, different evaluation schemes are needed in the early stage in which potential is being appraised. In that stage, the first question must be whether a substantial effect is produced in at least some circumstances—even if under hothouse conditions. In addition to this demonstration of effect achievability, a strong evaluation of potential will include some considerations of the ultimate deliverability of the treatment. This might come from a few preliminary tryouts in less sheltered conditions, or it might come from microstudies of what exactly students and teachers do when using the new tools. More generally, detailed descriptive studies are an essential adjunct of any large-scale evaluation effort—they help clarify our understanding of *why* a given treatment works. As suggested above, any randomized clinical trial can only be interpreted if there is a clear model of the factors that play a causal role in producing positive learning outcomes.

If we could accumulate a longitudinal database of innovation effectiveness studies, it might become possible to predict what contextual requirements various classes of innovations will have. That is, we could begin to have causal model templates that can be used as initial approximations of the causal model for a newly introduced innovation, with detailed observational studies then being used to refine the initial approximation.

To the extent that this is possible, it would facilitate the initial evaluation of hothouse demonstrations. For example, if a new innovation has a number of characteristics associated with innovations that have proven to be hard to implement except in areas of high socioeconomic status, a prudent manager might want to see early evidence that the innovation works in a low-SES population. In this way, one could achieve a mixed strategy of not killing good ideas prematurely while not sinking excessive money into projects that are not likely to work in real schooling environments. In the remainder of this chapter, I sketch out a model of how a contextualized evaluation might proceed in the investigation of the effectiveness of technology-supported innovations.

The Basic Scenario

Here is a rough sketch of how this approach might work for educational innovation.

1. A federal agency sponsoring innovative development might convene a *group of project leaders* who have been developing innovative educational technology or other innovative approaches.

2. Depending on the maturity of the innovations to be evaluated, the group might start by developing a *formative evaluation protocol* specifying core data elements and how they should be measured to facilitate sharing of data as the innovations are refined and put into pilot use.

3. Then, working with a previously selected *primary evaluation coordinator*, an investigator selected via a competitive process, the group of project leaders develops a plan for tracking a group of schools, teachers, and students over a multiyear period. The specific variables to be tracked, the basic rules for deciding who is and who remains in the sample, and the basic processes for gathering and maintaining the availability of the data are developed in the collegial atmosphere of this group. The coordinator is responsible for staffing the development of the data-gathering plan and for bootstrapping the process. The coordinator does all the work—but in the context of adapting the *longitudinal data-gathering process* to the needs of the various projects. Projects depend on the longitudinal effort for *context information* to be used in their *specific evaluations of their own innovations* and to track changes in the contexts in which their innovations need to operate.

4. The longitudinal sample becomes a *testbed* within which the various innovations are tested. Each member project makes its sample available for use by a few other projects, thus distributing the data-collection task.

All data are stored in a central repository maintained by the project coordinator. The project leaders group would share information about the evaluations they (or others) do of their innovations and would periodically meet (probably electronically) to decide on *smaller-scale studies* within the same testbed. The purpose of smaller-scale studies would be to confirm patterns evident in the longitudinal context data and perhaps also to refine the longitudinal measures over time.

Sufficient Analyses

It is important to keep in mind that the complete scheme sketched above is complex and expensive and requires a large sample size. This is especially true if multiple measures are to be used to estimate each of the factors deemed to be potentially important in predicting school outcomes. Such an approach may be suited for settling broad policy issues and for tapping the pattern of effects in well-established instances of innovation. However, it is not feasible to perform such complete studies every time a new innovation is first launched. Therefore, the remainder of this chapter focuses on what it is feasible to do routinely as part of the accepted process of developing and trying out an educational innovation.

Feasible Studies That Can Contribute to Policy

Several different kinds of studies are needed in a strong evaluation effort. These include studies of the necessary preconditions under which specific innovations are effective, studies of how contextual variables potentiate changes in each other, descriptive studies, studies of the cost–benefit ratio for components of a complex intervention, and assessments of the maturity of the systems of production for innovations (e.g., the maturity of a software development process).

Studies of Necessary Preconditions

Since educational technology is meant to serve learning goals, the central evaluation question for new innovations must be "What works when?" That is, what are the necessary preconditions needed for the innovation to produce the desired learning outcomes. If the central evaluation question is "What works when?" then it is essential to develop a standard means of specifying the *when* part of this formulation. While public health and education are different, the most useful policy information in both cases is a clear account of problem areas combined with demonstrated means for dealing with those problems conditioned on the overall context in which they occur.

When considering educational innovations, context-specific information has several important uses. First, it can tell us when a particular treatment might work by delineating the conditions under which the innovation has been demonstrated to be successful. Contextual conditions for success can be useful for another purpose as well. If we know something about the landscape of contextual variations, then we can begin to specify what sorts of changes in the implementation plans for an innovation are likely to improve its likelihood of success. For example, suppose that we discover in an evaluation that a certain minimal level of classroom process reform and of technological infrastructure is needed before a particular piece of software is likely to be productive. This would allow school systems interested in using that piece of software to plan the systemic changes needed before the software is likely to be beneficial.

The simplest way to get a rough cut on the preconditions question is to do an evaluation in which the four maturity scales are all used along with a similarly holistic measure of the learning outcome associated with the innovation. This could lead to findings like the following:

- This innovation works, but only when the technological infrastructure maturity is at least at stage 3.
- This innovation generally works, but it will fail if both technological infrastructure maturity and people maturity are low.
- This innovation is generally ineffective, but it can work if classroom process maturity and the maturity of subject-matter content goals are sufficiently high.

One way to make this precondition analysis more powerful would be to include some student input measures in addition to the maturity measures. Combined with the maturity measures, this would provide a usable picture of the preconditions necessary for an innovation to work.

Descriptive Studies

While it is essential to have simple, easily measured variables in order to conduct large-scale evaluations of innovations, it is also necessary to develop detailed models of *why* an innovation works. To do this, it is necessary to observe and document in detail the processes that occur in effective learning environments. Consequently, large-scale quantitative evaluations need to be supplemented by detailed observational studies, in which we can discover what really happens when a particular product is used or when a particular teaching approach is being followed. The intensity of such studies does not permit the large numbers needed to reliably confirm effectiveness, but such rich data are essential to help shape and validate simpler and more efficient evaluation schemes. When a descriptive study suggests a causal model of how an innovation is effective, larger-scale quantitative studies can confirm the basic causal pattern. And when a large-scale study finds a particular relationship between a measured context variable and desired outcomes, descriptive studies can help provide an interpretation of the observed statistical relationship.

One possible list of the kinds of preliminary and mostly observational measures worth gathering has been put forth by Tom Glennan (personal communication, 2000), who was considering how some of the activities of the University of Pittsburgh Institute for Learning might be evaluated, at least at a formative level. Glennan suggested that such a formative evaluation should provide the following types of information:

- A *description* of the intervention over time
- An assessment of the *degree of implementation* of the learning goals on which the work has focused in classrooms and schools over time
- A tracking of *contextual variables* that are likely to affect the levels of implementation or outcomes
- A tracking of *important school outcomes* through time
- An assessment of the reasons for high and low levels of implementation

These kinds of information can be gathered from a mixture of descriptive studies, studies of the effects of degree of implementation, and studies of why implementation is not uniform.

Degree of implementation is always an important factor, though there are pitfalls in assessing it. We can't expect an innovation to work if it isn't used. However, when outcomes are known, it can sometimes happen that the manner in which degree of implementation is measured produces a necessary correlation between degree of implementation and desired outcomes. This occurs when the terms of an implementation include outcome benchmarks. Suppose, for example, that I have a curriculum to produce runners for the 1-mile competition. If I specify the levels of implementation as ability to run a mile in 8 minutes, 7 minutes, and so on down to 5 minutes, I should not be surprised if level of implementation measured this way correlates with the desired outcome of speed for the 1-mile race! While the example seems trivial and extreme, it is not unknown for degree-of-implementation measures to directly or indirectly have necessary correlations with outcome measures.

Cost–Benefit Analyses

One aspect of evaluation that is seldom pursued completely is cost–benefit analysis. Researchers and research-based prototype developers have a tendency to ignore costs in their search for perfect educational paradigms. Often, the resulting products are just too expensive to produce, use, and maintain. Once an innovation has been shown to be effective, an important kind of evaluation is a study of the cost contributed by various product components and features and the learning outcome enhancements that can be attributed to these components. For example, I have developed several intelligent coached apprenticeship environments. Increasingly, those environments contain less student modeling (i.e., tailoring of the advice a student receives to estimates of his or her current knowledge). This is not because I believe that advice should not be tailored but rather because I have not found that the high cost of even modest student modeling is justified by the gains observed so far. In contrast, fidelity to the ongoing context of student work as students attack complex problems (so computer-generated advice is always relevant to what the trainee is thinking about) is also expensive, but it seems to pay off highly. Ideally, such observations would be subject to external assessment. Even a little of this kind of componential cost–benefit analysis would contribute substantially to educational improvement efforts around the country.

WHEN IT REALLY MATTERS

To conclude this chapter, I turn to the issue of what to do when a class of innovations is a serious public candidate for broad implementation. In that circumstance, it seems appropriate to sponsor long-term studies of the effectiveness of that class of innovations. In such studies, innovations should be nominated and selected through a process with wide participation of educational agencies and their professional staff, researchers, and policymakers. For each innovation, specific outcome measures should be developed in consultation with relevant stakeholder communities. In addition, a similar consultative process should be used to develop maturity models and associated scales for content maturity, process maturity, technological infrastructure maturity, and software product maturity.

The studies should be conducted over extended periods, both to permit extended use of the innovations and to track the long-term learning effects they might produce. Such long-term efforts would necessarily require highly efficient data-gathering procedures, that is, measurements that can be made quickly, reliably, and simply. In addition to this "backbone" that would extend over a period of years, microstudies should be conducted throughout the overall study period to better specify appropriate treatment, outcome, and context variables and to confirm findings about the influences of different maturity aspects on each other.

It is likely that a given long-term study would contain microstudies embedded within it, just as happens in the health sector. It is the interaction of these microstudies with the longer-term, broader-based activity that would generate much of the overall value of such an evaluation enterprise.

Study Costs and Benefits of a Longitudinal Context-Sensitive Evaluation of Educational Innovations

A sensible first step would be to gather a small group of experts together to refine the scheme proposed in this chapter, giving special attention (1) to tuning the mechanisms to be politically realistic (with respect to both general public reaction and the social structure of schools) and functional, and (2) to assessing the costs of different aspects of the proposed program.

Set Up a Coordinating Body

In contrast to many funded projects, implementing a systematic long-term evaluation effort will require a combination of competitively funded components and strong collaborations among a number of educational innovators. There are several ways this can happen. One possibility is to stimulate the creation of a separate entity to be the coordinator for the longitudinal effort. This approach is taken in some longitudinal studies in the medical area, such as the National Surgical Adjuvant Breast and Bowel Project (NSABP) (2000), which coordinates a collection of studies of different cancer therapies. The project is a collaboration of more than 300 institutions involved in cancer research. There is a common database and a single register of comparative treatment protocols, but there are dozens of studies, each involving different clinical centers and even different hypotheses about central treatment issues. Major researchers who are involved in a number of the clinical trials are represented in the advisory committees that coordinate the project. By funding various specific clinical trials and providing core funding to operate an operations management center and a biostatistical data center, the National Cancer Institute maintains federal control over how the resources are used.

It would be quite reasonable to place the coordinating center for a similar national educational technology innovation project at a specific institution, so long as the institutional agreement allowed the level of independence that this kind of longitudinal effort requires. It might also be possible to place this coordination and archival maintenance function in the National Center for Education Statistics, but a more plausible approach would be to hold a competition for this coordination center and establish it via a cooperative agreement. This would allow the U.S. Department of Education (or whichever agency is the primary sponsor) to have substantial approval control over the membership on the controlling advisory board for the project. Further, starting with the establishment of the coordination site would simplify other parts of the project, such as the holding of community meetings for investigators interested in using the longitudinal testbed as a base for evaluation of their innovations.

Develop Plans for the Longitudinal Testbed and Selecting Testbed Sites

Once a coordinating center is established, its first charge should be to develop a detailed plan for the longitudinal testbed that is to be the base for the project. Presumably, a preliminary plan for the testbed will have been part of the winning proposal for the coordination center. However, it is important that the final protocols for the longitudinal testbed and the data to be gathered result from a broad consultative process. The coordinating center should hold one or more workshops at which suggestions are made about which systems, classrooms, and students should be included in the longitudinal sample and what data should be gathered at each level.

An important part of the testbed establishment process should be the development of a standard process for obtaining consent from testbed teachers, students, and parents for individual studies. The sponsoring agency should attempt to work out with the U.S. Department of Health and Human Services an arrangement that expedites the consent process and assures both that true informed consent is secured for all studies and that neither participants nor investigators are subjected to redundant paperwork. Parents of disadvantaged students, in particular, are wary of signing forms, and some institutions are excessive in the kind of legalistic wording they require. Clear explanations of what will happen in studies and of parent and student rights are essential; redundant forms, arcane wording, and excessive numbers of forms are not.

Develop the Maturity Models

A critical step is the shaping of the maturity models that will be the basis for much of the testbed. It will require considerable integrative effort to take the shopping list of variables that one or another group would like to have measured in the longitudinal testbed and to group these into maturity scales for which scoring rubrics can be developed. Cooperation and participation of the potential users of the testbed will be critical in this process.

Specify Global Outcome Variables

Certain global outcomes might be desired for all or most innovations. For example, the Flashlight Project (*www.tltgroup.org/programs/flashlight .html*) identified four capabilities that it felt should be produced by the innovations they focused on:

- Being able to apply what was learned in the instructional program (i.e., what was learned was not sterile or shallow—the "graduate" would be seen to use the learning in real situations after completing the instructional program)
- Being able to work in teams
- Being able to use information technology appropriately and creatively in one's work
- Being able to manage one's own process of continuing learning

One could imagine a variety of generic outcomes—in the realm of communications, teamwork, technological skills, and analytic skills—that would be so commonly desired as long-term outcomes that they would be tracked routinely in the same way as the maturity models specified for baseline context.

Gather the First Round of Baseline Data and Develop Scoring Rubrics

The next step is to gather the first round of baseline data. It may be possible to do this in the context of the first innovation evaluations that use the testbed. If the procedures for gathering data are sufficiently clear, then individual investigators who are using the testbed can do some of the gathering of context and outcome data, conceivably even for innovations other than their own. An approach partly of this form is commonly used in major medical studies such as the NSABP discussed above. The medical world's experience suggests that it is extremely important to house all collected data in a central site—the project coordinator should handle this—though the actual center for data storage and analysis need not be in the same institution as the overall project coordination.

Begin Specific Innovation Evaluation Studies

As data accumulate, the testbed will become more valuable for evaluations of specific innovations. An ideal arrangement would have institutions competing for both the funding to conduct evaluation studies and access to the testbed as the site for these evaluations. The project coordinator would determine how many studies can be accommodated during a given period, and first access would be given to funded evaluations chosen through a peer-review process. The project coordinator's advisory group would approve any additional usage of the testbed.

Begin Microstudies of the Testbeds Themselves

The final component of the proposed scheme is to conduct microstudies focused on the context variables being collected from the testbeds. For example, it might emerge that movement to higher maturity levels on one maturity scale predicts subsequent movement to higher levels on another. The project coordination site should conduct systematic data mining aimed at revealing such relationships and should then propose focused studies to follow up on what is discovered. The coordinator could conduct such follow-up studies if relatively short term and low cost, or they could be targets for a funded competition.

CONCLUSION

As a country, we are not very systematic in gathering or preserving data that would help schools to figure out which innovations would serve them and to refine those innovations. But innovation is not unique to education. The medical world, also an area of rapid change, has developed powerful schemes for tracking various health measures over long periods of time. Further, major epidemiological studies and comparative studies of therapies are conducted in ways that maximize the value of the collected data for further research. It is time to bring the evaluation of educational innovations up to the same level of utility.

There are several basic problems in the production and testing of educational innovations that must be considered. These include the following:

- Large-scale data-collection efforts (e.g., the National Longitudinal Study, Third International Mathematics and Science Survey, and National Assessment of Educational Progress) are focused on benchmarking, policymaking, and accountability. Accordingly, they operate under political constraints that limit the kinds of information that can be gathered.
- Educational R&D, while experiencing growth in total federal funding, still tends to be allocated in ways that are fragmentary with respect to which people are involved in any project, how long the project lasts, and which federal entity or foundation is the sponsor. As a result, cumulative data are seldom available about the impact of a particular innovation. And each evaluative effort is idiosyncratic, so even meta-analysis schemes can only speak in the most global terms about effects that are generally highly context specific.

- The cost structure for large-scale studies in which details of learning context are recorded does not match well with the cost structures of relatively small-scale educational innovation efforts, so it is unusual to have evaluation data that include information on contextual requirements.

These problems would not be as critical if we were at a stage in educational R&D where we could produce innovations that worked well in all settings, but we are not. The existing clearinghouses and compendia of data on "what works" contain large numbers of innovations, but we generally do not know what the prerequisite conditions are for any of them. And, as a group, they are not sufficiently coherent that we can say "just do all this stuff and you'll be fine." What is needed is some ability to frame the context within which a given innovation has been shown to be effective, so that school leaders, teachers, and parents can have a sound basis for deciding which innovations to adopt.

A scheme such as that laid out in this chapter would permit systematic progress in educational innovation. It would go a long way toward ending the current situation in which studies conducted under nonstandardized conditions in poorly indexed populations produce competing results that simply confuse decision makers and the public and that produce a popular perception that no progress can be made in improving education except through exhortation and simplistic calls for harder work.

Acknowledgments. This chapter has benefited greatly from conversations I have had with Tony Eichelberger, Thomas Glennan, Gaea Leinhardt, Kevin O'Neill, Lauren Resnick, and Russell Schuh. They removed many of my misconceptions; they are not responsible for those that remain.

REFERENCES

Curtis, B., Hefley, W. E., & Miller, S. (1995). *Overview of the People Maturity Model^{SM}*. Technical Report CMU/SEI-95-MM-01. Pittsburgh, PA: Carnegie Mellon University, Software Engineering Institute.

National Council of Teachers of Mathematics (NCTM). (1989). *Curriculum and evaluation standards for school mathematics*. Reston, VA: National Council of Teachers of Mathematics.

National Surgical Adjuvant Breast and Bowel Project. (Retrieved May 2000 from http://www.nsabp.pitt.edu/)

Pearl, J. (2000). *Causality: Models, reasoning, and inference*. Cambridge, UK: Cambridge University Press.

Resnick, L. B. (1999). Making America smarter. *Education Week, 18*(40), 38–40.
Sibley, P. H. R., & Kimball, C. (1997). *Technology planning: The good, the bad and the ugly.* (Available 2 June 2000: http://www.microsoft.com/education/instruction/articles/planTMM.asp or http://www.edmin.com/article/goodbad2.cfm)
Simmons, W., & Resnick, L. (1993). Assessment as the catalyst of school reform. *Educational Leadership, 50*(5), 11–15.

Chapter 3

Achieving Local Relevance and Broader Influence

Katherine McMillan Culp
Margaret Honey
Robert Spielvogel

This chapter reviews a perspective on evaluation of educational technology that emphasizes the importance of locally valid and locally useful research designs. This perspective builds on our 20 years of experience as researchers at the Center for Children and Technology (CCT), investigating how technologies can best be integrated into high-quality educational environments. More specifically, it builds on our increased focus, over the past 6 years, on understanding how schools, school districts, and state and national educational authorities actually move through the process of investing in and implementing educational technologies.

INVESTIGATING NEW TECHNOLOGIES AT THE CENTER FOR CHILDREN AND TECHNOLOGY

Our work at the CCT brings us into contact with many different types of institutions. We collaborate with school districts, museums, individual teachers, college faculty members, after-school programs, and many others. These relationships take many different forms, but they always require us to value the needs and priorities of those individuals and institutions that are working with us. These partners are the subjects of our research, but they are also equally invested in the research, with questions and goals that exist in a complex relationship to our own questions, goals and interests. These relationships are often complicated, but we believe that they have pushed us, throughout our center's history, to challenge our own beliefs and expectations about how teaching and learning occur. Working closely with practicing educators, administrators, policymakers, and curriculum and tool developers has pushed us, as researchers, to reflect on and question our theoretical and methodological groundings, and to be both explicit and modest in stating the frameworks and assumptions that guide us in our work.

CCT has been asking questions about how technology can best support teaching and learning in K–12 schools and other educational contexts for 20 years. This work and the work of our many colleagues has led us to our current perspective on what is important about infusing technology into K–12 education. We have learned that when student learning does improve in schools that become technology rich, those gains are not caused solely by the presence of technology or by isolated technology–learner interactions. Rather, such changes are the result of an ecological shift and are grounded in a set of changes in the learning environment that prioritize and focus a district's or school's core educational objectives (Hawkins, Spielvogel, & Panush, 1997). For some districts, this may mean a focus on literacy, while for others it may mean using technology to support high-level scientific inquiry. We have seen that technology does not just bring change to a static set of tasks (such as typing on a keyboard instead of writing on paper or searching the Internet rather than an encyclopedia). Rather, technology enhances the communicative, expressive, analytic, and logistical capabilities of the teaching and learning environment.

Technologies offer a range of specific affordances that privilege types of communication, analysis, and expression by students and teachers that are important in two ways. First, technologies can support ways of learning that would otherwise be difficult to achieve. For example, they involve qualities such as dynamic and relevant communication with people outside the classroom; engagement with politically ambiguous or aesthetically challenging visual imagery; and habitual revision and reworking of original student work, written or otherwise. Second, technologies can support activities that are often held up in public discourse as kinds of learning experiences that all students should have the opportunity to achieve in all schools, such as visualizing complex scientific data, accessing primary historical source materials, and representing one's work to multiple audiences. It is this broadly defined quality of technology-rich learning and teaching experiences that we are placing at the core of CCT's research agenda.

We believe that this type of technology use will only happen when technology is viewed, at multiple levels of the educational system, as a set of valuable tools that must be put in the service of a broader vision of school change (Chang et al., 1998; Hawkins et al., 1997; Honey, Carrigg, & Hawkins, 1998). Therefore, a crucial part of an agenda for evaluating the impact of technology on K–12 schools will be committing to a body of work that investigates, establishes, and disseminates research findings that both reflect and speak to the complexity of the daily work of teaching and learning in U.S. schools and school districts. We privilege the creation of descriptive, complex models of the role technology can play in addressing chronic educational challenges. These models must take into account the contingency and the diversity of decision making and practice in schools (Robinson, 1998). They must be models that can help practitioners, policymakers, and the public make informed decisions and hold informed discussions about technology investment and infrastructure development. We believe that in order to accomplish these things, this body of evaluative knowledge must be built, in large part, from explorations of how technologies can help schools and districts respond to locally relevant educational challenges.

The guiding question for this chapter is, "How can researchers act as mediators, synthesizing the findings of locally generated evaluations to inform policy?" This question requires a response that links together two sets of goals: (1) finding scalable and substantive ways to support local school communities in thinking differently about evaluative questions and about evidence; and (2) finding equally substantive and effective ways to synthesize and disseminate local findings to a much broader policy community. Our answer to this question is outlined in a proposal for the development and refinement of a set of mediating strategies that can be used to support local evaluations, and a methodology for synthesizing and generalizing from local evaluation findings to feed into large-scale evaluation studies and to inform policy.

In this chapter we present CCT's Partnership Model of Evaluation. We will describe how it breaks with past research models—including shifts in the research methods that have traditionally been used. We will then describe how CCT has used design experiments to understand how technology innovations are adapted to the complex environments in which learning takes place. In response to our increased awareness of variables such as local educational leadership, funding structures, and the material realities of geography and physical plant, we have rethought the role of design experiments to take into account the complexity of the social factors that influence the school community. These developments have led to CCT's Partnership Model of Evaluation. The chapter culminates with a description of the new partnership approach and its application to evaluating the effectiveness of educational technologies. In this approach, results from locally relevant evaluations are synthesized across local settings in order to get a broader picture of the effects of technology. We outline how a network of intermediary organizations could work to review, synthesize, and generalize from locally generated evaluation studies, producing broad-based findings that could guide large-scale policymaking. We illustrate, with a hypothetical case, how local studies of students' use of technologies in history classes might contribute to a broad understanding of effective uses of technology in this discipline.

AN OVERVIEW OF THE CCT'S PARTNERSHIP MODEL TO EVALUATE EDUCATIONAL TECHNOLOGIES

We believe that evaluation research that is responsive to local concerns, constraints, and priorities can be structured and synthesized to produce knowledge about effective uses of educational technology that has both a high level of face validity within local communities and informs the much larger-scale projects of policymakers.

By building up from many small-scale studies that focus on particular technologies used in the service of particular learning goals and that take local contextual factors into account, researchers can have greater confidence that their findings are capturing relevant local variations, as well as addressing appropriately narrow questions about the particular affordances of particular technologies. Simultaneously, researchers can avoid the risks of action research—such as a lack of generalizability and idiosyncratic research practices—by establishing, through the mediating agency, structures and processes that will guide local research, as well as by conducting rigorous reviews and syntheses of the local findings.

Breaking with Past Research Models

Implicit in the kind of practitioner-focused research we are proposing is a rejection of past research models that treated schooling (at least for the purposes of study) as a "black box." Much of the early research attempting to answer the question "Does technology improve student learning?" eliminated from consideration everything other than the computer itself and evidence of student learning (which in this type of study was usually standardized test scores). Teacher practices, student experiences, pedagogical contexts, and even what was actually being done with the computers—all these factors were bracketed out in one way or another. This was done so that the researcher could make powerful, definitive statements about effects—statements unqualified by the complicated details of actual schooling (Kulik & Kulik, 1991; President's Committee of Advisors on Science and Technology, 1997).

Studies conducted in this way lack local validity, which is an inevitable result of the emphasis put on maximizing generalizability within the scope of individual research projects. By "local validity," we mean a face value, or an apparent relevance and interpretability, to school administrators, teachers, parents, or students reviewing their findings. These practitioners, rather than seeking out the commonalities between the subjects in the study and their own situation, are likely to believe that their school, or classroom, or curriculum is very different from those addressed in the study being reviewed, making research findings not obviously useful.

Such studies are not able to help practitioners understand those salient features of a technology-rich environment that they want to know about in order to translate the findings of that particular study at the classroom level. Educators are rarely either able or willing to replicate practices established as effective by researchers. Rather, they want to build up a body of knowledge that can guide them in making good choices among the options that are locally available to, and politically possible for, them. This requires access to a kind of information that is not established through traditional research designs—information about how the technological intervention fits in with all the other constraints and priorities facing a classroom teacher on any given day. This information is, of course, precisely the material that is excised from (or controlled for) in traditional experimental research paradigms (Norris, Smolka, & Soloway, 1999).

Without an ability to explain *why* one intervention is better than another, evaluation research is, at best, of passing interest to practitioners. The "why" that practitioners are looking for is not a theoretical one but a contextual one—what were the particular conditions of the implementation and what were the contextual factors that interacted with the intervention? Where researchers are motivated to see the commonalities across schools and classrooms, practitioners see difference, and only when research accounts for and acknowledges those differences will the research be relevant to them.

Of course, large-scale and summative evaluations have not traditionally been expected to answer questions about why an outcome occurred. But because both "educational technology" and "education" itself are such huge categories, we believe that only designs that include the "why" from the start will be able to inform decision making about the effectiveness of technology in educational settings.

Shifts in Research Methods

Some parts of the educational technology research community are recognizing that single-variable models tracking linear effects are an ineffective means for capturing an adequate picture of how and why change occurs (and doesn't occur) in schools and for communicating effectively with practitioners about how change might best happen. Consequently, researchers using quantitative techniques are, like their colleagues in other applied social sciences, relying increasingly on more complex research designs. They are combining quantitative and qualitative investigations; qualitative researchers are drawing on the theoretical progress in anthropology and cultural studies to structure more sophisticated questions about educational communities; and quantitative researchers are refining complex approaches to modeling complex situations, such as multidimensional scaling techniques (Rumberger, Chapter 8, this volume).

Some of these researchers in the educational technology community are increasingly interested in establishing theories which explain technology's effects, and not use of correlational studies to document what is working (diSessa, 2000). DiSessa points toward the need in technology evaluation research for better definition of the intervention (which technologies, how and why?), for more elaborated theoretical models of the imagined impact (how, exactly, is technology in general expected to improve learning and under what related conditions?), and for more strongly grounded arguments about the relationship between the intervention and the goal stated (how can we articulate an adequately complex model of the roles different types of computer use play in improvements in schooling?). The speed and scope of the introduction of digital technologies into schools have made it particularly difficult for researchers to develop the conceptual, theoretical, and methodological tools necessary to respond adequately to these challenges. But past research has clearly demonstrated our need for these tools by exposing the complexity of the technology integration process and the need to identify effective technology use as embedded in a larger process of school change.

This need for better frameworks, and the need for those frameworks to be derived from context-sensitive and application-oriented research, is echoed in Schoenfeld's broader discussion of the need "to think of research and applications in education as synergistic enterprises rather than as points at opposite ends of a spectrum, or as discrete phases of a 'research leads to applications' model" (Schoenfeld, 1999, p. 14). Schoenfeld describes the importance of putting research and practice in a dialectic with each other and the need for better theoretical elaborations of the complex social systems interacting in educational systems and of the conceptual units under study in research (such as curriculum, assessment strategies, and processes of change) (Schoenfeld, 1999). Each of these needs exists in the educational technology research community as well and, we argue, can best be met by moving, as Schoenfeld describes, toward research that seeks to link together the knowledge-building enterprise of research and its application to the challenges of educational practice.

We should be clear that we are not claiming that other approaches to evaluation research, such as large-scale controlled experimental studies, are impossible to conduct in working school environments. Further, we certainly concede the value of incremental knowledge building through systematic, controlled study of well-defined interactions with particular technologies. The mistake lies not in conducting this research but in relying on it exclusively, or even primarily, to guide effective decision making about investment in and implementation of technology in working educational environments.

Where We Want to Go Next

Past research has made it clear that technologies by themselves have little scalable or sustained impact on learning in schools. Indeed, the very urgency of the desire to find some way to produce these large, powerful statistical effects speaks to the inability of our community, so far, to produce such evidence. However, rather than further refining our experimental methods and analytic approaches in an attempt to achieve experimental success, we argue that it is far more appropriate and effective to confront the realities of schooling that have been so impervious to the requirements and constraints of experimental approaches.

It is clear that, to be effective, innovative and robust technological resources must be used to support systematic changes in educational environments. These systematic changes must take into account simultaneous changes in administrative procedures, curricula, time and space constraints, school–community relationships, and a range of other logistical and social factors (Fisher, Dwyer, & Yocam, 1996; Hawkins et al., 1997; Means, 1994; Sabelli & Dede, 2001; Sandholtz, Ringstaff, & Dwyer, 1997). Consequently, our approach to evaluation must respond to, rather than control, these complex aspects of schooling. As Jan Hawkins, a former director of CCT, wrote: "Rather than viewing interactive technologies as independent instruments with powers in themselves to reform schooling, our aim is to understand how to adapt them as coordinated components of new educational landscapes" (quoted in Hawkins & Collins, n.d.).

The pressure to learn more about how technologies contribute to student learning continues to build. However, there is a somewhat contradictory growth in popular understanding that technology is a crucial player in a complex process of change that cannot be accomplished by technological fixes alone. We believe that administrators, school boards, and many other stakeholders in this debate are far more open to alternative, and more realistic, explanations of the role technology can play in their schools than those that would be established by narrow proofs of the impact of specific technologies on specific student competencies. We believe that these stakeholders can best be spoken to by researchers who are asking questions about the following:

- How technology is integrated into educational settings
- How new electronic resources are interpreted and adapted by their users
- How best to match technological capacities with students' learning needs
- How technological change can interact with and support changes in other aspects of the educational process, such as assessment, administration, communication, and curriculum development

The remainder of this chapter takes two steps toward describing how the educational technology research community might establish more locally valid evaluations of impact, while also beginning to generate findings that could be both more persuasive at the policy level and more useful at the local level. We first describe an approach to conducting locally focused research that we are currently pursuing at our own center, which we call "partnership research." We then outline a vision for a national organizational infrastructure that could serve as a mediating presence for practitioners, researchers, and policymakers, both synthesizing locally grounded research to inform policy and supporting critical consumption of research information among practitioners.

PARTNERSHIP RESEARCH: MAKING EVALUATION MAKE SENSE ON THE GROUND

Our Starting Point: Design Experiments

CCT has historically worked on projects at the intersection of technology and school reform. The fundamental objective is to use technology to continually deepen student learning. The more we know about technology and learning, however, the more we understand how difficult achieving this objective is in actuality, given the institutional complexities of school communities. We believe that acknowledging this reality is crucial to constructing a successful research agenda that will truly allow us to understand the impact of technology in education. We believe that multiple research strategies must be brought to the table and that a strong presence in that mix must be research that begins from, rather than elides, the diversity of schools— not only in the populations they serve but in their practices, constraints, priorities, and available resources. This reality is not going to change—it is the way schools are and probably should be. Therefore, we must construct research and dissemination paradigms and practices that incorporate an accurate, rather than a wishful, definition of the object of our study—real, and messy, schools, teachers and students.

CCT's emphasis on seeking to understand the process of technology integration at the local level began from an academic interest in understanding the importance of social context in structuring and guiding students' learning. Our first systematic foray into addressing this issue was a series of research studies we called "design experiments," which were conducted between 1988 and 1993 as part of our work as the national Center on Technology in Education (funded by the U.S. Department of Education). In these studies we sought to understand how small teams of teachers, tailoring particular technological tools to fit into their project-based curricula, would move through the process of integrating technology into their teaching and how their students would make use of and learn from that technology-enriched curriculum. It is important to locate this work historically—at the time, technologically rich and educationally substantive learning environments were almost nonexistent and were typically unavailable in schools without the intervention of a researcher. We rarely if ever encountered a teacher who had appropriated complex technological tools into his or her own teaching without a strong initial partnership with a research group.

Starting from the local level—understanding the social context of use— was the task we pursued in this series of studies. We can most easily define design experiments by quoting at length from Hawkins & Collins (n.d.; see also Brown, 1992):

> Technology provides us with powerful tools to try out different designs so that instead of theories of education we may begin to develop a design science of education. The creation of a design science of education requires selecting and testing the most promising designs and elucidating how different designs contribute to these qualities of effective education (cf. Collins, 1990). Unlike the analytic sciences (e.g. physics or psychology), our approach more resembles design sciences like aeronautics or artificial intelligence. In aeronautics, for example, the goal is to elucidate how different designs contribute to lift, drag, maneuverability, and so forth. Similarly, a design science of education must determine how different designs of learning environments contribute to key qualities of effective learning. This design science must also take into account the interpretive nature of adapting innovations to the complex social settings in which learning takes place. (p. 8)

We and others learned a great deal from the design experiments (Means & Olson, 1995). Two of our key lessons were that (1) even under the watch of the most well-intentioned teacher, inequities related to race and gender persist in students' access to and ways of using the technology and (2) intensively supported, well-designed, technology-rich curriculum units, even when they are successful, do not necessarily spur teachers into becoming habitual users of technology throughout the curriculum.

Technological Changes

We have also learned a great deal since the conclusion of the design experiments, and the world around us has changed a great deal as well. Key technological changes since that time include the following:

1. Making technologies available in every classroom has become part of the national agenda, and they are consequently far more present in schools than they were prior to the advent of the Universal Service Fund for Schools and Libraries (E-Rate) in 1997.
2. The Internet has dramatically altered educator perceptions of the relevance and usefulness of technology in the classroom. Schools, which have always suffered from a scarcity of resources, can now get their hands on vast amounts of information and "learning opportunities."
3. The communications capabilities of the Internet make possible a whole range of collaborative work among educators.
4. The production and distribution capabilities of the Internet and other media have dramatically changed the potential relationship between students and their audiences.

These changes have both raised the stakes of research on educational technology and diversified how technologies are being used in the classroom. Both of these consequences have greatly increased the complexity of the research issues that we are seeking to address.

Partnership

There are elements of our approach to design experiment research that we have now significantly rethought. First, while design experiment research teams viewed themselves as "partners" with school personnel, the definition of the problem and the scope of the technological intervention were, in fact, largely determined by the outside research team. The resources, knowledge, and interests of school personnel in relation to educational technology have diversified greatly since the 1988–1993 period. Further, the political context—specifically, the current emphasis on "accountability" and high-stakes testing—has led schools to be, of necessity, far more self-determining in their definitions of their priorities, interests, and goals for student learning. Our theoretically driven vision of what constitutes "good" learning can no longer be imposed on schools uniformly as a condition of improvement, nor can researchers assume that effective learning is something the cognitive research community is well positioned to educate schools about.

The design experiments were also conceptualized as a step in the creation of a "design science of education." This "design science" was built on a highly iterative engineering model that focused on the improvement of the technological innovation, privileging the technological object over the classroom context, curriculum, and teaching practices. What we have learned since then is that the particular details of the technological tool are generally of far less importance in determining the success of the innovation than are social factors, such as local interpretation of the innovation, and outside constraints, such as pressures to improve test scores. Collins (1990) did emphasize that technologies were not to be expected to improve learning on their own but to become a part of a way of working—of teaching and of learning—that would facilitate the really important process, which was one of defining and pursuing a shared set of substantive and locally relevant learning objectives. This is a process that will always be fundamentally about people and involves building a set of shared understandings through long-term collaborative work. Consequently, we now see the engineering metaphor underlying the design experiments as less than ideal and prefer the more interpersonally focused metaphor of coaching.

Broadening and Deepening Our Understanding

Although the design experiments sought to address schoolwide change, in reality they typically studied a small group of teachers and classrooms within a single school. Because of the explosion of interest in technology throughout American society and in schools since the time of our design experiment work, we have since come to understand what it truly means to attempt to understand technology integration systemically. We now recognize the importance, and the difficulty, of looking across entire districts and even states to understand how the impact of technology in schools is mediated and largely determined by local educational leadership and vision, funding structures, school board politics, and material realities of geography and physical plant. While these topics seem far from the world of cognitive research that drives much of the evaluation work around educational technology, it has been made painfully clear to us that, again, these issues are core to the definition of the object of study in this field and that to ignore them is to design research that is flawed from the outset.

At the same time, we have also come to appreciate the importance of building-level priorities in shaping educational agendas and definitions of achievement and learning for students. Different schools have very different educational priorities and different educational constraints, and understanding what will and will not work in schools requires listening carefully to find out what the school community identifies as indicators of success. This process can perhaps be understood as one of diagnosis—an interpretive or deductive identification of how particular local qualities are working together. This image of diagnostic work is quite different from a more typical approach to educational research, which relies on experimental methods to identify what is uniform, consistent, or generalizable across schools.

Creating a New Approach

What we have preserved from the design experiments is a privileging of examining *types* of technology use that match some of the most promising affordances of technology with some of the most intractable problems facing educators. This level of examination is a midpoint between fine-grained studies of student learning with particular software tools and broad, generic evaluations of "the impact of technology" that group all technological objects as a single form of intervention and create some broad outcome indicator, which is typically disappointingly difficult to change. For example, we have a sustained interest in working with history teachers to explore how digitized primary source materials, combined with authoring tools, can best support sustained historical inquiry among high school students and in collaborating with science teachers to explore how simulation and modeling tools can support students in understanding complex, multivariate interactions in complex systems. In each of these situations, a particular set of technological affordances—manipulating previously unavailable historical resources, or visualizing and manipulating data representing physical phenomena—are well matched to specific teaching and learning challenges that are persistent and familiar to teachers.

However, even these relatively well-defined topics cannot be studied in isolation, apart from the school context in which teaching and learning are occurring. The extension and enrichment of learning—through activities such as those just described—consistently encompass two issues of systemic sustainability: helping teachers reflect and expand on their own practices and scaling up innovative uses of technology to the larger school community. We have learned through our work with a variety of schools that numerous factors influence a school's ability to use technology effectively for student learning. These factors include the following:

- Leadership and vision at multiple levels of the system
- School- and districtwide goals and expectations for the use of technology in the classroom context
- School culture and climate
- Teachers' beliefs about students and their potential for learning
- Ongoing professional development for teachers

- Teachers' prior experience with technology
- Availability of technology resources (both infrastructure and human) in the school

Schools attempting to undertake broad-based programs of educational reform and restructuring face a great number of challenges. Schools are being asked to implement higher standards for all students and at the same time to meet state proficiencies in a number of core subject areas. Well-designed and thoughtfully deployed technologies need to be enlisted as essential partners in the reform process. CCT's research and development work in this area focuses on the ways in which schools can use technological tools to do the following:

- Deepen subject-matter teaching and learning
- Support and sustain the ongoing professional development of teachers
- Build communities of learners that extend the traditional boundaries of learning in schools
- Analyze and reflect on a wider range of evidence so that administrators and teachers can develop a broader vision of accountability and performance
- Develop analytical skills that cultivate students' ability to perform the essential analytical, communicative, and authoring tasks made possible by digital media

How, then, can we do this locally relevant research? Building on our experience with the design experiment work and other projects, we need to define a set of strategies for developing collaborative research projects with schools that are neither research for research's sake nor direct service. We are trying to define a "third way" between being academic researchers and being service providers that has the following characteristics:

- Collaborations with teachers and administrators are at the core of the process of defining research and innovation.
- The research grows out of felt needs and important challenges that districts and schools are facing.
- The collaboration sets goals that are both practical and generalizable— that are helpful to the immediate community and informative to the larger community.
- As researchers, we benefit from the process by being consistently exposed to, challenged by, and forced to learn from the complexities of real school situations.
- Educators benefit by gaining experience in using reflective, critical lenses on their own experiences to learn about the strengths and weak-

nesses of their current practices and to identify paths toward successful change.

This kind of partnership research has the advantage of privileging the
knowledge that both entities bring to the task at hand and allowing for variation in school culture to inform work. It puts process first, and, unlike the
design experiments, is not looking for strategies that at the outset are going
to lead to uniformity of information across sites. This is not to say, however, that this kind of extrapolation can't take place after the fact—in fact,
we now understand this to be crucial.

We have also learned, though we sometimes forget, that we need to
balance our respect for local realities with a clear and explicit statement of
the base of knowledge that we, as researchers, are working from. CCT's
perspective on teaching and learning remains constructivist and rooted in
our early years as a part of Bank Street College of Education. As such, it
includes a set of beliefs about how learning occurs and about how technology can support learning. First, learning is understood broadly, as the ability to use one's mind well in framing and solving open-ended problems in
original ways and in coordinating complex activities with others. Collaboration among students is privileged; students help each other to learn, and
they share data and knowledge in ways that model the work of real scientists and other communities of learners. Teachers play crucial roles in selecting goals and materials and act as guides and intellectual coaches to students.
Teachers make broad subject-matter decisions, but students, who also play
a role in determining performance criteria, make more local decisions.

Technology's role in this context is to serve as a catalyst and support for
an extended classroom inquiry that is open ended and "messy," involving
guessing, debate, and multiple materials. It is integrated with other tools and
media, as students learn using many different resources—including books,
libraries, museums, videos, and adult experts—in the school and beyond.

A DESIGN FOR THE FUTURE

We propose the creation of a network of technology evaluation teams.
These teams could be located in each state, or regions of large states, in already existing entities such as the Regional Technology Assistance Centers.
Each team would be made up of researchers focused on a set of thematic or
disciplinary areas identified as high priorities within the larger project of
determining the effectiveness of technology in education. For example, we
would initially propose the following thematic areas:

- English as a second language: How can technology effectively support multilingual students in effective communication and mastery of written and spoken English?
- Early grades literacy: How can technology effectively support emergent reading and writing skills?
- Middle and high school humanities and social sciences: How can technology effectively support critical thinking, writing, and interpretation across a wide range of content areas?
- Early and middle grades science: How can technologies help students develop empirical skills, acquire analytic concepts such as categorization, and begin to conduct scientific inquiry?
- High school science: How can technology support the analysis of complex systems and the pursuit of scientific inquiry?

The role of the area specialists would be multiple and would include the following:

- Synthesizing the existing and emerging research in their domain, both with regard to technology specifically and in the educational area more broadly, and disseminating that knowledge
- Deriving, and iteratively modifying, key research questions within their thematic area
- Creating templates for research methods and instruments and sharing them with local researchers
- Supporting local researchers in their work
- Collecting and reviewing the results of local research
- Synthesizing local research with reference to key research questions, in collaboration with other area specialists working in other technology evaluation teams across the country

This "area specialist" role would likely require a team of researchers, some more skilled in providing technical assistance to local researchers and others more skilled in meta-analytic techniques that would allow them to synthesize across large numbers of local research studies.

Our organization and many others like us are already being called upon to play this role informally. It requires sharing with local educators a set of processes that can become embedded within the operations of a school, a district, or some programmatic effort. Its primary purpose is to support local participants in a complex ecology undergoing change, such as a district's integration of information and communications technologies, by generating valid and robust findings about the effectiveness of their investments.

An important, but secondary, goal is the synthesis of findings like these, collected from multiple sources. Synthesis will initially focus on generating more refined hypotheses about the conditions affecting successful implementations and outcomes within the various high-priority areas. Gradually synthesis will be able to focus in on the identification of emerging patterns and conclusions about the interrelationship of various contextual factors and the technological intervention. These emerging results can then be shared with practitioners and subjected to further study under the mechanisms described above, leading to either verification or practical guidelines (Baker & Herman, Chapter 4, this voume; Lesgold, Chapter 2, this volume).

Given this premise for supporting and utilizing evaluation, there are several functions that need to be performed by the research entity:

- Developing a body of processes and tools for producing evidence of impact on learning, teaching, and organizational functioning at the near, mid, and far term
- Sharing and exchanging these methodologies with other researchers and mediating organizations
- Standardizing some of the specific methodologies so that compilation and synthesis can be done across environments
- Providing assistance to schools (or informal education institutions) in framing outcome indicators that are relevant to the organization, its use of technology, and its main goals and aspirations
- Working with the organization to put in place instrumentation of various sorts to provide ongoing feedback that can triangulate information relevant to the identified indicators
- Analyzing the information jointly with the partner organization and creating mechanisms for sharing the analysis with stakeholders in the organization
- Combining the emerging information from multiple organizations that are working on similar problems or within similar ecologies to get a broader picture.

An organization playing this mediating role can also serve as an intermediary in the implementation of other, large-scale research initiatives. For example, key survey questions being asked across a large sample could be added to surveys being used in various early grades literacy studies by the technology evaluation teams, and results could be shared with other institutions conducting other types of studies.

The mediating strategy implied by this structure is different from both traditional research approaches and the strategies of existing outreach organizations. While it contributes to and helps spread large-scale results, it performs a more immediate role of helping to ensure that local practices are infused with the capacity to collect and leverage information directly relevant to the utilization of technology within their specific context. This model greatly speeds up the time it takes for research to get back to practitioners while also increasing the amount of research with a high degree of specificity and face validity that is available to the policymaking community.

A Possible Scenario

A history teacher from Washington High School has attended a summer workshop at the Library of Congress about using digitized primary source material in his American history class. This teacher, Mr. Smith, is very concerned because while his students do learn the basic facts of American history, they are not acquiring a strong ability to ask critical questions about history or to think about how historical narratives are established. In his summer workshop, he created a 2-week unit on post–Civil War migration patterns in the United States. The unit requires students to examine newspaper articles, photographs, and journals from the period that are available at the Library of Congress website. He then guides students through a process of analysis and interpretation that leads to a final product of a small website in which students present their competing views of the period, using the artifacts from the Library of Congress as evidence for their conclusions.

Mr. Smith is excited about this unit and is hopeful that it will contribute to an improvement in his students' ability to think critically about historical narratives. His department chair is interested in the new ideas Mr. Smith has brought back to the school, but he is dubious that all of the students who take American history will be able to do such sophisticated work. Mr. Smith and the department chair begin to discuss how they might figure out whether it is worthwhile for them to support all of the other history teachers in using this unit with their students and perhaps even offer districtwide workshops.

Mr. Smith looks at the Department of Education website, wondering whether he might find guidance there about how to answer the questions he has about the effectiveness of this unit. He finds a link to a number of technology evaluation teams, each focused on a different topic. He goes to the humanities area within the technology evaluation network and finds a series of reports on promising applications of technology in the history classroom. He also finds a set of benchmarks for student learning that draw on the National History Standards, rubrics for scoring student work in history, sample surveys for teachers and for students, and guidelines for beginning to design the kind of investigation he is interested in. He discovers that if he is willing to document his work and write up what he finds, he can join a network of other humanities teachers in his part of his state who are investigating similar questions. This group meets regularly with the humanities adviser from his local technology evaluation team, who works with them to design, conduct, and draw conclusions from their research.

Over the course of the year, Mr. Smith and his department chair, with support from their network, collect student-learning data from four American history classes that have used the unit that Mr. Smith created. They find that these students are able to formulate good critical questions about history. When they look at schoolwide data from the standardized tests that they use, they find that this is an area where their students typically do very poorly. They find this encouraging, but it also raises new questions—how much did these students' improvements have to do with the novelty of the task or with the particular teachers they had? They are already devising new studies to carry out next year to learn more. However, their initial results were encouraging enough to convince their district technology coordinator to allocate more powerful, Internet-ready computers to all of the humanities classrooms for the next schoolyear.

Alternative Scenario

Now consider the same scenario from the point of view of the humanities coordinator for that local technology evaluation team. This researcher considers her main job to be accumulating the best possible evidence from schools in her region to help the national humanities team determine how technology can most effectively be used to support high achievement among students, as measured against the National History Standards. She is pleased when Mr. Smith joins her network, because she knows that a number of teachers from other parts of the country who have taken the same workshop at the Library of Congress have already conducted evaluations of their own. She shares their strategies and tools with Mr. Smith and helps him to conduct an appropriate study. When his write-up is delivered and is lacking in detail, she makes a trip to his school and spends a day collecting all of the contextual information she needs about the students he teachers, the kinds of curriculum standards that are used in the school, and so on.

This researcher shares her own summary of Mr. Smith's findings with her counterparts in other technology evaluation teams around the country. They have found, so far, that many projects similar to Mr. Smith's can lead to improvements in students' ability to think critically about historical narratives and historical source material. But they are now trying to determine how robust that effect is and what contextual factors are most important in creating that effect. One of their main debates this spring has been whether or not to require all of their local practitioner partners to involve their colleagues in a brief survey that would allow them to collect some background information on these teachers that would make it easier to draw conclusions across the many different sites.

The eventual goal of the humanities-area specialists is to create a summary report on the promise of this type of technology-rich activity that will go to policymakers and will explain that, with particular contextual supports in place (such as teachers with adequate training with the tools and substance of the project) but regardless of other factors (such as students' previous exposure to technology), this activity is an effective response to an educational problem—supporting high-level historical thinking—that has previously seemed solvable only in the most sophisticated and resource-rich high schools. Their group will most likely then move on to a new set of questions, determined by emerging new technologies, new interests among their network of practitioners, or interests expressed by policymakers.

CONCLUSION

This example glosses over many of the details and complexities of each individual research situation. But those complexities are exactly the challenge that researchers need to take on in evaluating the impact of technology in education. By inviting practitioners into the process of discovering what does and doesn't make a difference in their classrooms, we will both increase the validity of the research and engage teachers in a critical examination of practice that will encourage effective applications of technology and discourage unthinking adoption of ineffective innovations.

Making visible the processes of change that are required to make technology investments make a difference in schooling is an enormous challenge, but it is important. The pedagogical changes, the shifts in classroom practice, and all the other changes that need to be funded, supported, and developed at the school level cannot be elided if the research is to be meaningful or have sustained impact.

REFERENCES

Brown, A. L. (1992). Design experiments: Theoretical and methodological challenges in creating complex interventions in classroom settings. *The Journal of the Learning Sciences, 2*(2), 141–178.

Chang, H., Henriquez, A., Honey, M., Light, D., Moeller, B., & Ross, N. (1998). *The Union City story: Education reform and technology—Students' performance on standardized tests.* Technical report. New York: EDC/Center for Children and Technology.

Collins, A. (1990). *Toward a design science of education.* Technical report. New York: EDC/Center for Children and Technology.

diSessa, A. A. (2000). *Changing minds: Computers, learning and literacy.* Cambridge, MA: MIT Press.

Fisher, C., Dwyer, D., & Yocam, K. (Eds.). (1996). *Education and technology: Reflections on computing in classrooms.* San Francisco: Jossey-Bass.

Hawkins, J., & Collins, A. (Eds.) (n.d.). *Design experiments: Integrating technologies into restructure schools.* Unpublished manuscript.

Hawkins, J., Spielvogel, R., & Panush, E. (1997). *National study tour of district technology integration summary report.* Technical report. New York: EDC/Center for Children and Technology.

Honey, M., Carrigg, F., & Hawkins, J. (1998). Union City online: An architecture for networking and reform (pp. 121–140). In C. Dede (Ed.), *The 1998 ASCD yearbook: Learning with technology.* Alexandria, VA: Association for Supervision and Curriculum Development.

Kulik, C., & Kulik, J. (1991). Effectiveness of computer-based instruction: An updated analysis. *Computers and Human Behavior, 7,* 75–94.

Means, B. (Ed.). (1994). *Technology and education reform.* San Francisco: Jossey-Bass.

Means, B., & Olson, K. (1995). *Technology's role in education reform.* Menlo Park, CA: SRI International.

Norris, C., Smolka, J., & Soloway, E. (1999). *Convergent analysis: A method for extracting the value from research studies on technology in education.* Commissioned paper for the Secretary's Conference on Educational Technology, July, 1999. Washington, DC: U.S. Department of Education.

President's Committee of Advisors on Science and Technology, Panel on Educational Technology. (1997). *Report to the president on the use of technology to strengthen K–12 education in the United States.* Washington, DC: U.S. Government Printing Office.

Robinson, V. M. J. (1998). Methodology and the research-practice gap. *Educational Researcher, 27*(1), 17–26.

Sabelli, N., & Dede, C. (2001). *Integrating educational research and practice: Reconceptualizing the goals and policies: "How to make what works, work for us."* (Available: http://www.virtual.gmu.edu/ss_research/cdpapers/policy.pdf)

Sandholtz, J., Ringstaff, C., & Dwyer, D. (1997). *Teaching with technology: Creating student-centered classrooms.* New York: Teachers College Press.

Schoenfeld, A. H. (1999). Looking toward the 21st century: Challenges of educational theory and practice. *Educational Researcher, 28*(7), 4–14.

Chapter 4

A Distributed Evaluation Model

Eva L. Baker
Joan L. Herman

The purpose of this chapter is to consider the reciprocal relationship between evaluation and the educational use of technology, with an eye toward improving both endeavors. We intend to do this by focusing first on the purposes and challenges involved in the evaluation of technological advances intended for use in education and training settings. Here we will explicitly describe the broad range of purposes thought to be served by formal evaluations. We will also briefly consider common approaches to technology evaluation and reflect on their strengths and limitations. In particular, we will review questions related to the overall conceptions of evaluation guiding such studies, the evaluation designs appropriate to constraints of technology development and use, the quality of measures, and the validity of inferences ultimately drawn from evaluation studies. We will treat each of these subareas in medium depth.

After laying bare the limits of familiar evaluation approaches, we will outline a model of technology evaluation that might be considered to be an evolution of current practice. The approach, *distributed evaluation*, will be described in relation to its likely sensitivity to the range of known and unknown technological innovations, its focus on simultaneous data interpre-

The work reported herein was supported under the Educational Research and Development Centers Program, PR/Award Number R305B60002, as administered by the Office of Educational Research and Improvement, U.S. Department of Education. The findings and opinions expressed in this report do not reflect the positions or policies of the National Institute on Student Achievement, Curriculum, and Assessment, the Office of Educational Research and Improvement, or the U.S. Department of Education.

tation by multiple users, its reliance on an indicators approach to data configuration, and its dependence on technology. We will also acknowledge areas of uncertain effects and other potential risks of this approach. Throughout, we will provide examples of what we mean in order to stimulate full consideration of this and other alternatives.

EVALUATING TECHNOLOGY: WHY?

To the layperson, the formal examination of the impact of technology may seem to be largely a make-work endeavor. With the dizzying array of new technological options, the rapid expansion of functions served by software and devices, and the head-snapping obsolescence of platforms, operating systems, and programs, much important evaluation gets conducted on the fly by individual adopters. Consumer evaluation, a daily occurrence using multiple criteria and contexts, leads to broadly generalizable and actionable interpretations in the realms of customer satisfaction, types of use, choice, and competitive advantage of products. Clean designs are not needed for this kind of work. In fact, the tension caused by the remarkable speed of technological change has raised huge questions about the fit of evaluation (and other research) methods and technology as an object or process of study.

PURPOSES OF EVALUATIONS

Formal evaluation of technology nonetheless remains an enterprise with considerable support. Let us look at some of the reasons such evaluations continue to be of interest and review the interlocking purposes that they serve.

Soothe and Rationalize

Some evaluations of technology may be undertaken because of the need to soothe the anxiety of the older generation of decision makers, those more suspicious of newfangled stuff. There are a significant number of educators who still regard technology as an added attraction rather than as a part of the main feature. They may be partly right because of the persistent paucity of high-quality curriculum supporting goals for which schools and students are rewarded. Technology should come to be considered a routine part of the modern world of education, almost rivaling math problems and lunch. Evaluation may always be needed to rationalize large and recurring expenditures of resources; and technology, technology support services, and various applications appear to be relatively expensive, especially when they are compared to other nonsalary categories of cost. Evaluations of this sort may be conducted and almost immediately filed away, to be recalled in the event that investments are challenged.

Broad Media Contrast

One frequent purpose of technology evaluation is pertinent to a most general question: What is the evidence that educational technology is better than no technology? This question has a summative ring to it (Bloom, Hastings, & Madaus, 1971; Scriven, 1974); that is, answers to such a question will guide general propensities as well as decisions about whether to adopt or not to adopt a set of particular practices. In the case of technology, these practices may involve not simply a program but the creation of an environment that will support, presumably, a wide and changing range of implementations. Policymakers remain interested in the comparative effects of technological interventions with present practice. They persist in this desire despite the decades-old analyses identifying the logical flaw in studies focused on comparisons of one or more media with some type of poorly defined but available form of present practice (Hovland, Lumsdaine, & Sheffield, 1949; Leifer, 1976; Lumsdaine, 1965). Because the important part of the "treatment" is often not what is most salient (a keyboard and screen) but rather what is embedded in the software (a type of instructional strategy in a particular set of content), interventions are usually confounded and, as a result, inferences about effectiveness may be in error.

In any case, most inferences cannot wholly apply to the entire class of media. Designs to show computer technology to be superior to lecture or television in general are not valid because studies sampling the full range of implementations could not be done. Even with randomized, experimental designs, people could, at best, infer that *in the past* results favored one particular treatment compared with another. Generalization beyond that statement, especially to new kinds of technology, is logically impossible.

With the advent of the use of meta-analytic approaches (Glass, McGaw, & Smith, 1981), a more powerful tool became available to answer in a general sense the question of impact about a class of interventions, such as tutoring, bilingual programs, or technology. Retrospective looks across a range of studies became possible, and a way of counting up the positives and negatives grew in acceptance. Meta-analysis summarizes across many studies, each of which embodies a particular view of the intervention (for instance, computer-based instruction) and procedures for defining the variables, the context, and the control or comparison groups. Although individual studies vary in terms of their rigor, size of differences, designs, quality of measures, and so on, meta-analyses of technology nonetheless have had some impact on the overall debate (Fletcher, 1990; Kulik, 1994). These studies helped in answering general questions about impact on students and have been useful in the continuing discussion about technology effects. Yet, because they are necessarily dependent on an available set of prior studies, they point in a general direction. Given the rapid developments in the field, meta-analytic studies, relying as they do on retrospective summaries, show their age rather rapidly, and their relevance similarly decays. Even though meta-analysis provides a handy tool, its availability does not supplant the requirements for careful design of evaluations directed to the impact of specific technological interventions. In fact, future meta-analyses will be strengthened by careful attention to such studies.

Evaluating Effects of Particular Implementations

In addition to general comparisons, evaluations often have the purpose of investigating the quality and effects of competitive implementations so that decisions can be made to expand or contract services of a particular category. These evaluations (also summative evaluations, in the sense of Scriven, 1974) may be focused on an impending decision and may use both implementation and outcome data. Because of vagaries of evaluation design and choice of measures, many of these studies have not lived up to their potential utility.

There are, of course, continuing legitimate interests in evaluating the impact of specific interventions, with the goal to tie technology investment to student performance. Support for such studies grows in part from that necessary evil, the overstatement and overpromising to boards or legislators that occur in the plea for significant new resources. It is natural for such oversight groups to be interested in effects obtained so as to verify the legitimacy of original claims and perhaps to assess the credibility of proponents. The cycle of exaggerated promises and weak findings is not unique to technological innovation in education; it is unfortunately a feature of most reform cycles, a side effect of our funding mechanisms. Perhaps it is time to raise the question of whether technology investment should be treated in the same way as any other intervention—for example, expanded summer school funding. Is it wise for policymakers to treat technology in this way? Probably not. However, for the most part, it is still the case that policymakers feel the need for formal evaluations of technology because of the annual surprise—that outcomes didn't meet claims.

Implementation

Technology evaluation is usually undertaken to determine the particular impact of technology on students, in a particular subject area, or as a piece of a larger set of program elements. To interpret effects, the actual use of the technology or system needs to be examined. How do the technology, systems, or software actually get used? Many such questions of implementation can be raised. For instance, is there truly differential access of subgroups based on socioeconomic class to technology (Wenglinsky, 1998)? Even if the problem rapidly diminishes in the light of reduced prices, it remains a significant ethical concern nonetheless and a key question involving implementation decisions. A second type of implementation evaluation emphasizes understanding the relationship between processes (as implemented) and obtained outcomes. Of particular interest are the explicit interactions of technology with teachers' and students' behaviors. A companion concern to the earlier question of differential access to technology by student groups is whether there is differential use of technology by significant subgroups of students and the relationship of such use and outcomes.

Evaluation studies targeting technology implementation have been handled in a number of ways, all with their own unique difficulties. These include studies of the degree of implementation using a particular plan or strategy (e.g., Chung, O'Neil, & Herl, 1999; Herl, O'Neil, Chung, & Schacter, 1999; Klein, Yarnall, & Glaubke, 2003; Schacter, Herl, Chung, Dennis, & O'Neil, 1999), analysis of the level of implementation using a model such as Kirkpatrick's (1994), or, most frequently, reports of simple descriptions of technology use: what it has been used for and whether the respondents are pleased or dissatisfied with it for particular purposes. The great preponderance of technology evaluation studies to date depend on relatively weak survey measures of implementation—single-item scales, for instance, that rely on the self-report of members of user groups.

There are obviously other, more powerful ways to investigate implementation. One strategy requires a frank look at an obvious enabling condition for any study of implementation: Did the technology stuff get to where it needed to be on time and in usable form? Embarrassing stories abound, and many carefully designed evaluations of technology are unable to obtain quality data because of failures to meet delivery schedules, underestimates of electrical requirements, and missing pieces of hardware and software. Such shortfalls may be the fault of the program designer or the authorities supervising the study; as a result, some of these problems may not be forthrightly reported in an effort to save embarrassment.

Formative Evaluation—Information to Improve Processes and Outcomes

Evaluation has often been advocated for its ability to provide decision makers with information on a timely basis as a means to assist them with impending judgments. Especially valued is information that can be used for formative purposes where the force of findings can be used to revise current programs or conditions of use. The advocacy of using data to improve education is part of the policy fabric of U.S. educational policy (Improving America's Schools Act, 1994). In reality, the quality of the data obtained in evaluation governs the degree to which appropriate inferences can be drawn (Herman & Gribbons, 2001; Mitchell & Lee, 2000).

Formative evaluation is an unassailable goal, but the true power of such information is often curtailed by a number of aspects of the setting or the system under study:

- Measures (test information that doesn't provide enough guidance about changing instruction or technology options)
- Timing (data that are too late to make a change)
- Inflexibility of revision options (systems that are fixed rather than revisable)
- Insufficient guidance about who needs to make the change (teachers, supervisors, designers)
- Lack of resources to make needed adjustments (limits on professional development days, for example)

The logic of formative evaluation assumes that feedback leads to productive change. Its constraints are that the information provided must be relevant, targeted, and useful.

Evaluative Research

Fifteen years ago, a new kind of impact evaluation was developed in educational technology settings, where attention was paid to specific technology interventions that were intended to affect educational outcomes or processes. The Apple Classrooms of Tomorrow was a case in point (Fisher, Dwyer, & Yocam, 1996). Other interventions served as proofs of concept, and their evaluation was expected not only to shed light on the specific implementation but also to provide a prototype for the development of a broad set of new technology applications (Baker & O'Neil, 1994; Burns, Parlett, & Redfield, 1991; O'Neil & Baker, 1994; O'Neil, Baker, Ni, Jacoby, & Swigger, 1994). At that point, the evaluation questions expanded from "Is *x* better than *y* for *z*?" to interest in longer-term questions: What could be learned about teaching, learning, and assessment through the application of technology (e.g., Geisert & Futrell, 1999; Gooden, 1996; Perkins, Schwartz, & Wiske, 1997)? How did serious technology use affect the roles, functions, and expertise of teachers and students (e.g., Gearhart, Herman, Baker, Novak, & Whittaker, 1994; Sandholtz & Ringstaff, 1997)? What effects did technology use have on attitudes and beliefs (e.g., Dwyer, Ringstaff, & Sandholtz, 1991; Ertmer, Addison, Lane, Ross, & Woods, 1999; Hansen, 1995; Medcalf-Davenport, 1998)? How were organizations changed because of the introduction of technology (e.g., Kerr, 1996; Salisbury, 1993)? And, of course, as a coda for all evaluations, could the goals of learning be addressed as well or better by using technology (e.g., Clark, 1994; Jonassen, Campbell, & Davidson, 1994; Kozma, 1994; Kulik, 1994; Kulik & Kulik, 1991)? Studies with a blend of research and evaluation goals are fundamentally useful to the research and development community but may often appear to be too diffuse to help decision makers with their immediate problems.

Another modal pattern of evaluation study involves the use of shallow, large-scale studies and deeper interview or observation data collection, which are principally used to interpret or to validate findings from the larger data collection. An illustration of this approach is the Urban and Suburban/Rural Special Strategies for Educating Disadvantaged Children Project (Stringfield, Millsap, & Herman, 1997). It is likely that such studies will persist. However, it is our intention to explore whether an alternative approach to evaluation could provide deeper information on a broader set of cases or participants. Such evaluations should furnish both objective and interpretative information and do so taking into account the impact of the evaluation on the participants. The evaluation strategy we propose is frankly reactive (Campbell & Stanley, 1963, p. 176) in that we expect it to positively affect outcomes that it will subsequently measure. We want evaluation procedures that influence the thoughtfulness of users in the application of technology. We want evaluation to be directly relevant to improvement. Before turning to a description of this alternative evaluation approach, we will review shortcomings of current practice, including limitations in the conceptions of evaluation, evaluation designs, and instrumentation.

LIMITATIONS OF CURRENT APPROACHES TO THE EVALUATION OF TECHNOLOGY

Embedded in our discussion has been a raft of limitations that have plagued studies of educational practice in general and of technology specifically. Limitations are likely when any single intervention (for instance, a specific technology program) must have a series of requirements in place for it to be implemented correctly:

1. The availability of the equipment
2. The support of the management
3. Skilled use by teachers, if it is to be used as part of formal educational experiences
4. Necessary prior knowledge and skills of students
5. Appropriate timing and integration in the curriculum

Failure on any one of these points could easily make an evaluation of effects useless. Even under the rare conditions of effective implementation, it is difficult to think about evaluation purposes, to assure that the measures used will be potentially sensitive to the intervention, and to create appropriate and feasible designs that will yield interpretable data. Unless these features are part of the study, the validity of the findings may be highly suspect.

When the intervention is not something as direct as the application of a technology-based system or software suite, the difficulty in undertaking evaluation simply multiplies. Often the "impact" of technology—in general—is the object of study; for instance, answering a question such as how reducing the ratio of users to computers from 8:1 to 5:1 affects outcomes. In such a case, the application of technology will vary in myriad ways. As a result, the types of implementation will not be subject to easy comparison and perhaps not easily documented. The technology could be applied differentially to a variety of subject matters or to different students. The wary evaluator may have no option but to fall back on the reported happiness of the users as the safest and perhaps most attainable piece of hard data. In the next section, we will briefly highlight the key issues in the conception of evaluation, designs, and measures as they potentially affect validity interpretations of findings.

Limitation: Conception of Evaluation

As noted above, distinctions between formative and summative evaluation have figured prominently in conceptions of evaluation. Formative studies, meant to provide a basis for intervention revision, are usually aimed at designers and users. These studies are typically long on sensitivity to local context and interests but, except in the case of experimental contrasts, short on methodological rigor. The situation with so-called summative evaluation, usually addressed to decision makers, has been just the reverse: long on technical rigor but short on sensitivity to local context. The reality is that to be valid and useful, evaluations indeed must be both technically rigorous and sensitive to programs in context. Because most evaluations are actually expected to give information useful for a range of purposes and for multiple audiences, including policymakers and user groups, the hidebound formative–summative distinction is a false dichotomy.

That evaluations of large-scale technology reform efforts have rarely taken a longitudinal view of outcomes presents another design limitation. Additionally, in an attempt to assess the big picture of implementation and impact, evaluation attention has focused on what's common across a diverse set of sites and has concentrated on common measures that can easily be aggregated across sites and levels. While there is merit to this view from the perspective of power and quantitative research, the exclusive attention to common measures gives short shrift to what may be unique and most promising at individual sites and may lead to measures that are modestly responsive to all but effectively sensitive to none. We need to consider "value-added" conceptions, where value is imputed from longitudinal designs and where the content of the measures provides some opportunity to demonstrate the unique value added by individual sites and programs.

Finally, as we have noted above, technology does not stand still. It is evolving at an astronomically rapid rate. We cannot expect programs or approaches that integrate technology to remain stable over the period of time we have come to expect serious evaluation to take. "Technology-push" (Glennan, 1967) means that programs and strategies are evolving even as we try to assess them. We need a conception of evaluation that can respond to these rapid cycle times, not 5-year studies whose results are irrelevant long before they are released.

Limitation: Designs

The realistic possibilities for evaluation designs offer another set of important limitations in the evaluation of technology. Yes, randomized samples of treatment and comparison groups are theoretically possible, but in reality they are very difficult to accomplish. The allure of technology in the eyes of many parents and the demand for equal access make such assignments impractical. At the same time, for classroom-based innovations, technology's differential allure to individual teachers and teachers' variable comfort and capacity with new technological approaches, not to mention differential home support and resources, confound attempts at clean designs likely to yield clear findings. Even with the luxury of a very large sample of classrooms and an attendant luxurious evaluation budget, collective bargaining limits what may be asked of teachers—both in their participation in new projects and in the data demands that may be placed on them. Both randomized designs and good information with which to monitor teachers' and students' progress

are thereby limited. And were these impediments not enough, the highly laud-
able requirements of protecting human subjects effectively provide additional
limits. Participation and data provision require informed consent, and data
may not be compelled from anyone—regardless of injuries to the randomized ideal.

While these are not insurmountable obstacles, certainly very creative strategies are required to overcome these design limitations, including lots of conversation, extended negotiation, and trust building. In the absence of such
efforts and with the reality of limited evaluation resources, much evaluation
effort devolves to messy studies involving volunteer teachers and schools.

Limitation: Measures

Given these challenges, it should come as no great surprise that many
evaluations of technology come down to surveys of implementation and
teachers' and students' self-reports of impact. Did the equipment come? Did
you receive enough training? Did you like "it"? Do you think it has affected
your learning? Would you recommend it to a friend or a colleague? These
indeed are common issues that transcend specific programs, but the smile-
test instrumentation that often results lacks credibility, particularly given
social desirability and the gee-whiz quality of many technology programs.

How do we get closer to accurate measures of impact on students' or
adults' learning? Unfortunately, there are no easy answers given the state of
both technology and measurement practice. It is axiomatic that to be sensitive to effects on learning and attitudes, outcome measures must be aligned
with intervention goals. The alignment issue presents multiple difficulties
(Herman, 1994). On the one hand, for too many technology innovations,
the intended outcomes are unclear, making it impossible to define sensitive
measures. In other situations, the intended goals are variable across individual
settings (schools, classrooms, homes, other organizational levels or institutions). Yet even where student or adult outcomes are clearly specified, the
availability of sensitive measures is likely to be problematic. Policymakers'
and the public's proclivity for standardized test results aside, these measures
have been developed to provide a general barometer on student performance
in basic academic skills—reading, language arts, mathematics, basic knowledge of science, social studies/history, and so on. While certainly it is the case
that some technology initiatives have been developed to address these skills,
such programs seem to constitute the minority, not the majority, of technology use. And it is noteworthy that those programs that have been designed
to improve these basic academic skills—for example, learning systems—are
indeed one of the relatively few examples of technology impact on student
learning (see, for example, Kulik, 1994; Kulik & Kulik, 1991). But why would

we expect standardized tests to show the effects of initiatives directed at other outcomes—how students learn, the depth of their problem solving in a subject matter, their access to and use of resources, and their facility with technology, to name just a few?

Certainly, the last decade of performance assessment has tried to make a dent in the assessment of these latter capabilities, and the generalizability and technical quality of some of these measures have been improving (Baker, Freeman, & Clayton, 1991; Baker, Linn, Abedi, & Niemi, 1996; Baker & Mayer, 1999). Well-intentioned assessment developers, steeped in program intents and learning theory but not measurement, have toiled mightily in coming up with homegrown measures that attempt to get at specific technology goals. Though these measures are high in face validity and apparent alignment with intended outcomes, they tend to be short on validity and reliability. The current choice then tends to be between measures that are credible and technically sound but irrelevant to program goals and measures that are aligned with technology goals but inadequate technically. Neither will do the job.

Our evaluations have also typically taken a restricted view of what the outcomes of technology should be. Certainly, some initiatives aim for improved student learning in traditional areas of curriculum. And for these, longitudinal studies with comparison groups, and with expectations that the technology groups will outperform the nontechnology groups, may be justified. But the implementation of technology has a range of other potential goals as well, and these goals call for different designs, different instrumentation, and different expectations, for example:

- Achieving existing curriculum goals more efficiently or cost effectively
- Developing technological capacity and fluency (Baker & O'Neil, 2003; Fulton, 1997)
- Achieving new goals that were not possible without technology (e.g., inferences from seismic readings; new forms of collaboration, communication, and teamwork)
- Achieving new goals unattainable and unmeasurable without technology (e.g., web-search skills)

There also are goals that transform the nature and functions of the teaching and learning process, such as the following:

- Increasing teachers' subject-matter knowledge and understanding through new systems, or otherwise providing students with access to expert knowledge and coaching
- Providing the capacity to develop integrated standards, instruction, and assessment systems through mapping technologies

- Automating the assessment capacity for educational and training programs (e.g., assessment of student writing, assessment of critical dimensions of assessment process)
- Creating new forms of technology and knowledge transfer, including professional development

The point is one we have tried to make repeatedly: Technology is changing rapidly and changing the ways and possibilities for conducting education and training. New goals are emerging, requiring new approaches to evaluation and assessment. Traditional designs are not doing the job, nor are they really providing the control expected of them. Similarly, traditional measures, while technically credible, cannot capture the outcomes we most want to achieve with new technological interventions, and these tend to be variable across and even within specific initiatives. Traditional evaluation and measurement have been developed with generalization in mind—but generalization to what, in the face of the intricacies and complex and varying goals of technology? We argue that it is time for a new paradigm that puts power in the hands of those who can best understand the meaning of their initiatives and the meaning of the data and provides good information, sensitive to program implementation and outcomes as they evolve, to the various decision makers who need it.

Of particular concern in the evaluation of technology is whether or not there is anything like a stable treatment to be assessed and, if so, for how long. Rapid changes in technology are likely to impact any setting, albeit schools last of all. Furthermore, what one starts to evaluate may soon be obsolete. At one level, such a state of affairs suggests that long-term, massive studies ought not to be conducted. Rather, a strategy should be developed to optimize ongoing data collection and used as a means to monitor technology impact. Do we have a solution for you!

IMPROVING EVALUATION OF TECHNOLOGY

From the foregoing discussion, let us agree that the enterprise of technology evaluation can be improved. The goal of our evaluation model is to link quality information—information that is credible and objective—with processes that lead to deeper understanding of the causes and effects of particular relationships uncovered in an evaluation and to more rapid improvement. This next section describes the attributes and beginning examples of a model of evaluation that might be useful for the evaluation of technology as well as for other interventions. Any approach will have some strengths and weaknesses, and we will try to anticipate what they may be for our recommended approach.

Both Formative and Summative Evaluation of Technology

We start with the assumption that the fundamental purposes of most technology evaluations have both summative and formative components. The summative component—the question "Does the intervention work?"—may actually be targeted to an element of the intervention rather than to the total technology investment, answering questions such as "Is the math program selected helping children to reach their goals?" or "Was the professional development effective for teachers?" It is far more likely that a technology investment will generate formative evaluation questions—"How can the system be improved?" "Who needs to receive more (help, training, attention, equipment)?" The likelihood that technology will be regarded as an option that could be discontinued shrinks daily.

Technology-Sensitive Characteristics of Evaluation

One goal of evaluation is to match it to the conception of the intervention. This concept is called "ecological validity" (Cole, 1999). The idea is that the evaluation strategy, data collection, and measures should be consonant with the intervention at hand and sensitive to the context and process as they exist.

Yet many evaluations of educational technology lack such ecological sensitivity by ignoring at least four interrelated characteristics of technology initiatives: (1) the distributed nature of the intervention, (2) flexibility of local implementation, (3) rapid change in the nature of the technology, and (4) the multiple user audiences evaluation data should address. That is, for many technology initiatives, there may be a general set of goals and implementation strategies, but much of the responsibility for specific implementation is left to individual teachers, schools, and/or sites. With this responsibility comes discretion in the choice of particular applications, uses, and emphases, and some variation in the specific goals that are likely to be accomplished. For example, technology reform in many school districts has started with a general vision of integrating technology with curriculum to improve student learning and has provided technology, professional development opportunities, and software resources for school-level personnel. Yet whether, how, and what technology is actually used in the curriculum is very much the choice of an individual school or teacher. But there is a clear trade-off between local sensitivity and potential wider generalization about the impact of effect under varying circumstances.

The local character of implementation demands flexibility in evaluation, a need that is accentuated by the changing nature of technology itself. These same characteristics also suggest the multiple audiences who can benefit from evaluation. Three major groups require information:

- Those at the local level, who best know what they are attempting to accomplish and who are actually engaged in the specifics of technological change
- Those at higher institutional levels who may be responsible for wider planning and improvement support
- Policymakers and members of the public who are interested in impact and effectiveness

DISTRIBUTED EVALUATION

We suggest an evaluation model that accounts for these technology characteristics. This approach has the added credibility of relying on technology itself to support the evaluation approach. The idea of a distributed evaluation system places responsibility for evaluation at the multiple levels at which evaluation data are needed. It supports a coordinated system across levels that allows for flexibility and unique emphases at individual sites. The model assumes a system where all players/levels buy in to a general set of goals and an approach to evaluation that features a longitudinal design and the analysis of appropriate indicators over time. Such indicators include measures that are common across local sites, as well as those that are unique to the interests and emphases of each individual site. A special strength of the model is its giving over to individual sites and schools the responsibility and capacity to define their local goals. Because feedback and reporting are functionally instantaneous, users do not need to wait for external evaluation data in order to get useful and timely feedback on questions that bear directly on their improvement aims. The system facilitates the communication of data to various audiences in the local community. With an exporting function, data from sites can be communicated to central stations, such as program managers or evaluators, for aggregation and analysis of the intervention.

Four key attributes are at the center of our model: First, evaluation purposes and goals need to be understood by all players—the sponsor, the evaluators, and the users of information—at every level. Second, as mentioned, we believe an indicators approach is essential not only to provide evaluation with the comparable measures needed for certain purposes but also to be adaptive and flexible to local implementations that may vary dramatically from classroom to classroom, from school to school, and so on. Longitudinal designs are fundamental to our indicators approach. Third, we believe that distributing responsibilities for data collection and analysis to local sites provides a number of benefits. Sites can get information on a timely basis and may have special questions or intervals on which they wish to obtain information. Fourth, feedback must be distributed to the program evaluators, the institution funding the enterprise, and the users themselves. If data collection is distributed, it is possible to get immediate feedback about findings to those who are operating the program. Let us consider each of these points in turn.

Clarity on Purposes and Goals

Clarity about the purposes of an evaluation is essential in order to develop an efficient plan that obtains the relevant information. In general, clarity is discussed as part of the bargain between the evaluator and the sponsor (Alkin, Daillak, & White, 1979; Joint Committee on Standards for Educational Evaluation, 1994), and although the rules may change as boundaries shift, understanding intentions can guide evaluation action. In a period of increased accountability and risk, even benign general research studies may generate the suspicion, and sometimes the resistance, of teachers. Low response rates, socially desirable responses, and the charge of irrelevant "paperwork" are among the milder responses of individuals. When data or information is collected for general or unspecified use, there is a growing resistance to participating in research and evaluation studies, and agreements are now made in school districts limiting the number or extent of mandatory data collections for teachers. It is for this reason that we believe that the formative evaluation purposes of an evaluation should be emphasized and made clear.

A second, linked responsibility is that the information collected actually gets used to refine or revise the intervention(s) under study. In addition to collecting information in order to revise and improve a system or intervention, we would add one additional purpose: Distributed evaluation, because it requires involvement of the participants, can also serve the goal of increasing local capacity to use information to improve local practices. As a clarification, the dictum that all users should understand the evaluation purposes is solemnly put forth. Intentionally it means everyone—students (above the age of reason, whenever that is), teachers, administrators, sponsors, and evaluators. This public recognition of the intention of data collection works to assure that serious questions are asked and quality data obtained. It also pushes the task of reflection down the system and makes it the responsibility not only of the evaluator–sponsor pair. To make evaluation work in the way we wish, we have to rely on technology.

Indicators and Measures

The system relies on an indicators approach that includes both quantitative and qualitative measures. It builds up from an individual-level student database to create composites that reflect student demographics and other school context issues, instructional process and opportunity-to-learn indicators, and multiple measures of student performance. In our view, these performance measures can and should run the gamut from general measures of academic performance, such as standardized test results, to more detailed classroom and curriculum-embedded measures. For instance, collections of assessments and student work can help teachers and schools explore the strengths and weaknesses of student understanding and progress because these measures are directly connected to instruction. And we believe that technology and R&D in assessment in the near term will enable teachers and schools to create such measures—measures that are sensitive to schools' and teachers' instructional goals and that also are technically credible.

It would be altogether another treatise to discuss how the existing and commonly used measures are likely insensitive to interventions such as technology. For instance, if technology facilitates hypothesis generation, search-strategy development, and organization of knowledge, most of the available measures touch only tangentially on these issues. At the Center for Research on Evaluation, Standards, and Student Testing (CRESST), we have developed a stream of research and development on measures of achievement that is based on a set of families of cognitive demands: content understanding, problem solving, teamwork and collaboration, metacognition/self-regulation, and communication. CRESST has developed models for each of these families and has used them to guide our assessment design across multiple subject matters and grade levels (e.g., Baker, 1996; Baker et al., 1991; Baker, Niemi, et al., 1996). We have developed computer-supported implementations of these models in problem solving, knowledge representation, and search (Chung et al., 1999; Herl et al., 1999; Schacter et al., 1999). Key to these models are expert system-based scoring approaches and a design that permits the reimplementation of the assessment model in different topics and subject matters, for administration in paper-and-pencil or technologically supported settings. Our vision, only partially realized, is the creation of a suite of authoring systems that would allow individual curriculum developers, managers, and teachers to create and use measures easily. We believe we will be able to build in sufficient constraints to strengthen validity for classroom and program evaluation purposes.

Even with improved strategies for developing and administering tests, schools and programs will not need to spend all their time assessing. Indeed, we envision a system where all sites commit to assessments in a limited number of areas and then choose to spend more effort on domains of special interest. To reduce the burden for the common measures, matrix sampling could be used for the many instances where individual data are unnecessary for valid inferences. Likewise, technology itself can reduce some of the logistic and scoring burden. For example, indicators of student performance, collected in a web or other online setting, can be automatically scored, and the database of performance can be transferred into the evaluation system.

Longitudinal Design

One characteristic of indicator approaches—whether single, reconfigured, or composite in nature—is that they gain meaning by their use over time. Thus, consistent with remedying a design flaw in many evaluation studies, we propose approaching at least some of the evaluation using a longitudinal strategy, where changes in indicators are monitored over time.

The longitudinal constraint has raised concern in some venues. To look at value added, it is thought that one must monitor the exact indicator over time, and this may be the case for empirical indicators on which we want to make sound comparisons over time. However, our conception of longitudinal analysis is broader, unwilling to sacrifice rich measures for more standard ones. As many in the performance assessment debate have pointed out (Herman, Aschbacher, & Winters, 1992; Linn, Baker, & Dunbar, 1991), standardized tests may trade off efficiency and technical credibility for instructional sensitivity and utility for teaching and learning. Not all measures need to be reduced to numbers; indicators could also be more qualitative. As suggested above, monitoring the quality of assignments given by teachers can suggest the extent to which technology use was raising instructional standards. Rather than using exactly the same measure from data collection to data collection, a sample of assignments could be scanned into the system and displayed on an annual basis. Even without sophisticated analysis of the cognitive demands of such tasks (Clare, Pascal, Steinberg, & Valdez, 2000), local communities could observe and reflect on the value added (or not) of the implementation.

Distributed Data Collection

Imagine a system where the following is in place. In a first category, common measures to be used in the evaluation are either available or delivered over a network to sites being evaluated. These measures might consist of particular questionnaire items, interview prompts that could be completed via telephone, logs of utilization, or special achievement measures. A second category includes implementation-specific questions; for instance, questions about collaborative learning, if that is a part of the local strategy. A compendium of other measures of potential interest to different sites is also available. This compendium might include different measures of classroom practice, measures of beliefs about or efficacy of the technology, or questionnaires for students and parents. A third category, which could be either mandatory or discretionary, includes procedures for sites to use in collecting examples of student work, screen shots, or products that students of various backgrounds and experience have built. Procedures for scanning and reporting such data are provided. From the system, instruments are printed, or completed online, during the dates or window specified. The system time-stamps data.

The benefits of this approach are that it is possible to manage data collection on-site, rather than having it be an external activity. Data entry can be accomplished with far less error and on a far more timely schedule, especially as it is a locally controlled enterprise. This approach really is the only choice for web-based implementations that may be accessed from a variety of computers, not just those in a particular location. The limitation of this approach is that access to the instruments may be more open. It is possible that respondents will game the system on the basis of this extended knowledge. On the other hand, they may wish to game the system and provide inaccurate information anyhow.

Feedback to All Audiences

A common complaint about school-focused evaluation and research is that it is neither timely nor understandable. The evaluation system we propose allows information to be arrayed in a longitudinal file, by student or classroom. The system has the capacity to disaggregate information so that eight separate filters can be employed simultaneously. The data-analytic capability can generate simple reports showing relationships among variables and relationships to standards or targets. The capability of the system enables immediate feedback to be provided to local sites related to their own data. This information may involve data that are common across various sites and data that are unique to a particular site. The nontechnical analytic displays make it easy to understand what the findings have been and to query the system about potential relationships of interest—for example, performance of subgroups using particular software.

An export function allows school data to be transmitted to the program evaluator or program manager. Transmitted findings are controlled at the site. Thus, if particular information were collected at one site, there would be no requirement that it be transmitted to the central evaluator. Depending on the terms of the agreement, the central evaluator could provide performance indicators back to individual sites. These could be based on average performance across groups. Or profiles of all sites could be shared, protecting the identity of individual sites. The data could similarly be arrayed in a simple-to-understand graphic or iconic representation. This process could be repeated as frequently as the site or program manager had negotiated. It would be possible, for instance, for local sites to develop their own specific evaluation questions, collect data locally, include it in the system, and provide local-only analyses on a more frequent basis than the central evaluation team.

Summary of Features—A Real System

The system features we have outlined—indicators-based with flexible measures, distributed data collection, longitudinal design, reporting to all audiences in graphic or iconic displays—remedy at least some of the flaws we have observed in the evaluation of technology, especially those evaluations conducted at schools. Such a system is in the process of being developed in the context of a charge to evaluate a diverse set of distance-learning courses, launched from multiple institutions in various contexts. The intent is to provide a common template of questions and instruments that can be adapted to the unique target offered by each course and provide information at different levels of granularity for local and policy uses.

Our initial set of common evaluation questions represents the various types of questions that are typically subject to inquiry:

1. How well does the course or module meet its goals?
2. What are the effects of the course on students' learning?
   - Is there evidence that the course supported growth in learning, improved performance, or retention of skills?
   - What specific skills were learned? Over how many different contexts or situations do they generalize?
3. How are students' attitudes and motivations affected?
   - What attitudes and motivations were exhibited during the course (e.g., eagerness to learn, to improve performance, to compete)?
   - What attitudes or beliefs were affected by the course (e.g., self-monitoring, self-efficacy)?
4. How much time do participants invest?
   - How much time was spent in coursework or structured activities?
   - How much time was spent in collaborative (team) activities?
   - How long did it take to reach criterion (or meet exit criteria)? Did that time vary systematically by topic, group characteristics, or preferences?
5. How do trainees and experts judge the quality of the application(s)?

6. Compared to plausible alternatives, how did the distance learners perform?

7. What costs are associated with the program?
   - What are the direct costs of the program? Of alternatives to the program?
   - What are the opportunity costs?
   - What are the costs of failure?

At the local level, each of these questions can be addressed purposefully from multiple perspectives to serve formative purposes, with data collected using standard instrument templates and participants' observations and judgments providing alternative points of entry and interplay. Multiple representations of results, using automatically generated iconic and standards representations, can help to support such conversations. For large-scale policy and decision purposes, standard cross-site measures can be easily summarized and exported to create comparable indicators for cross-site analyses and aggregated to make judgments about cross-program impact.

The measures used in the system will be a blend of standards and customization. For example, measures of participants' reactions and judgments would feature a standard set of items to solicit students', teachers', and experts' reactions to specific aspects of course components and applications, as well as their suggestions for improvement, but the specifics of the components and applications would, of course, be unique to each course. Measures of student learning and performance would draw on specified measurement approaches that were also common across sites, such as concept mapping and structured explanation tasks (e.g., Baker et al., 1991; Harmon, Chung, & Baker, 2001; Herl, Baker, & Niemi, 1996) to address understanding of complex knowledge and simulation-based measures of problem solving, but the specifics of the measurement would be adapted to the unique targets of learning at each site. The latter might include targets that were common across a number of sites (e.g., communication objectives that might be common across disciplines), as well as those that were distinctive to each. Similarly, students' self-report measures of their efficacy, effort, and acquired expertise, as well as measures of metacognitive and conative constructs, would each employ a standard set of items that were adapted to the specific course targets.

An example from our work is the evaluation of distance-learning instructional systems and instructional gaming. The evaluation frameworks specify analysis of the relationship between goals and strategies, developed from research-based guidelines, in instruction, learning support, and assessment, for instance. Projects are given modules for assessment to employ, and the evaluator helps to refine the assessments and assure the technical quality of domain-specific assessment elements.

Problems Remaining

The system in and of itself does not solve every problem in technology evaluation. One continuing problem is the question of whether the intervention can be evaluated. Has it been in place long enough or used with enough regularity to warrant an analysis of its implementation and impact? Second, what standard will be used to determine impact or need for revision? Often evaluations are conducted in a procedural way, and the answer obtained is rationalized in a variety of ways. One of the benefits of clear experimental comparisons is that a normative judgment is reached about the extent to which a version of an intervention is as effective as, or more effective than, a competing alternative. Without discussing some of the reasons why such comparisons are difficult (and they are, in school settings with a changing "treatment" and population), we note that they do provide a standard against which to make a judgment of merit.

A third, knotty issue is the selection of measures. In our model, we advocate emphasizing measures that match the implementation. Certainly all schools may administer standardized tests to children, and the evaluator may have access to that information. However, we believe that such measures will show serious impact only over time and that, it is therefore wise, in the first stages of an evaluation, to emphasize either indicators related to practice or those connected to curriculum-based outcomes. We term these *leading indicators*, and they should have characteristics such as the following:

- Being under control of the actors (e.g., students, teachers)
- Being predictive of longer-term impact
- Being sensitive to intervention

A second level of indicators would show impact at the intermediate point—for instance, better attendance (of students or teachers, presumably because of interest or productivity), quality of student work or teacher assignments, or performance on curriculum-embedded measures such as final examinations or curriculum-focused tests. The last set of indicators, which we call *trailing indicators*, have the greatest credibility among policymakers because they are the best known. They include standardized or statewide tests, graduation rates, completion of college-bound requirements, and so on. These types of indicators, as we have suggested, also generally bear the least connection to particular interventions, are most correlated with student background characteristics, such as economic or language status, and as a result may be less likely to detect intervention effects.

REFERENCES

Alkin, M. C., Daillak, R., & White, P. (1979). *Using evaluations: Does evaluation make a difference?* Beverly Hills, CA: Sage.

Baker, E. L. (Ed.). (1996). A focus on educational assessment [Special issue]. *Journal of Educational Research, 89*(4).

Baker, E. L., Freeman, M., & Clayton, S. (1991). Cognitive assessment of history for large-scale testing. In M. C. Wittrock & E. L. Baker (Eds.), *Testing and cognition* (pp. 131–153). Englewood Cliffs, NJ: Prentice-Hall.

Baker, E. L., Linn, R. L., Abedi, J., & Niemi, D. (1996). Dimensionality and generalizability of domain-independent performance assessments. *Journal of Educational Research, 89,* 197–205.

Baker, E. L., & Mayer, R. E. (1999). Computer-based assessment of problem solving. *Computers in Human Behavior,15,* 269–282.

Baker, E. L., Niemi, D., Herl, H., Aguirre-Muñoz, A., Staley, L., & Linn, R. L. (1996). *Report on the content area performance assessments (CAPA): A collaboration among the Hawaii Department of Education, the Center for Research on Evaluation, Standards, and Student Testing (CRESST) and the teachers and children of Hawaii* (Final Deliverable). Los Angeles: University of California, National Center for Research on Evaluation, Standards, and Student Testing.

Baker, E. L., & O'Neil, H. F., Jr. (Eds.). (1994). *Technology assessment in education and training.* Hillsdale, NJ: Erlbaum.

Baker, E. L., & O'Neil, H. F., Jr. (2003). Technological fluency: Needed skills for the future. In H. F. O'Neil, Jr. & R. Perez (Eds.), *Technology applications in education: A learning view* (pp –265). Mahwah, NJ: Erlbaum.

Bloom, B. S., Hastings, J. T., & Madaus, G. F. (1971). *Handbook on formative and summative evaluation of student learning.* New York: McGraw-Hill.

Burns, H., Parlett, J. W., & Redfield, C. L. (1991). *Intelligent tutoring systems: Evolutions in design.* Hillsdale, NJ: Erlbaum.

Campbell, D. T., & Stanley, J. C. (1963). Experimental and quasi-experimental designs. In N. L. Gage (Ed.), *Handbook of research on teaching* (pp. 171–246). New York: Rand McNally.

Chung, G. K. W. K., O'Neil, H. F., Jr., & Herl, H. E. (1999). The use of computer-based collaborative knowledge mapping to measure team processes and team outcomes. *Computers in Human Behavior, 15,* 463–493.

Clare, L., Pascal, J., Steinberg, J. R., & Valdez, R. (2000, January). *A framework for examining the quality of classroom assignments* (LACE Education Briefs). Los Angeles: University of California/University of Southern California/Los Angeles Compact on Evaluation.

Clark, R. E. (1994). Media will never influence learning. *Educational Technology Research & Development, 42*(2), 21–29.

Cole, M. (1999). Ecological validity. In R. A. Wilson & F. Kiel (Eds.), *MIT Encyclopedia of the cognitive sciences.* Cambridge, MA: MIT Press/Bradford Books. (Retrieved November 8, 2000, from http://cognet.mit.edu/MITECS/Entry/cole2)

Dwyer, D. C., Ringstaff, C., & Sandholtz, J. H. (1991). Changes in teachers' beliefs and practices in technology-rich classrooms. *Educational Leadership*, 48(8), 45–52.

Ertmer, P. A., Addison, P., Lane, M., Ross, E., & Woods, D. (1999). Examining teachers' beliefs about the role of technology in the elementary classroom. *Journal of Research on Computing in Education*, 32(1), 54–72.

Fisher, C., Dwyer, D. C., & Yocam, K. (Eds.). (1996). *Education and technology. Reflections on computing in classrooms.* San Francisco: Jossey-Bass.

Fletcher, J. D. (1990). *Effectiveness and cost of interactive videodisc instruction in defense training and education* (IDA Paper P-2372). Alexandria, VA: Institute for Defense Analyses.

Fulton, K. (1997). *Learning in a digital age: Insights into the issues. The skills students need for technological fluency.* Santa Monica, CA: Milken Family Foundation, Milken Exchange on Education Technology.

Gearhart, M., Herman, J. L., Baker, E. L., Novak, J. R., & Whittaker, A. K. (1994). A new mirror for the classroom: A technology-based tool for documenting the impact of technology on instruction. In E. L. Baker & H. F. O'Neil, Jr. (Eds.), *Technology assessment in education and training* (pp. 153–172). Hillsdale, NJ: Erlbaum.

Geisert, P. G., & Futrell, M. K. (1999). *Teachers, computers, and curriculum: Microcomputers in the classroom* (3rd ed.). Boston: Allyn & Bacon.

Glass, G. V., McGaw, B., & Smith, M. L. (1981). *Meta-analysis in social research.* Beverly Hills, CA: Sage.

Glennan, T. K., Jr. (1967). Issues in the choice of development policies. In T. Marschak, T. K. Glennan, Jr., & R. Summers (Eds.), *Strategies for research and development* (pp. 13–48). New York: Springer-Verlag.

Gooden, A. R. (1996). *Computers in the classroom: How teachers and students are using technology to transform learning.* San Francisco: Jossey-Bass.

Hansen, R. E. (1995). Socialization in technological education. *Journal of Technology Education*, 6(2), 34–45.

Harmon, T. C., Chung, G. K. W. K., & Baker, E. L. (2001, June). *Evaluation of a simulation and problem-based learning design project using constructed knowledge mapping.* Paper presentation at the 2001 ASEE Annual Conference & Exposition, Albuquerque, NM.

Herl, H. E., Baker, E. L., & Niemi, D. (1996, March/April). Construct validation of an approach to modeling cognitive structure of U.S. history knowledge. *Journal of Educational Research*, 89, 206–218.

Herl, H. E., O'Neil, H. F., Jr., Chung, G. K. W. K., & Schacter, J. (1999). Reliability and validity of a computer-based knowledge mapping system to measure content understanding. *Computers in Human Behavior*, 15, 315–333.

Herman, J. L. (1994). Evaluating the effects of technology in school reform. In B. Means (Ed.), *Technology and education reform: The reality behind the promise* (pp. 133–167). San Francisco: Jossey-Bass.

Herman, J. L., Aschbacher, P. R., & Winters, L. (1992). *A practical guide to alternative assessment.* Alexandria, VA: Association for Supervision and Curriculum Development.

Herman, J. L., & Gribbons, B. (2001). Lessons learned in using data to support school inquiry and continuous improvement (CSE Tech. Rep. No. 535). Los Angeles: University of California, National Center for Research on Evaluation, Standards, and Student Testing.

Hovland, C. I., Lumsdaine, A. A., & Sheffield, F. D. (1949). Experiments on mass communication. Princeton, NJ: Princeton University Press.

Improving America's Schools Act of 1994, P. L. No. 103–382, 108 Stat. 3518 (1994).

Joint Committee on Standards for Educational Evaluation. (1994). The program evaluation standards (rev. ed.). Thousand Oaks, CA: Sage.

Jonassen, D. H., Campbell, J. P., & Davidson, M. E. (1994). Learning with media: Restructuring the debate. Educational Technology Research & Development, 42(2), 31–39.

Kerr, S. T. (Ed.). (1996). Technology and the future of schooling. Ninety-fifth yearbook of the National Society for the Study of Education, part 2. Chicago: University of Chicago Press.

Kirkpatrick, D. L. (1994). Evaluation training programs. The four levels. San Francisco: Berrett-Koehler.

Klein, D. C. D., Yarnall, L., & Glaubke, C. (2003). Using technology to assess students' web expertise. In H. F. O'Neil, Jr. & R. Perez (Eds.), Technology applications in education: A learning view (pp. 305–320). Mahwah, NJ: Erlbaum.

Kozma, R. B. (1994). Will media influence learning? Reframing the debate. Educational Technology Research & Development, 42(2), 7–19.

Kulik, C.-L. C., & Kulik, J. A. (1991). Effectiveness of computer-based instruction: An updated analysis. Computers in Human Behavior, 7, 75–94.

Kulik, J. A. (1994). Meta-analytic studies of findings on computer-based instruction. In E. L. Baker & H. F. O'Neil, Jr. (Eds.), Technology assessment in education and training (pp. 9–33). Hillsdale, NJ: Erlbaum.

Leifer, A. D. (1976). Teaching with television and film. In N. L. Gage (Ed.), Psychology of teaching methods: NSSE yearbook (pp. 302–334). Chicago: University of Chicago Press.

Linn, R. L., Baker, E. L., & Dunbar, S. B. (1991). Complex, performance-based assessment: Expectations and validation criteria. Educational Researcher, 20(8), 15–21. (ERIC Document Reproduction Service No. EJ436999)

Lumsdaine, A. A. (1965). Assessing the effectiveness of instructional programs. In A. A. Lumsdaine & R. Glaser (Eds.), Teaching machines and programmed learning: A source book: Vol. II. Data and directions (pp. 267–320). Washington, DC: National Education Association of the United States.

Medcalf-Davenport, N. A. (1998, November). Historical and current attitudes toward and uses of educational technology: A work in progress. Orlando, FL: WebNet 98 World Conference of the WWW, Internet and Intranet Proceedings. (ERIC Document Reproduction Service No. ED427721)

Mitchell, D., & Lee, J. (2000, April). QSP software and school data driven decision-making. Paper presented at the annual meeting of the American Educational Research Association, New Orleans.

O'Neil, H. F., Jr., & Baker, E. L. (Eds.). (1994). Technology assessment in software applications. Hillsdale, NJ: Erlbaum.

O'Neil, H. F., Jr., Baker, E. L., Ni, Y., Jacoby, A., & Swigger, K. M. (1994). Human benchmarking for the evaluation of expert systems. In H. F. O'Neil, Jr. & E. L. Baker (Eds.), *Technology assessment in software applications* (pp. 13–45). Hillsdale, NJ: Erlbaum.

Perkins, D. N., Schwartz, J. L., & Wiske, M. S. (1997). *Software goes to school: Teaching for understanding with new technology*. New York: Oxford University Press.

Salisbury, D. F. (Ed.). (1993). Designing and implementing new models of schooling [Special issue]. *International Journal of Educational Research, 19*(2).

Sandholtz, J. H., & Ringstaff, C. (1997). *Teaching with technology: Creating student-centered classrooms*. New York: Teachers College Press.

Schacter, J., Herl, H. E., Chung, G. K. W. K., Dennis, R. A., & O'Neil, H. F., Jr. (1999). Computer-based performance assessments: A solution to the narrow measurement and reporting of problem solving. *Computers in Human Behavior, 15*, 403–418.

Scriven, M. (1974). Evaluation perspectives and procedures. In J. W. Popham (Ed.), *Evaluation in education: Current applications* (pp. 3–93). Berkeley, CA: McCutchan.

Stringfield, S., Millsap, M., & Herman, R. (1997). *Urban and suburban/rural special strategies for educating disadvantaged children: Findings and policy implications of a longitudinal study*. Baltimore, MD & Cambridge, MA: Johns Hopkins University Press & Abt Associates.

Wenglinsky, H. (1998). *Does it compute?: The relationship between educational technology and student achievement in mathematics*. Princeton, NJ: Educational Testing Service.

MEASURING IMPORTANT STUDENT LEARNING OUTCOMES

Barbara Means
Geneva D. Haertel

Addressing the question of how best to investigate the effects of technology on student learning requires explicating both what is meant by "technology" and what is encompassed in "student learning." The prior section dealt with issues surrounding the specification of a technology-enabled instructional innovation, as well as some contrasting views on the purposes research should serve and how to approach study design. In this section we turn to consideration of the kinds of student learning that should be investigated and how that learning should be measured. Answers to both of these questions have implications for study designs.

WHAT KINDS OF LEARNING OUTCOMES
SHOULD BE MEASURED?

There is a wide range of opinion in the education research and policy communities concerning both the educational outcomes that are most important in general and those that are most important to examine when gauging the value added by technology. One argument would give priority to the fundamental basic skills, principally reading and mathematics, that are driving assessment and accountability systems nationally and in most states. These enabling skills are capabilities that nearly everyone believes are important and for which we have a fairly well-understood, reasonably cost-effective assessment strategy in the form of standardized, multiple-choice tests. Indeed, some policymakers have expressed the view that investing in technology for our nation's schools is worthwhile if, and only if, this investment increases student achievement scores in reading and mathematics.

In some cases the focus on this kind of learning and assessment makes sense because the measures are a good match to the technology innovation under study. Integrated learning systems (ILSs), which provide extended individualized drill and practice on reading and mathematics skills, became very popular in schools, particularly those receiving federal compensatory education funds, in the middle and late 1980s. These systems were designed to improve students' reading and mathematics skills and in fact incorporated assessment items very much like those found on standardized tests. While ILSs have declined in popularity, newer forms of basic skills drill-and-practice software, such as SuccessMaker and Math Blaster, continue to have a strong foothold in schools.

In many cases, however, schools are using technology for quite different purposes. A 1998 national survey of teachers found that the most common technology uses were for word processing followed by Internet research (Becker, Ravitz, & Wong, 1999). Thus, measures of composition and editing skills are more relevant than reading and math achievement test scores to evaluations of *typical* school technology use. While we might hypothesize that these activities would have some positive effect on students' reading comprehension, that is certainly not the most direct outcome of the activity.

Some proponents of technology argue that we should focus not on the most common school applications of technology but on those that use technology to best advantage. We should be looking for enhancements to students' learning in the academic-content areas, especially in academic areas that have traditionally been difficult for many students to master. When the research question is of this nature, it is important to think through the essential concepts and skills in the academic area and to have measures of student learning that tap them. Many have argued (e.g., Means & Haertel, 2001) that widely available standardized tests are better able to capture factual knowledge and discrete procedures than the reasoning, problem solving, and complex performances involved in such traditionally difficult areas as higher mathematics, science inquiry, or historical analysis.

Another viewpoint concerning what we need to know about student learning focuses on the skills students develop in using technology. Many argue that technology has become such an important part of our world in general, and such an important part of the jobs with the best prospects for economic return and professional growth in particular, that our schools need to ensure that all students develop facility with computer technologies. In this case, the focus is not on the academic content learned with supporting technology tools but on students' ability to choose appropriate technologies and to use them efficiently. Many states have embraced the goal of ensuring that their students have acquired technology skills, and several (e.g., North Carolina and Kentucky) have mandated assessments of these skills.

WHAT KINDS OF LEARNING OUTCOMES HAVE BEEN MEASURED?

Above we discuss kinds of learning outcomes that research on educational technology might want to incorporate. The reader might wonder what learning measures are used in existing research. Henry Jay Becker (from the University of California, Irvine) and Barbara E. Lovitts (an independent consultant) suggest in Chapter 5 that the research examining the effects of technology on student learning can be divided into two basic categories. The first, what they call "development-linked research," is typically performed by learning technology developers as they seek to learn what is and what is not working in their prototype innovation. These developers are typically interested in the potential of new technologies to support learning in various content areas. They have incorporated student-learning measures into their research and development on systems to support students' learning in areas such as physics (Hunt & Minstrell, 1994; White, 1993), algebra (Koedinger, Anderson, Hadley, & Mark, 1997), and geometry (Wertheimer, 1990). In many cases, the measures of student learning used in these investigations were themselves part of the instructional software. From the standpoint of providing convincing evidence of technology's effects, two problems arise with respect to learning measures in these development-linked studies. First, because the assessments are developed by those who developed the instructional innovation, they can be suspected of being idiosyncratic in content and limited in their generality. It is not clear that anyone who had not been exposed to the instructional program would have had exposure to the same content and would understand what was being asked. The assessment is not likely to be anything with recognized value in the education community or among the public at large. When the assessment is incorporated into the learning software, this problem is compounded by the fact that students who did not receive the technology-based instructional program may not have access to the assessments or, if they do, may lack facility with the technology tools needed to complete them.

The second type of learning technology evaluation in Becker and Lovitts's dichotomy is comparative studies, in which students, classrooms, or schools with and without technology are compared. In contrast to the development-linked research, these studies have typically employed externally developed learning measures, most often standardized tests. In cases where the technology under evaluation is geared toward facilitating acquisition of the kind of content covered on standardized tests, such outcome measures are convenient and credible. For example, a large-scale evaluation conducted in West Virginia looked for effects of the state's investment in basic skills drill-and-practice software on its elementary school students' performance on standardized tests (Mann, Shakeshaft, Becker, & Kottkamp, 1999). But in many cases, the technology-supported innovation of interest targets learning outcomes that are not tapped by widely available standardized tests—outcomes such as middle schoolers' understanding of the mathematics of change or principles of genetics, or high school students' ability to reason about complex systems. In such cases, there is no strong reason to predict a difference between groups on standardized tests of reading and mathematics performance, and yet there is the temptation to use those outcome measures, largely because they are available. In other cases, researchers have given up on directly measuring student learning and instead relied on teacher or student reports of how much they think they have learned. Clearly, a more rigorous assessment approach is needed, with learning measures that are valued and matched to the content of instruction in both technology-using classrooms and those without technology supports.

Many developers of learning technologies, while sensitive to Becker and Lovitts's assertion that technology-embedded assessments of student learning are not compatible with research designs comparing experimental and control groups, argue that the focus of research should be precisely those learning outcomes that cannot be achieved without technology. Technology is changing both jobs and academic disciplines, they argue, making analyses and information manipulations that were unfeasible before the age of powerful computers and visualization and modeling tools not only possible but mundane. If we are to prepare our children for the 21st century, we need to rethink the content of our curriculum, including these new areas that can only be taught—and assessed—with technology tools.

WHAT ADVANCES ARE NEEDED?

Many evaluations of technology effects suffer from the use of scores from standardized tests of content unrelated to the intervention, while others suffer from the substitution of measures of opinion, implementation, or consumer satisfaction for measures of student learning.

Evaluations of technology-supported interventions need a wide range of student-learning measures. In particular, performance measures are needed that can more adequately capture higher-level problem-solving skills and the kinds of deeper understandings that many technology-based innovations are designed to enhance. Measures within specific academic subject areas might include level of understanding within the subject area, capability to gain further understanding, and ability to apply knowledge in new contexts. Other competencies that might be assessed are relatively independent of subject matter, such as (1) acquiring, evaluating, and using information and (2) collaboration, planning, and leadership skills.

Technology proponents are not alone in calling for assessments with these features. Education reformers have made similar pleas for decades. There have been attempts to serve this need through the development of alternative assessment techniques such as performance assessments and portfolios. In contrast to the typical standardized test in which little or no context is provided for individual test items (typically of a multiple-choice or short-answer format), performance assessments are actually tasks given to individuals or small groups of students. These tasks typically include both a context and a multipart problem, both intended to mimic a performance that might be required in the real world (e.g., design an experiment to test the effect of a pendulum's weight on its rate of swing). Performance assessment developers see advantages in this form of assessment because it can incorporate the following:

- Extended, complex performances
- Mechanisms for students to reveal their problem-solving strategies, to describe their rationale for proceeding through the task, and to document the steps they follow
- Opportunities to demonstrate social competencies and collaboration
- Scoring rubrics that specify important attributes of performance

Because performance assessment tasks are more complex and take longer to administer, fewer "items" are administered. Performance assessments require well-specified criteria for rating student performance, and a single task can produce multiple scores reflecting different aspects of the student's performance (e.g., whether the student's experiment controlled all extraneous variables; whether the procedure was described clearly enough that another student could execute it, etc.).

An alternative approach to capturing complex performances is the use of portfolios. In this case, examples of students' work, often with self-reflections or teacher comments, are compiled in a portfolio much as an artist might build a portfolio of sketches or photographs. The most rigorous application of assessment portfolios involves the development and application of detailed scoring rubrics for the kinds of work included in the portfolio. In practice, this degree of systematicity is rare.

In recent years, electronic versions of both performance assessments and portfolios have been developed (Means & Haertel, 2001; Pellegrino, Chudowsky, & Glaser, 2001). Despite the perception of the promise of such technology-supported assessments, researchers need to be cognizant of unsolved problems. Earlier attempts at using nonelectronic forms of performance assessments were often stymied in their efforts to obtain the technical ("psychometric") quality needed for assessments used on a broad scale. Shavelson and his colleagues (Shavelson, Baxter, & Gao, 1993; Shavelson, Baxter, & Pine, 1991) have investigated the generalizability and reliability of performance assessment scores for individual students. While careful development of scoring rules ("rubrics") and rater training and calibration can produce adequate reliability for such measures, the generalizability problem has not been solved (Shavelson et al., 1993). A student's performance on a particular performance assessment task tells us less than we would like about how that student would perform on a different performance assessment task presumed to tap the same kinds of skill and knowledge.

Technology developers who have incorporated assessments into their instructional software have rarely paid attention to the issue of the psychometric quality of their items. Their assessments have generally been both very particularized to their specific software environments and focused on a narrow slice of content as well as being of unknown reliability and validity (Quellmalz & Haertel, 1999). The problem of an assessment's technical quality is of great importance when scores from performance assessments are to be used to make consequential decisions about the education of individual students (e.g., promotion or qualification for graduation). In Chapter 5, Becker and Lovitts argue that when assessments are used for research where the results will be aggregated across groups of students, relaxing the reliability requirements is of less consequence. However, even in this kind of research context, researchers will often want to be able to measure change (growth) in student skills over time, and assessments with weak reliabilities can result in unstable growth scores.

Robert J. Mislevy from the University of Maryland and his colleagues have been working on an approach to systematic development of assessment tasks designed to mitigate this problem (see Chapter 6). This approach brings a strong psychometric foundation, in combination with evidentiary reasoning, to the measurement of complex cognitive performances. Expanding the repertoire of research-quality instruments, if successful, would be an important step toward more meaningful evaluations of technology's effects on students.

Mislevy and his colleagues use principled assessment design, which relies on assessment developers' articulation of student, evidence, and task models, to make the assessment argument. Specifying these models helps the developers relate the student knowledge, skills, and abilities to be assessed with the evidence to be collected and with the features of the assessment tasks to be administered. Making the relationships among these elements of the assessment design clear and logical means that the validities of the assessment increase. Such principled assessments can provide better measures of the complex performances that are needed to truly measure the effects of technology.

REFERENCES

Becker, H. J., Ravitz, J. L., & Wong, Y. T. (1999). *Teacher and teacher-directed student use of computers and software.* Irvine, CA: Center for Research on Information Technology and Organizations

Hunt, E. B., & Minstrell, J. (1994). A cognitive approach to the teaching of physics. In K. McGilly (Ed.), *Classroom lessons: Integrating cognitive theory and classroom practice* (pp. 51–74). MIT Press/Bradford Books.

Koedinger, K. R., Anderson, J. R., Hadley, W. H., & Mark, M. A. (1997). Intelligent tutoring goes to school in the big city. *International Journal of Artificial Intelligence in Education, 8*, 30–43.

Mann, D., Shakeshaft, C., Becker, J., & Kottkamp, R. (1999). *West Virginia story: Achievement gains from a statewide comprehensive instructional technology program.* Santa Monica, CA: Milken Family Foundation.

Means, B., & Haertel, G. (2001). Technology supports for assessing science inquiry. In *Proceedings of the Workshop on Technology and Assessment* (pp. 12–25). Washington, DC: National Academy Press.

Pellegrino, J., Chudowsky, N., & Glaser, R. (2001). *Knowing what students know: The science and design of educational assessment.* Washington, DC: National Academy Press.

Quellmalz, E., & Haertel, G. D. (1999). *Breaking the mold: Technology-based science assessment in the 21st century.* Manuscript submitted for publication.

Shavelson, R. J., Baxter, G. P., & Gao, X. (1993). Sampling variability of performance assessments. *Journal of Educational Measurement, 30*, 215–232.

Shavelson, R. J., Baxter, G. P., & Pine, J. (1991). Performance assessments in science. *Applied Measurement in Education, 4*, 347–362.

Wertheimer, R. (1990, April). The geometry proof tutor: An "intelligent" computer-based tutor in the classroom. *Mathematics Teacher*, pp. 308–317.

White, B. (1993). Thinkertools: Causal models, conceptual change, and science education. *Cognition and Instruction, 10*, 1–100.

Chapter 5

A Project-Based Approach to Assessing Technology

Henry Jay Becker
Barbara E. Lovitts

With frustration in her voice, Linda Roberts, former director of the U.S. Department of Education's Office of Educational Technology, often recounts her experience of being asked by Ted Koppel, host of ABC's *Nightline*, to defend the level of public expenditure on computers for schools, given that most of the evidence provided has been anecdotal. With all of the millions of dollars that schools have spent on computers, asked Koppel, where is the "national objective study . . . by someone who doesn't have an axe to grind" that shows that all this money has made a difference? How do we know that kids and teachers are better off for it (Koppel, 1998)?

Whenever large amounts of public funds are invested—school reform funds that might be used in other ways—it is understandable that popular sentiment and the people responsible for making legislative and administrative policy decisions will phrase their concerns by asking "What are the effects?" and "At what cost compared to other avenues of investment?"

These seemingly simple questions mask an underlying complexity. A teacher's classroom use of computers may be more or less effective depending on his or her pedagogical approach; the convenience, density, and quality of the technology and software available; the teacher's and students' technical expertise in using computer software; and a whole host of other factors. Still, the underlying question about effectiveness, even when phrased conditionally and delimited by specific circumstances and applications, has several qualities:

- It is a legitimate question.
- It is one that needs to be addressed at an appropriate level of generalization so as to provide evidence for decision making at legislative and administrative levels from the Congress to individual school principals and teachers.
- It is inherently comparative—that is, compared to other alternatives that are available and plausible for reaching chosen outcomes.

Although there are many different learning outcomes that could be examined, including students' skills in using technology tools per se, the type of public policy question that we address concerns competencies that could be acquired *without* use of computer resources, thus leading to Koppel's demand for evidence that the computer approaches are superior. These competencies include:

- Students' levels of understanding in the academic subjects of the school curriculum, their ability to gain further understanding in these areas, and their ability to apply what they know in practical ways
- Students' capacities to undertake a wide variety of tasks in various work, citizen, and community roles that involve integration of diverse competencies and understandings—competencies that are largely independent of specific subject-matter disciplines and include skills in acquiring, evaluating, and using information as well as skills in working in groups to solve problems and accomplish tasks

RESEARCH IN EDUCATIONAL TECHNOLOGY: WHY ARE THESE QUESTIONS NOT BEING ANSWERED?

If we grant that there is a legitimate public interest behind Koppel's question about the "effects" of investing in technology for schools, we must ask why research on educational technology has not addressed this issue to date. Are the patterns of educational technology's effects so idiosyncratic that we cannot provide empirically based guidance for school, district, state, and federal decision makers regarding the consequences of different policies for investing in computer technology? Are the student outcomes achieved with computers so unique that they can't be compared to outcomes for students given other educational experiences? If educational research is not providing information that informs these policy decisions, what evidence *is* it providing, and why doesn't it assist policymakers?

Development-Linked Research

The research literature in educational technology spans a number of genres. In one common approach, developers of unique computer-based tools present theoretical arguments for how their software product helps students to acquire understandings or skills not typically addressed in traditional curricula—for example, by making difficult concepts meaningful to students who would otherwise be treated as insufficiently prepared to grasp these ideas, or by displaying new forms of patterns among ideas so that insights arise that might generally not occur. To the extent that this development-oriented literature reports on *empirical* studies of the consequences of use of these software tools, one typically sees three types of evidence.

One type of evidence is anecdotal in nature and illustrative in intent. This includes descriptions of individual students' use of the software or "screen shots" of students' work that demonstrate the researcher's perceptions of how students' viewpoints develop as they use it. See, for example, Roschelle, Kaput, and Stroup's (2000) portrait of a student's use of SimCalc, software designed to make the ideas of calculus accessible to younger students; or Lamon, Reeve, and Caswell's (1999) description of the use of CSILE, an instructional model and supportive software for collaborative inquiry and knowledge building.

A second type of evidence involves a longitudinal examination of the same students' ability to demonstrate competencies putatively associated with the software being studied. For example, researchers at the Educational Testing Service studied a group of several dozen secondary school teachers' implementation of STELLA, software designed for evaluating and creating causal models of social and physical systems. Paper-and-pencil instruments were used on several occasions to assess students' ability to understand "systems concepts," and students were asked to write essays that would enable the researchers to determine how well they could build a model of a particular system (Mandinach & Cline, 1994, 1996).

A third and related type of study contrasts teachers who implement the same technology-based innovation in different ways (either naturally evolving differences or systematically prescribed variations). An example of this type of research is Allen and Thompson's (1995) study of four classes in one elementary school that participated in the Apple Classroom of Tomorrow's long-term demonstration of high-density technology classrooms. In this study, the word-processing products of students in two classes were communicated to an outside audience for feedback via e-mail, and the quality of their writing was compared with the products of word processing done in two other classes in the same school where the work was turned in for traditional teacher comments.

In its best instantiations, development-linked research displays the following qualities:

- It is premised on a cumulative research program derived from well-informed and empirically validated cognitive research principles.
- It self-consciously employs a variety of reflective and formative evaluation techniques to assess and improve both the underlying model and its implementation.
- It is sensitive to the specific circumstances in which it is being implemented and adapts to these circumstances without breaking with its theoretical principles.
- It provides carefully researched and well-elaborated models for using technology resources and tools in ways that can significantly improve children's depth of understanding of important academic content.

Development-linked research makes a contribution to the quality of computer-based tools for learning and instruction. However, development-linked research neither provides the kinds of direct information that would help policymakers set legislative policy nor helps school decision makers make investment decisions.

Research associated with software development is, for the most part, designed either to help explain the rationale and functioning of the program to an outside audience or to assist the designers themselves in fine-tuning the product and its implementation. When systematic empirical research is conducted around development products, the outcomes studied tend to be defined in ways specific to the technology involved or tend not to be measured in classroom settings where the technology is not being used. As a result, the notion of *comparing* students who did not participate in the project with those who did founders on the lack of a common benchmark or common tools for making these comparisons.

Computer Versus Noncomputer Comparisons: Standardized Testing Environments

In contrast to development-linked research, the other type of research widely present in the educational technology literature *is* inherently comparative—research that explicitly compares students who have used computers in school with students who have not. Most of this research is based on standardized norm-referenced tests. However, this research, too, is unsatisfactory for purposes of policymaking or for understanding the actual effects of students' computer experiences.

This research has been criticized elsewhere on methodological grounds for failure to employ random-assignment designs or carefully matched control groups (e.g., Murphy et al., 2002). Here we focus on a less commonly discussed limitation of these studies—the bias inherent in the way they measure student learning.

The generic competencies measured in these standardized tests, such as "mathematics computation" or "language arts mechanics," are carefully designed around uniform testing conditions in which students are given a minimal set of materials and information, specific directions, and identical (or statistically equated) multiple-choice or short-answer questions. Indeed, providing a common information environment, identical (and necessarily limited) materials and tools, and identical tasks has been the hallmark of sophisticated assessment models. These assessments are designed to provide highly reliable information about individual students' abilities to recall knowledge, demonstrate an understanding of subject-matter concepts, and employ related skills on demand.

Such an approach to assessment makes sense for measuring enabling skills, such as reading comprehension and algorithmic work in mathematics. For these types of skills, students are likely to perform at levels that approach their underlying competence, despite being given little contextual information or other resources. Standardized testing environments may also usefully measure students' ability to recall factual and conceptual knowledge as long as that knowledge could reasonably be assumed to have been a topic of instruction across diverse schooling environments.

However, there are many competencies for which such a strictly limited information and resource environment would *underestimate* the competencies of many students, making their use in evaluating the effects of technology on student learning unfair. In particular, for competencies such as the ability to gain new knowledge or to apply knowledge to new contexts—as opposed to the ability to repeat ideas or facts previously remembered—it would seem to handicap students to have to demonstrate their competence without being able to use those technology tools and resources that they had come to rely on. Thus, the assessment setting for standardized tests defines away any possible utility of computer-based tools and resources by preventing their use during the assessment situation. What is being tested, then, is whether the use of computers in learning has any residue that carries over to intellectual challenges students may face without being able to call upon technology tools or resources. In Salomon, Perkins, and Globerson's (1991) terms, norm-referenced outcome measurements test the effects "of technology" rather than the effects "with technology."

Although it is possible that prior computer experience results in some understandings and abilities that can be demonstrated subsequently in the absence of computer resources, for the most part when we examine the information-gathering, analysis, communication, and problem-solving tasks that computer-experienced *adults* engage in, it is *their ability to employ computers during those tasks* that indicates whether their computer experience assists them in demonstrating relevant underlying competencies. Moreover, in the scholarly writing about educational computing, there appears to be a strong consensus that the most powerful consequences of computer use in academic classes involve "effects with"—the enhancement of learning and performance capacity provided by knowledgeable access to and use of computer tools and resources (Cognition and Technology Group at Vanderbilt, 1996).

Part of the common reluctance to allow computers into the assessment setting is the perception that access to such tools may give computer-using students an unfair advantage. Yet that is precisely the question that a study of the effects of computer use would seek to answer: To what extent does experience with computers result in improved performance on competencies that are deemed important outcomes of schooling? At the same time, it is clear that it is the academic and generic problem-solving competencies that are the outcomes to be measured, not students' competencies in using computer tools and resources themselves.

Thus, an assessment must be able to define outcome measures in a way that is formally independent of students' ability to use computer tools. What is needed are assessments for which the use of computers does not, by definition, result in stronger performance (as a measure of underlying competencies and understandings) but which permit use of the *affordances* (Gibson, 1977; Norman, 1988) that computer tools and resources provide. By "affordances that computers provide" we mean that the assessment tasks should be those for which computer tools and resources afford students an opportunity to demonstrate greater competency in a given area than they might otherwise. The availability of the computer tools and resources (even if exploited) should neither guarantee superior performance nor provide an exclusive route to demonstrating superior competency. The primary criterion of an assessment task should still be that it embodies measurement of the underlying academic or generic skills and understandings thought to be important and relevant to classroom instruction in the school subject at hand.

Summary of the Problem with Existing Research

Thus, existing educational technology–related research that contains student outcome measures fails us. Although some of this research is valuable for documenting and evaluating developing efforts to use computers to add richness to the school curriculum, that type of research generally does not provide comparative data for large-scale decision making. Its outcome measures are usually too narrow for our purposes, often defining the measurement objectives in terms of computer-specific competencies or providing a protocol for measuring student outcomes that requires the use of specific computer programs. The other type of educational technology research on outcomes assumes that the only effects worth measuring are effects "of computers"— effects that manifest themselves as competencies in the absence of computers. That research operationally defines outcome measures in ways that make computer skills irrelevant at the time of assessment—or at least prohibits their use in the interests of standardization of the assessment setting.

If we accept the legitimacy of the goal of informing public policy—that is, making generalizations about the comparative consequences of computer-based approaches to school-directed learning—then it is worth investigating whether approaches can be developed that can plausibly address these weaknesses of existing assessments and designs.

USING PROJECT-BASED ASSESSMENTS TO INVESTIGATE THE EFFECTS OF TECHNOLOGY

A clearer picture of what a research design using project-based assessment would look like may come from considering the design of a particular study. In 1999–2000, the authors led a design team from the American Institutes for Research (AIR) that, under contract with the U.S. Department of Education, proposed a set of longitudinal studies of the effectiveness of sustained and intensive uses of educational technology in U.S. schools (Lovitts, 2000). One of the studies proposed as part of that contract is described here to illustrate an approach to student assessment and comparative studies that could address Koppel's question.

This approach, which we call technology-afforded, teacher-involved, project-based assessment (shortened to technology-afforded assessment, or TAA), is intended to supplement more conventional student achievement data that seem unlikely to identify the most important consequences for students of having a technology-rich educational experience. Its goal is to maximize attention to the outcomes most likely to be affected by a high-intensity computer experience while employing a design that systematically controls for other variables that might be correlated with computer use in class and are also likely to affect student achievement—for example, how much time students spend on an assessment task and the nature of their teachers' approach to instruction.

In the TAA approach, each student (or small group) and each classroom undertake work of a similar nature on the same curricular topic. However, the specific tasks that each student performs and the specific questions that a student investigates are permitted to vary from student to student and from classroom to classroom across the classes participating in the study. Nevertheless, the research design systematizes how these variations manifest themselves so that differences in performance can be attributed to the extent of a student's computer technology experience rather than to other variables distinguishing classes and their teachers from one another.

A reasonably close approximation to the type of assessment structure involved in TAA is the one used when independent student work is being judged competitively, as in science fair project competitions and other situations that involve recognition or monetary rewards based on the comparative merit of students' accomplishments. In these situations, comparative judgments can be made about students' products and the quality of thinking behind their products even though each student focuses on different content. The key is that criteria and standards for judgment are made publicly available ahead of time, as are the ground rules for what constitutes an equitable set of procedures for the completion of assessed student work.

Traditionally, "rigor" in assessments prescribes that students undertake identical tasks about identical content. Although it is easy to see why those are desirable attributes of an assessment design, there are three reasons why variability is also desirable: (1) to maximize the motivation and effort of the participants; (2) to appropriately measure certain outcomes that require initiative; and (3) most importantly, to more fully cover the domain of applicable content and skills.

The Value of Variability Across Classrooms and Students

Practically speaking, the most important criterion for accomplishing valid research on student project work is the investment that teachers and students make in doing that work. Calling on teachers to have their students devote several days to several weeks to a research project over which they have no subject-matter control would make it very likely that a high percentage of teachers selected to participate would decline to do so. In contrast, enabling teachers to be closely involved in selecting the content for student project work would make it more likely that teachers would see the work as fulfilling their own curriculum-coverage goals rather than interfering with them. By selecting teachers in the same state, and possibly the same district and school, the TAA design would seek to minimize differences between project content among classes involved in a given comparison.

A second reason for not specifying project tasks and specific content in detail is that the outcomes to be studied (that is, outcomes hypothesized to be related to expert use of computer technologies) include competencies related to students' defining problems, identifying and obtaining needed information, and carrying out tasks independently. A project defined in too great detail would eliminate those important dimensions of student achievement from the purview of the study.

The third reason for building into the design systematic variability in tasks among students is to enable a project-based study to adequately tap a wide range of concrete manifestations of the underlying competence domain. In multiple-choice tests, this goal of domain-content coverage is accomplished by having each student address a large number of test items. In a project-based assessment design, this broad sampling of the underlying competencies and understandings is accomplished by having different subject-matter content for different subsets of assessed subjects. Because our interest is in assessing the differences in the average levels in discipline-related abilities that are associated with high-intensity technology experiences versus more typical levels of student technology competence, we think it advantageous to measure these demonstrated abilities across a wide range of substantive problems and conditions. Indeed, it is this broad sampling of the domain of application of general discipline-related competencies that is an advantage of project-based assessment.

The Basic Comparison Unit: Four Teachers Systematically Varying in Computer Use and Pedagogy

The study we envision calls for multiple replicates of *matched sets of four teachers* who teach the same subject to students at the same grade level. Within a matched set, each of the four teachers would be selected to represent a different combination of intensity of technology use and pedagogical style. A matched set, in other words, would consist of one technology-intensive teacher with a student-centered (constructivist) pedagogy; one technology-intensive teacher with a content-centered (skill-based and transmission-oriented) pedagogy; one teacher with "typically limited technology use" and a student-centered pedagogy; and one limited technology user who had a content-centered pedagogy.

This design examines pedagogical style along with intensity of technology use because of the accumulating research showing that high-intensity technology-using teachers are disproportionately constructivist in their orientation (e.g., Riel & Becker, 2000) and the potential of that association to otherwise confound conclusions about the effects of a high-intensity technology experience on student outcomes. Furthermore, in order to measure the effects of high-intensity technology experience under reasonable conditions, technology-intensive teachers would be selected based on their having sufficient personal experience and knowledge about computers and having adequate levels of support for computer use at their school.

The selection of teachers to participate in this study (and their distribution into matched sets) would have to be based on other factors besides having contrasting levels of technology use and contrasting pedagogies. They must teach students the same subject at roughly the same grade level, from similar socioeconomic backgrounds, and having similar prior levels of school achievement. In addition, for a TAA assessment design to have internal validity, it is also essential that there be a match between each teacher's implementation curriculum and the content of the particular project which their matched set is using for assessment.

By having a *multiplicity* of matched sets of classrooms, each set engaged in somewhat different projects, working under somewhat different conditions, and measuring somewhat different products and performances, but within a set minimizing these same differences as far as possible, a far fuller range of content knowledge would be studied than when a single assessment task is to be performed in all research settings. A further advantage of such a design is that some tentative understanding may be gained of the impact of variations in study conditions, types of projects, and content areas on the effects of pedagogy and of technology intensity on student outcomes.

Student Outcomes and a Construct-Centered Approach

In many performance assessments, the students' tasks are developed first, and then outcome measures and scoring rubrics are designed in terms of each specific task. Messick (1994) argues for a construct-centered assessment approach instead. In construct-centered assessments, the set of student competencies to be studied is defined first, and then tasks are developed that provide a reasonable opportunity for those particular competencies to be exercised. The TAA model is based on the latter approach, although the particular set of competencies to be evaluated for any particular matched set of teachers in the study would be a subset of a larger set of student outcomes.

The larger set of outcomes is a library of outcome descriptions that are selected as those most likely to be affected by a high-intensity technology experience in the subject matter and grade level under study. Roughly, they are likely to encompass each of the following:

- Attributes of the work process (e.g., initiative, metacognitive insight, project planning, collaboration, and leadership)

- Attributes of student products (e.g., completeness)
- Apparent levels of skill, knowledge, understanding, quality of reasoning and thinking, valuation and motivation, and learning (i.e., increases over time in those attributes) in areas most likely to be affected by their use of computer resources and tools—that is, information acquisition; analysis, synthesis, evaluation, and application of information; and writing and communication

Defining the Project for a Matched Set of Classes

The measurement of these student outcomes would occur in the context of a well-defined project whose overall topic (or short list of alternative topics) is selected by (and developed in conjunction with) teachers of each matched set. The topic and set of project questions would be selected for a matched set based on the planned curriculum of the four classes. It could be seen as a capstone activity that enables the application of information learned in all of the curriculum units during the year. The topic of the project would break new substantive ground for all classes in the matched set, but it would enable students in the four classes to apply the skills, tools, resources, and content knowledge taught in their previous units. The project work would occur during April or May, at approximately the same time in the four classes in a matched set.

A small library of possible topics and component projects would be provided, and the matched set of teachers would select one or more of these, or modify one to better match their setting and curriculum for the year. The critical requirement is that all four teachers in a set consider the defined project to be feasible and equally appropriate for the curriculum and skill sets taught in their respective classes.

Defining student project tasks and questions so that they are equally relevant to classes with different learning experiences is just one of many procedural challenges that must be overcome in order to conduct a project-based assessment that controls on "irrelevant" factors that might distinguish classes with different technology experiences. Another obvious design decision is whether students conduct the project work independently or in teams of two, three, or four students. Also, the procedures for constituting teams need to be predefined—for example, how teams balanced by student ability would be created and how prior friendships, gender similarities, and so forth would be taken into account in constructing teams.

These decisions are among the ground rules for the "competition" among the four classes in any one matched set, so that all four classes work under the same constraints. Other obvious ground rules include the amount of class time to be devoted to student project work, the types of assistance that the teacher or other adults (e.g., parents) are permitted to provide, how much the work is contributing to students' class grades, and so forth.

In the proposed design, an initial pass at these ground rules would be made by the researchers, but they would be subject to modification based on a consensus of the teachers participating in a matched set. Basically, the idea is to reason out what appears to be an optimum arrangement, given the particular topic and set of project assignments defined, but then to incorporate the situational wisdom and perspectives of the participating teachers who, in the end, will be conducting the activity themselves.

Mechanisms for Assuring Equal Relevance Within a Matched Set

The selection of teachers to participate in a study of this type (and their distribution into matched sets) is based on many factors that are independent of the project-based assessment—for example, having teachers with contrasting levels of technology use and expertise and contrasting pedagogies who teach the same subject to students at the same grade level, from similar socioeconomic backgrounds, and with similar prior levels of school achievement. However, for the design to have internal validity, it is also essential that there be a match between each teacher's implemented curriculum and the content of the particular project that their matched set is using for assessment. Composing matched sets of teachers from the same school district is one means of achieving roughly equal curricular relevance.

The matched sets of teachers and classes could be created by gathering information about teachers and their classes through questionnaires, interviews, and an examination of teaching materials and assignments. Then, once the matched sets have been created, the research team could propose to the four teachers one or more of the prepared projects along with their derived assessment structures (e.g., outcomes and scoring rubrics) and a set of ground rules regarding the conduct of the task.

Data Analysis Design

Analyzing the outcomes of this kind of study requires a regression-oriented approach to data analysis that also incorporates multilevel analysis. Five types of variables would be at the core of this analysis:

1. There are dependent variables that can be measured in the same way across different matched sets—for example, academic and career plans and attitudes towards schoolwork studied through questionnaire surveys or structured diary reports.

2. There are dependent variables that can be measured in the same way across matched sets but whose measurement may differ among matched sets because their operational definitions are dependent on the specific tasks undertaken by students in that set of classes. These include content knowledge about the specific subjects studied; information-handling skills, including acquisition of information, evidence of analysis and synthesis accomplished, and written communications and oral presentation competencies; and particular attributes of the products constructed in performing the assessment tasks. These somewhat varying scoring criteria can nevertheless be combined (e.g., through creating z-scores) to study the impact of design factors and other variables on the general underlying outcomes.

3. The primary independent variables are built into the student design—technology intensiveness and teacher pedagogical practice. These dimensions are treated as dichotomies for purposes of selection of contrasting cases, but large differences will inevitably exist among teachers within any one category—and systematic differential effects within the design categories are likely. For example, high-intensity technology environments may have different average impacts depending on how accessible and how sophisticated their computer equipment is and how much prior expertise the students and teachers bring to the task. Similarly, students may be more accomplished on project outcomes if their teacher's practice typically involves the use of student projects than if their teacher has less experiences in that approach, even if both teachers score equally highly on a more generalized measure of "student-centered" or "constructivist" pedagogy. These and other variations within the same "cell" in the four-cell design can be measured through surveys and used in analysis of subgroups of similar cases.

4. There are control variables. Four classes selected to represent contrasting technological and pedagogical environments will certainly be different in many other ways, both in terms of their setting and—despite every effort to create identical testing conditions—in how the assessment tasks are undertaken. Teachers may differ in teaching expertise, classrooms may vary in how much technical assistance they need (and have available) to complete projects, and so forth. These differences become less significant the larger the sample size (individual differences balance out in large aggregates), even in nonrandomized designs like this one, but they are potentially more problematic when variations in how the assessment specifications are *implemented* are themselves correlated with design variations. For example, there may be insufficiently matched socioeconomic differences between high- and low-intensity technology settings in terms of the amount and type of *non*computer resources that students use, and this might be manifested in differential access to use of computer resources at home or through the resources of their peer network; or there may be systematic differences in cells across matched sets in the amount of out-of-class

time spent on project work or the amount of access to outside help (expertise) that students have (within the agreed-upon constraints governing that particular matched set). A substantial data-collection effort (primarily through questionnaires and periodic form completion) should be undertaken to measure a wide variety of ways in which classrooms *within* sets might systematically vary in undesirable ways that are nevertheless permitted in the study design.

5. Finally, another set of variables are conditions of the project-based assessment that do not vary *within* a matched set but do vary *between* sets. These variables are measured in order to study the conditions where the design variables—pedagogy and technology intensity—may have disproportionately more or less impact. Here we would include such dimensions as the relevance and requirements that different assessment products have in terms of cognitive skills and competencies; the individual or collective nature of products and student team formation rules and team size; the amount of time given to project work during class, time limits for completing tasks, and similar ground rules; the extent to which the negotiated assessment project permits students latitude in curricular content or in the nature of assessed products; and the contribution that project work plays in the students' course grades.

The Nature and Size of the Effort Required to Understand the Effects of Computers

This enumeration of the many variables relevant to an empirical study of the effects of computer technology use on student academic outcomes raises the question of the feasibility of such a study. Two elements are at issue: (1) the size and diversity of the sample of sites and the variety of project content necessary to draw general conclusions about effects and (2) the magnitude of expenditure that any single investigation of this type would require.

Clearly, the effectiveness of computer use on student achievement varies substantially across subject matters, student characteristics, teacher instructional styles, the nature of access to computers and computer resources, and the nature of different student outcomes being measured. The only way that the general question about the effectiveness of school investments into computers can be answered is for many different studies to be undertaken, each one with sufficient depth and size to be informative for educational investment decisions.

This chapter was written with the belief that general statements about the effectiveness of computer-based approaches to teaching *are* possible within certain limits. The limits that we believe are reasonable to consider consist of a single academic subject (as defined by the curriculum coverage common across a majority of states and districts) taught to students within a two to three grade-level range from a broad range of socioeconomic backgrounds and with a broad range of abilities (e.g., two population standard deviations each), and for teachers who span a similarly broad range in their basic approach to teaching.

We also postulate that, for those limits, a reasonable and reliable measure of effectiveness of computer-intensive classroom experience could be provided by a study that included 25–30 matched sets of four teachers and their classes (one class each), each set within a single school district (or other administrative unit providing curricular uniformity within a state), and each set matched carefully with regard to student SES and prior achievement levels and both matched and contrasted carefully in terms of teacher pedagogy and technology infusion into instructional practice.

To conduct such a study, the research would include (1) a screening process for selecting states and districts that are implementing content standards in a way that directs teachers toward common curricular objectives but that permits wide latitude in instructional approaches; (2) a screening process for selecting schools and individual teachers that permits close matching in terms of student and teacher characteristics as well as close matching and clear contrasts in terms of the teacher pedagogy and in-class computer-use practices needed to fill each of the four cells in a matched set; (3) collection of baseline data (self-report survey data from teachers and students and test score data from the district) confirming the initial selection and matching process and providing for replacements when expected fit is not confirmed; (4) a negotiation process within each matched set for clearly defining the curriculum content, project work, assessment criteria, and project ground rules; (5) initial tests of students' technology competencies and discipline-based content knowledge; (6) periodic diary entries and completion of forms by teachers on the progress of related instruction and project work; (7) periodic reports from students regarding their project work, including mini-questionnaires and possibly diaries; (8) end-of-year questionnaires from teachers and from students; and (9) outcome data including tests of both content knowledge and technology skills and, more saliently, a variety of student work products related to their demonstration of competencies, as provided by and defined in the protocol for that particular matched set of classes.

Planning did not proceed far enough to determine what the cost of such a study might be. However, we suspect that it is likely to be on the order of $2 million to $3 million. In comparison to most funded research, this is a substantial sum of money. However, compared to the funds spent annually on technology and on multiple-choice testing of a narrow range of student achievement outcomes, this does not seem like much money.

A PERSPECTIVE ON RELIABILITY AND GENERALIZABILITY

The objective of assessing a broad range of student outcomes by using performances more complex than multiple-choice tests has been generally

praised as worthwhile by assessment researchers, theoreticians, and practitioners. Nevertheless, the literature has been cautionary with respect to reliability (whether measures of student performances and products are sufficiently
consistent across different judges and scoring procedures) and generalizability
(whether measurements of a student's single performance or product sufficiently
generalizes to a broader class of theoretical instances in which common underlying attributes might be measured). Researchers have repeatedly raised the
concern that scoring of individual student work products and performances is
subject to too much variability unrelated to the underlying dimensions being
assessed for this to be a useful approach to assessing student skills, factual
knowledge, understandings, competencies, and dispositions.

These cautions derive in part from empirical studies (Baxter & Shavelson,
1994; Gao, Shavelson, & Baxter, 1994; Koretz, Stecher, Klein, McCaffrey,
& Deibert, 1993; Shavelson, Baxter, & Gao, 1993; Shavelson, Baxter, & Pine,
1991). These studies have found that a well-defined and well-monitored scoring procedure produces limited variability in scoring of specific tasks, but
that measuring the general competency or knowledge underlying its mani-
festation on any one task requires a great number of diverse tasks ranging
across the relevant content or procedural domain. These results apply most
clearly to judgments about individual students; however, even reliability at
the level of classrooms may require a substantial number of discrete tasks to
achieve adequate reliability.

Given the problems with making reliable generalizations, why would one
continue to recommend assessments of complex student performances? We
have several reasons, and they relate to the following issues:

- The level of aggregation at which findings are desired, and the level
  of reliability needed for the purpose of the assessment
- The importance of measuring the full range of important student outcomes, which traditional measurement is seen as largely incapable of
  doing
- The importance of student and teacher motivation and effort for
  achieving performances of appropriate quality relative to underlying
  competencies

The literature on performance assessment focuses on three different types
of assessment programs, each with its own characteristic purposes and other
attributes:

- Performance assessments developed or used by individual teachers and
  schools to provide student-level diagnosis and adjustment of a teacher's
  own instructional practices

- Performance assessments incorporated into large-scale testing programs that have a variety of purposes, such as evaluating teachers, assessing school-level accountability, and providing individual student scores on dimensions of academic skill and knowledge
- Studies of the consequences of alternative instructional practices, curricula, or features of school organization, such as the consequences of sustained use of computer technologies

From a perusal of this literature, one inescapable conclusion can be reached: Very little research on the reliability and generalizability of performance assessments is focused on research on instructional programs and practices. Nearly all of it concerns the quality of teacher-developed instruments for diagnosis and instructional planning or the quality of large-scale performance assessments for purposes of evaluating individual students, teachers, and schools. Thus, the requirements of assessment measures for research studies has simply not been addressed.

In both teacher-based diagnostic assessments and in large-scale assessments that have the goal of providing individual student scores, the reliability that matters is at the level of the individual student. Teachers need to know on an absolute scale what individual students are able to accomplish and understand; school administrators communicating student scores to parents want to accurately rank students with respect to national samples or rate them with respect to a clearly understood standard of accomplishment. The concern with student-level reliability, valuable for both statewide assessments and teacher-diagnostic efforts, seems to involve misplaced precision when applied to research activities aimed only at the general problem of distinguishing whether computer-based approaches yield greater academic knowledge, understanding, and performance compared to other instructional approaches.

A study, for example, that involves 20 pairs of classes of students, contrasting classes where computers are used to a great extent with similar classes that do not use computers, needs only to determine to what extent the 500 students in one group of classes have different levels of skill, knowledge, depth of understanding, general competencies, and dispositions than the 500 students in the other group of classes.

For generalizability, again the requirement is that appropriate conclusions be made concerning the differences between two or more study populations in the aggregate, not differences among individual students. To address the problem of generalizability, one might use a procedure in which each student undertakes only a limited number of tasks (e.g., as few as one), but where the content (or conditions or procedures) varies substantially across different individuals or classrooms in the study population (but does *not* vary between the two contrasting study populations). Thus, domain coverage of content and other important conditions is maintained without increasing the burden on any one student to supply the variety of data necessary.

Consequently, it is unreasonable to hold to the reliability standards met by psychometrically sophisticated multiple-choice tests when conducting assessments that do not require the precision of individual-level measures. A great deal can be learned from research that addresses questions where there is great interest even when measures are "sloppy," in a psychometric sense.

Take, for example, survey data from questionnaire and interview studies of adults. Although, in some cases, survey researchers will use item analysis and exploratory factor analysis to develop indices that have a reasonable level of internal-consistency reliability, this subfield tends to focus much more on issues of domain coverage than on redundancy, both in index construction and in questionnaire construction as a whole. Often, the analysis of survey research data proceeds from single-item measures, even simple dichotomies, with substantial analysis involved in looking at differences between subgroups in the percentage of sample cases that responded with, for example, the answer "yes" rather than "no."

We do not argue that such analysis is superior to well-refined scales with high standard deviations—only that much useful research can be accomplished with simple, if highly imprecise, measurements. In research studies of programs and practices, we think that the need to measure all the relevant variables in the causal system (e.g., teachers' instructional practices and philosophy, their use of technology resources, and their work environment) outweighs the importance of having the relative scores of respondents on any individual dimension measured with a high degree of precision.

CONCLUSIONS AND A FINAL COMMENT

For too long, comparative assessments of student academic accomplishment have been limited to short-duration paper-and-pencil tests. Such standardized tests are not likely to provide accurate assessments, either on an absolute scale or on a relative one, of the ability of secondary students to apply basic skills and domain knowledge in concrete contexts that more closely resemble real-life work. An examination of how computer technologies are being used in schools suggests that, in particular, it is necessary to develop assessment structures that permit students to use computer skills, tools, and resources in order to demonstrate their ability to do this real-life work—to plan investigations, to acquire information, to analyze data, to articulate reasoning, to collaborate with others, and to present findings to an audience.

Extended-in-time small-group research projects around a curriculum-relevant topic can provide a structure for conducting these resource-friendly assessments. By focusing assessments of student project work on academic outcomes for which computer expertise may be helpful, and by permitting, but not mandating, students to use computer tools and resources to accomplish their project tasks, we can conduct research on the consequences of providing students with a high-intensity technology school experience.

The design presented in this chapter for a research-oriented, project-based assessment is an effort to stimulate thinking into how an expanded and more appropriate set of student competencies might be incorporated into the toolbox of researchers (and also perhaps of large-scale assessment specialists). Because of our interest in providing a more appropriate range of outcome measures for studying the effects of sustained and intensive school computer experiences, we were drawn to extended-in-time performance assessments, seeing the amenability of such assessments to incorporating the use of computer tools and resources. However, the technical problems with such free-ranging assessment structures need much more assessment expertise than we can provide.

Policy decisions about investments in school computers will not be made on the basis of appropriate information about the consequences of student computer use until established testing organizations, and the broad array of public bodies that support them, develop assessment procedures built around both standardization and variability in the use of resources. Our goal here is to attempt to provide a model of how this can be done and the benefits that can be obtained when it is done. It is our hope that others, including those with greater technical expertise in student assessment, will build on and implement these ideas, so that an answer to Ted Koppel's question can be provided.

REFERENCES

Allen, G., & Thompson, A. (1995). Analysis of the effect of networking on computer-assisted collaborative writing in a fifth grade classroom. *Journal of Educational Computing Research*, 12(1), 65–75.

Baxter, G. P., & Shavelson, R. J. (1994). Science performance assessments: Benchmarks and surrogates. *International Journal of Educational Research*, 21, 279–298.

Cognition and Technology Group at Vanderbilt. (1996). Looking at technology in context: A framework for understanding technology and education research. In D. C. Berliner & R. C. Calfee (Eds.), *Handbook of educational psychology* (pp. 807–840). New York: Macmillan.

Gao, X., Shavelson, R. J., & Baxter, G. P. (1994). Generalizability of large-scale performance assessments in science: Promises and problems. *Applied Measurement in Education*, 7, 323–342.

Gibson, J. J. (1977). The theory of affordances. In R. E. Shaw & J. Bransford (Eds.), *Perceiving, acting, and knowing* (pp. 67–82). Hillsdale, NJ: Erlbaum.

Koppel, T. (1998, September 30). *Will computers improve public education* [TV program transcript]. ABC News, *Nightline*.

Koretz, D., Stecher, B., Klein, S., McCaffrey, D., & Deibert, E. (1993). *Can portfolios assess student performance and influence instruction? The 1991–92 Vermont experience.* Washington, DC: RAND Institute on Education and Training and Los Angeles: National Center for Research on Evaluation, Standards, and Student Testing.

Lamon, M., Reeve, R., & Caswell, B. (1999, April). *Finding theory in practice: Collaborative networks for professional learning.* Paper presented at the American Educational Research Association, Montreal.

Lovitts, B. E. (2000). *Sketch for a design for a study of high-intensity technology settings.* Washington DC: American Institutes for Research.

Mandinach, E. B., & Cline, H. F. (1994). *Classroom dynamics: Implementing a technology-based learning environment.* Mahwah, NJ: Erlbaum.

Mandinach, E. B., & Cline, H. F. (1996). Classroom dynamics: The impact of a technology-based curriculum innovation on teaching and learning. *Journal of Educational Computing Research, 14*(1), 83–102.

Messick, S. (1994). The interplay of evidence and consequences in the validation of performance assessments. *Educational Researcher, 23*(2), 13–23.

Murphy, R., Penuel, B., Means, B., Korbak, C., Whaley, A., & Allen, J. (2002). *E-DESK: A review of recent evidence on discrete educational software.* Menlo Park, CA: SRI International.

Norman, D. (1988). *The psychology of everyday things.* New York: Basic Books.

Riel, M. M., & Becker, H. J. (2000, April). *The beliefs, practices, and computer use of teacher leaders.* Paper presented at the American Educational Research Association, New Orleans.

Roschelle, J., Kaput, J. J., & Stroup, W. (2000). SIMCALC: Accelerating students' engagement with the mathematics of change (pp. 47–75). In M. J. Jacobson & R. B. Kozma (Eds.), *Innovations in science and mathematics education: Advanced designs for technologies of learning.* Mahwah, NJ: Erlbaum.

Salomon, G., Perkins, D. N., & Globerson, T. (1991). Partners in cognition: Extending human intelligence with intelligent technologies. *Educational Researcher, 20*(3), 2–9.

Shavelson, R. J., Baxter, G. P., & Gao, X. (1993). Sampling variability of performance assessments. *Journal of Educational Measurement, 30,* 215–232.

Shavelson, R. J., Baxter, G. P., & Pine, J. (1991). Performance assessments in science. *Applied Measurement in Education, 4,* 347–362.

Chapter 6

Improving Educational Assessment

Robert J. Mislevy
Linda S. Steinberg
Russell G. Almond
Geneva D. Haertel
William R. Penuel

Interest in complex and innovative assessment is expanding nowadays for several reasons. Advances in cognitive and educational psychology broaden the range of things we want to know about students and possibilities for what we might see to give us evidence (Glaser, Lesgold, & Lajoie, 1987). We have opportunities to put new technologies to use in assessment, to create new kinds of tasks, to bring them to life, to interact with examinees (Bennett, 1999; Quellmalz & Haertel, 1999). We are called upon to investigate the success of technologies in instruction, even as they target knowledge and skills that are not well measured by conventional assessments. But how do we design complex assessments so they provide the information we need to achieve their intended purpose? How do we make sense of the complex data they may generate?

In this chapter, we describe the use of principled assessment design as a means of addressing these questions. Three assessments will be used to illustrate the tenets of the design process. The first of the assessments is the Graduate Record Exam (GRE). This assessment was selected as an example since its purposes, format, and content are familiar to many, thus making it easier to apply the tenets of principled assessment design. In many institutions of higher education, a student must take and perform sufficiently well on the

GRE in order to matriculate to a graduate program. The second examination that is described is a simulation-based assessment of problem solving in dental hygiene. It is referred to as DISC, which is the acronym for the Dental Interactive Simulation Corporation (Mislevy et al., 1999, 2003). This prototype examination was selected for inclusion because it was designed using principled assessment design. The third examination is a hypothetical online performance task that was being designed by researchers to evaluate Classroom Connect's AmericaQuest instructional program (Penuel & Shear, 2000). It was included in this chapter to illustrate how technology and principled assessment design could be combined to provide powerful supports that could enhance the design and presentation of complex assessment tasks.

We begin by presenting vignettes that highlight how these three assessments are delivered to examinees and the nature of the examinees' assessment experience.

THREE ASSESSMENT VIGNETTES

The GRE

Amy, a recent graduate from a 4-year college, signs up to take the Graduate Record Examination (GRE) as part of her application to a postgraduate degree program in chemistry. As she begins to prepare for the examination, she has to plan her time wisely. She must review her verbal, quantitative, and analytic writing skills and, since the GRE is now administered via computer, she must identify effective test-taking strategies that can be applied to computer-delivered assessments. After she arrives at the test center on the day of her examination, she takes a seat at a personal computer. As the exam begins, she reads the instructions on the computer monitor and then moves on to the first question, which is followed by a list of possible answers. After she answers the first question, her response is cataloged, and then the next question appears on the screen. The computer supplies the second question at a level that takes into account Amy's success on the first item. If she answers the question correctly, the next question that appears will be more challenging. If she fails to choose the correct response, the subsequent question will be less difficult. The particular selection of GRE items that Amy will respond to depends on her performance on the prior GRE item as well as on the percentage of correct responses she has made to the prior questions. Amy will work for approximately 3½ hours at the computer to complete the examination. She will know within minutes of completing the GRE what scores she received.

DISC

Miguel graduated from Calvert County Community College's training program in dental hygiene this June, and he has already passed the multiple-choice content-knowledge test and the clinical examination on his way to becoming a licensed dental hygienist. Today he is taking the computer-based simulation assessment of problem-solving and decision-making skills. After checking in, he sits down at the computer to begin working his way through interactions with eight simulated patients. The first begins with a video clip of Elsa, a middle-aged woman who is seeking dental attention for the first time in 5 years. Miguel proceeds to take a patient history, asking Elsa questions on a checklist and following up problematic answers. He orders radiographs and finds probing depths. He summarizes his findings in terms of a dental insurance form, noting cues on which he based his hypotheses and notes to the dentist. Other simulated patients will present different challenges in treatment, evaluation, and education. Each one reminds Miguel of patients he has seen in the Calvert County clinic, and the experience feels surprisingly familiar. If Miguel has difficulties with the simulations, he will receive a summary of the aspects of patient care in which he needs additional study. But if he has done well, he will soon receive that long-awaited letter from the state board with his license.

MashpeeQuest

In a hypothetical scenario, Duanli, an American history teacher, introduces her honors class of 26 middle school students to what it means to offer evidence of proof of a historical fact. Working in groups, the students generate a list of historical truths about Native American tribes in the United States. Duanli asks, "How do you know what is true?" A discussion ensues in which students talk about history, its recording, and how scholars and writers document historical facts.

Duanli assigns a research project to the class. The assignment provides students with an experience in using primary historical documents and in developing and presenting an argument about what is true and what cannot be proved. As part of the research project, students will use their computers to access several primary sources to answer the question, "Do the Mashpee Wampanoags people qualify for official tribal recognition given the accepted guidelines as specified by the United States government?" In order to answer this question, students must determine what the guidelines are for tribal recognition and which criteria the Mashpee Wampanoags people meet under these guidelines, using evidence from the primary sources.

Duanli must supervise student research and measure students' ability to analyze and synthesize information from several primary sources and to develop a reasoned, verifiable argument. She will assess student performance on this complex research project using a hypothetical online performance task design entitled "MashpeeQuest." This performance assessment links to an array of primary source documents, including census data, personal testimony, and observational accounts of tribal customs, property deeds, and other government documentation. Duanli is interested in being able not only to score the student's performance but to trace the processes in which students engage as they complete the assessment task.

Therefore, embedded in the MashpeeQuest assessment task are online tools for measuring students' abilities to use multiple sources, to evaluate these sources, to synthesize information, to formulate hypotheses, and finally to construct an argument. The task design does this by tracking the students' solution path, how many documents students review, how often they revisit these documents, the notes they take, the questions they ask as they learn new information, and the foundations they use to substantiate their suppositions.

These vignettes provide a glimpse of the nature and essence of the three assessments (although the MashpeeQuest is hypothetical) to which we will apply principled assessment design. In the following sections of this chapter we present the principles of evidentiary reasoning that underlie familiar assessments and that are a special case of more general principles. Moreover, these principles can help us design and analyze new kinds of assessments, with new kinds of data, to serve new purposes.

The first half of the chapter reviews an "evidence-centered" (Schum, 1994) framework for designing assessments (Mislevy, Steinberg, & Almond, 2003). The second half discusses, through the lens of this framework, how and where advances in cognitive psychology and technology can be brought to bear to improve assessment. We draw on the three examples presented above to illustrate ideas throughout.

EVIDENCE-CENTERED ASSESSMENT DESIGN

There are two kinds of building blocks for educational assessment. Substantive building blocks concern the nature of knowledge in the domain of interest, how students learn it, and how they use their knowledge. Evidentiary-reasoning building blocks concern what and how much we learn about students' knowledge from what they say and do. How do we assemble these building blocks into an assessment? This section reviews Mislevy, Steinberg, and Almond's (2003) "conceptual assessment framework" (CAF). We will then use the structure of the CAF to discuss where and how advances in psychology and technology can be put to work to improve the practice of assessment.

Figure 6.1 is a high-level schematic of the CAF, showing three basic models we suggest must be present, and must be coordinated, to achieve a coherent assessment. A quote from Messick (1994) serves to introduce them:

> A construct-centered approach [to assessment design] would begin by asking what complex of knowledge, skills, or other attribute should be assessed, presumably because they are tied to explicit or implicit objectives of instruction or are otherwise valued by society. Next, what behaviors or performances should reveal those constructs, and what tasks or situations should elicit those behaviors? Thus, the nature of the construct guides the selection or construction of relevant tasks as well as the rational development of construct-based scoring criteria and rubrics. (p. 17)

The Student Model

"What complex of knowledge, skills, or other attributes should be assessed?" Configurations of values of student-model variables are meant to approximate, from some perspective about skill and knowledge in the domain, certain aspects of the infinite configurations of skill and knowledge real students have. It could be the perspective of behaviorist, trait, cognitive, or situative psychology. But from whichever perspective, we encounter the evidentiary problem of reasoning from limited evidence. Student-model variables are the terms in which we want to talk about students, to determine evaluations, make decisions, or to plan instruction—but we don't get to see the values directly. We just see what the students say or do and must use this as evidence about the student-model variables.

The student model in Figure 6.1 depicts student-model variables as circles. The arrows connecting them represent important empirical or theoretical associations. These variables and associations are implicit in informal applications of reasoning in assessment, such as a one-to-one discussion between a student and a tutor. In the more formal applications discussed in this chap-

Figure 6.1. Three Basic Models of Assessment Design

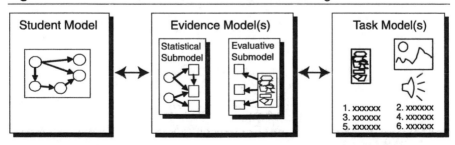

ter, we use a probability model to manage our knowledge about a given student's (inherently unobservable) values for these variables at any given point in time. We express our knowledge as a probability distribution, which can be updated in light of new evidence. In particular, the student model takes the form of a fragment of a Bayesian inference network, or Bayes net (Jensen, 1996).

A conception of competence in the domain is necessary for determining the number and nature of the student model variables to use in a given application, but it is not sufficient. This will also depend on the purpose of the assessment. A single variable that characterizes overall proficiency might suffice in an assessment meant to support only a summary pass/fail decision. But a coached practice system to help students develop the same proficiency would require a finer-grained student model in order to monitor particular aspects of skill and knowledge for which feedback is available. When the purpose is program evaluation, the grain size and the nature of the student-model variables should reflect ways in which a program may enjoy more or less success, or promote students' learning in some ways as opposed to others. The purpose of the MashpeeQuest assessment is to gather information about students' information-gathering and synthesis skills in a technological environment. It follows that the student model should include variables that concern aspects of these skills, to be defined more concretely by the kinds of observations we will posit constitute evidence about them.

It requires further thought to decide whether to include student-model variables for aspects of these skills as they are used in nontechnological situations, to be informed by observations from nontechnological situations. There are two reasons one might do this, and both revolve around purpose. First, if we want to talk about differential impacts in different environments, we must be able to distinguish skills as they are used in different technological environments. This might be done with a multivariate student model with variables that disentangle such effects from the same complex performances or with multiple but distinct assessments with different sources of evidence and each with its own student-model variables. Second, if we want to compare students in the targeted instructional program with students not in that program, we will not be able to obtain evidence from the latter with ways of collecting evidence that depend on being familiar with technologies specific to the program.

Example 1: The GRE. The student model that underlies most familiar assessments is a single variable, typically denoted ▦, that represents proficiency in a specified domain of tasks. We use as examples the paper-and-pencil and the Computer Adaptive Testing (CAT) versions of the GRE, which comprise domains of items for verbal, quantitative, and analytic reasoning skills. The

You can get involved in
Reach Out and Read and
help pediatricians bring books and
a love of reading into the lives of
young children and their families!

■

Donate on-line at
www.reachoutandread.org
$27.50 purchases 10 beautiful,
new books for a child

■

Join the Friends of
Reach Out and Read

■

Donate your gently used
children's books to ROR

■

Conduct a book drive
in your community

■

Volunteer to read
at a ROR clinic

■

Join our mailing list
to learn of special events
in your community

FOR INFORMATION VISIT OUR WEBSITE:
www.reachoutandread.org

Reach Out and Read®

Making Books Part of a Healthy Childhood

Our Mission:

Reach Out and Read makes literacy promotion a standard part of pediatric primary care so that children grow up with books and a love of reading.

Our Model:

■ In the exam room, trained doctors and nurses talk to parents about the importance of reading aloud.

■ At each check-up from 6 months to 5 years, the child receives a new book to take home.

■ Clinic waiting rooms are transformed into literacy rich areas with volunteer readers modeling techniques of reading aloud.

student model for the GRE (quantitative, verbal, and analytic writing) is represented as ▥ → θ. The first symbol represents the probability distribution that expresses current belief about a student's unobservable status. At the beginning of an examinee's assessment, the probability distribution representing a new student's status will be uninformative. We update it in accordance with responses to GRE verbal test items.

We can describe this model in terms of Bayes nets. In assessment, a Bayes net contains both student-model variables, the inherently unobservable aspects of knowledge or skill about which we want to draw inferences, and observable variables, about which we can ascertain values directly and which are modeled as depending in probability on the student-model variables. The student-model variables are a fragment of this complete network. Another kind of fragment contains one or more observable variables as well as pointers to the student-model variables they depend on. As discussed in the section below on "The Evidence Model," we can combine ("dock") the student-model (SM) Bayes net fragment with an appropriate evidence-model (EM) fragment when we want to update our beliefs about the student-model variables in light of data (Almond & Mislevy, 1999).

The GRE was developed using concepts from trait psychology. From this psychological perspective, traits—the targets of inference—are believed to influence student performances in many situations. The student model is quite simple. The traits represented in the GRE student model are verbal, quantitative, and analytic reasoning—just one trait for each section of the test, with all the items in that section contributing to the measurement of that trait. However, the other two examples that will be presented (DISC and MashpeeQuest) are based on student models that represent advances in cognitive and situative psychologies. In these psychological perspectives, the students' expertise is reflected in patterns, skills, knowledge, and abilities that evolve with the accumulation of competence.

Example 2: DISC. The Educational Testing Service (ETS) is working with the Chauncey Group International (CGI) to develop a scoring engine for a prototype of a simulation-based assessment of problem solving in dental hygiene, under contract with the Dental Interactive Simulation Corporation (DISC). We are working through student, evidence, and task models with DISC, and consequently examining the implications for the simulator. Two considerations shaped the student model for the prototype assessment. First was the nature of skills DISC wanted to focus on: the problem-solving and decision-making skills a hygienist employs on the job. The second was the purpose of the assessment: a licensure decision, with some supplementary information about strengths and weaknesses. We will therefore refer to the student model described below as an "overall proficiency + supplementary feedback" student model. While the use of the DISC example falls outside of K–12 education, we include it in this chapter because its student model is more complex than those presented for the GRE and MashpeeQuest. This complexity reflects understandings drawn from the theory and methods developed as part of advances in the psychologies of cognition and information processing. The assessment design approach and the character of the models and the tasks would be appropriate for simulation-based problem solving in mathematics and science.

Adapting cognitive task analysis methods from the expertise literature (Ericcson & Smith, 1991), we captured and analyzed protocols from hygienists at different levels of expertise as they solved a range of tasks in the domain (Johnson, Wohlgemuth, Cameron, Caughtman, Koertge, Barna & Schultz, 1998). We abstracted general characterizations of patterns of behavior—a language that could describe solutions across subjects and cases not only in the data at hand but also in the domain of dental hygiene decision-making problems more broadly. An example was using disparate sources of information. Novice hygienists were usually able to note important cues on particular forms of information, such as shadows on radiographs and bifurcations on probing charts, but they often failed to generate hypotheses that required integrating cues across different forms. We defined student-model variables that would characterize a hygienist's tendency to demonstrate these indicators, overall and as broken down into a small number of facets that could also be reported to students. Figure 6.2 is a simplified version of the student model we are presently using.

The ovals in Figure 6.2 are the SM variables. Two toward the upper right are *Assessment*, or proficiency in assessing the status of a new patient, and *Information Gathering/Usage*. The small boxes with grid lines represent conditional probabilities for the variables they point to, given the values of the variables from which they emanate. The full model further elaborates *Information Gathering/Usage* into variables for knowing how and where to obtain information, being able to generate hypotheses that would guide searches and interpretations, and knowing how to gather information that would help confirm or refute hypotheses.

Example 3: MashpeeQuest. Our third example is a hypothetical online performance task designed by researchers from SRI International to evaluate Classroom Connect's AmericaQuest instructional program. AmericaQuest aims to help students learn to develop persuasive arguments, supported by evidence they acquire from the course's website or their own research. MashpeeQuest poses a problem that gives students an opportunity to put these skills to use in a web-based environment that structures their work. Thus, this example illustrates how technology-based assessments provide

Figure 6.2. Simplified DISC Student Model

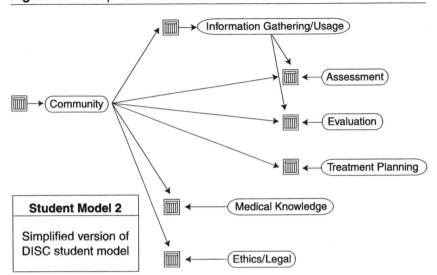

web-based environments that support the delivery of heavily contextualized assessment tasks that reflect new understandings from situative or psycho-cultural psychology. Furthermore, the recent advances in web-based technologies provide a means of capturing detailed evidence of students' performances that can be used in scoring students' proficiencies on the variables specified in the student model.

The design of the MashpeeQuest performance task was motivated by the goals of the evaluation. It assesses a subset of the skills that the AmericaQuest program is meant to foster:

- *Information analysis skills.* Ability to analyze and synthesize information from a variety of sources; ability to evaluate/critique both content and sources
- *Problem-solving skills.* Ability to synthesize disparate ideas through reasoning in a problem-solving context; ability to offer reasoned arguments rather than brief guesses; ability to formulate creative, well-founded theories for unsolved questions in science and history

Figure 6.3 illustrates two possible student models that are consistent with the preceding description. They differ in their specificity, or grain size. The first, which contains just two variables, would be used to accumulate information about students in terms of just Information Analysis Skills and

Figure 6.3. Two Possible MashpeeQuest Student Models

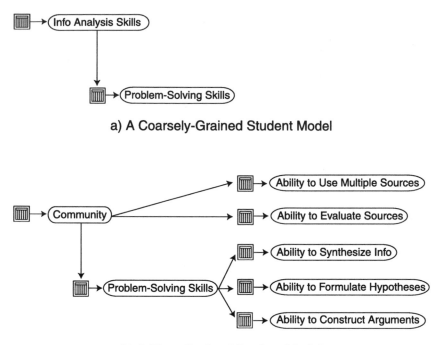

a) A Coarsely-Grained Student Model

b) A Finer-Grained Student Model

Problem-Solving Skills. The arrow between them indicates that they may be correlated in the population of students being addressed. The second student model includes variables for subskills so that evidence may be accumulated separately for them and used to identify for students or teachers more specific areas of strengths or difficulties. Deciding which of the two models to use would require (1) weighing the more detailed information in the finer-grained model against its lower accuracy and (2) examining the empirical correlation among the subskills, since the more highly they are correlated, the less that is gained by modeling them explicitly.

The effective meaning of any of these student-model variables will be determined by choices about the observations that are deemed to constitute evidence about them. In the MashpeeQuest task, students will have to weigh evidence they might find in online visits to cities in the northeastern United States to help decide a court case involving recognition for the Mashpee Wampanoags, a Native American tribe in Massachusetts. A band of people claiming Wampanoag ancestry have been trying for more than 20 years to gain recognition from the federal government as a tribe that still exists. In 1978, a federal court ruled against the Mashpee Wampanoags' claim, arguing that the tribe could not prove that it had a continuous claim to territory in Mashpee. The tribe is seeking recognition a second time in court. The assessment asks students to take a position on the case and to identify places where a Quest expedition team should go based on information about the kinds of evidence they might find there. Students will be asked to investigate the evidence, select sites that provide evidence to support their claim, and justify their choices based on the evidence. In addition, they will be asked to identify one place to go to find evidence that doesn't support their claim and to address how their theory of what happened to the Mashpee Wampanoags is still justified.

The developers of the Mashpee task had to tackle the issue of how to define student-model variables in the evaluation of a technology-based program. This task was designed specifically for use with students who have become familiar with the vocabulary and affordances of the technological environment of AmericaQuest. It obtains evidence about how well they can apply the skills they have been presumably developing in the AmericaQuest environment, but on other problems. This task's role in the evaluation is providing evidence about whether the students in the program can in fact use skills they have been working on, rather than comparing these students with other students from different programs or even with themselves before they began the program. Other components of the evaluation have been designed to produce evidence that can be compared across groups whether or not they are familiar with the environment and conventions of AmericaQuest.

The Evidence Model

"What behaviors or performances should reveal those constructs," and what is the connection? The evidence model lays out our argument about why and how the observations in a given task situation constitute evidence about student model variables. Figure 6.1 shows two parts to the evidence model, the *evaluative* submodel and the *statistical* submodel. The evaluative submodel extracts the salient features of the work product—whatever the student says, does, or creates in the task situation. The statistical submodel updates the student model in accordance with the values of these features, thus synthesizing the evidentiary value of performances over tasks (Mislevy & Gitomer, 1996).

The Evaluative Submodel. In the icon for the evaluative submodel in Figure 6.1, the work product is a rectangle containing a jumble of complicated figures at the far right. It is a unique human production, as simple as a mark on an answer sheet or as complex as a series of evaluations and treatments in a patient-management problem. The squares coming out of the work product represent "observable variables," the evaluative summaries of the key aspects of the performance. The evaluation rules map unique human productions into a common interpretative framework. These mappings can be as simple as determining whether the mark on an answer sheet is the correct answer or as complex as an expert's evaluation of multiple aspects of a patient-management solution. They can be automatic or require human judgment. An evidence rule based on the GRE example follows (see Figure 6.4).

What is important about this evidence rule is that a machine can carry it out. This technological breakthrough slashed the costs of testing in the 1940s. But the new technology did not change the essential nature of the evidence or the inference. It was used to streamline the process by modifying the student's work product to a machine-readable answer sheet and having a machine rather than a human apply the evaluation rules.

In the second example, based on DISC, the cognitive task analysis (CTA) produced "performance features" that characterize patterns of behavior and differentiate levels of expertise. They were the basis of generally defined, reusable observed variables. The evidence models themselves are assemblies of student-model variables and observable variables, including methods for determining the values of the observable variables and updating student-model variables accordingly. A particular assessment case will utilize the structures of one or more evidence models, fleshed out in accordance with specifics of that case.

The evaluation submodel of an evidence model concerns the mappings from examinees' unique problem solutions into a common framework of evaluation—that is, from work products to values of observable variables. What is constant in the evaluation submodels for tasks that are built to conform with the same evidence model are the identification and formal definition of observable variables and generally stated "proto-rules" for evaluating their values. Adequacy of examination procedure is an aspect of any assessment of any new patient, for example; we can define a generally stated evaluative framework to describe how well an examinee has adapted to whatever situation is presented. What is customized to particular cases are case-specific

Figure 6.4. An Example Rule Taken from the GRE Example

IF the response selected by the examinee matches the response marked as the key in the database,
THEN the item response IS correct
ELSE the item response IS NOT correct.

rules, or rubrics, for evaluating values of observables—instantiations of the proto-rules tailored to the specifics of case. The unique features of a particular virtual patient's initial presentation in a given assessment situation determine what an examinee ought to do in assessment and why.

The hypothetical MashpeeQuest task, which is the third example, requires students to demonstrate a particular set of information analysis skills and problem-solving skills that form the student model. While the task provides only a single-problem context in which students may demonstrate these skills, it provides multiple opportunities for students to demonstrate different aspects of information analysis skill, in different ways, in different parts of the problem. The observable variables defined to give evidence of information skills all demonstrate more generally cast skills one needs to use the Internet to conduct research or inquiry: comparing information from multiple sources by browsing and reading different web links, constructing texts that compare information gleaned from these sources, and evaluating the credibility of that information. The observables evidencing problem-solving skills are specific to the AmericaQuest instructional program, but all have strong parallels to the argumentation skills required of students in other innovative web-based learning programs (e.g., Linn, Bell, & Hsi, 1999). These include using information on the Internet as clues to solving a discrete problem and generating theories, based on consideration of evidence and counterevidence, related to a controversy in history and anthropology.

Technology plays two roles in the evaluative component of the evidence model for the MashpeeQuest task. The first is conceptual: The information analysis skills to be assessed and the behaviors that evidence them are embedded within the web-based assessment environment. The MashpeeQuest task intentionally takes a specific context for analyzing information—the World Wide Web—and tests a model of information analysis that involves performances specific to using the web for research and inquiry (e.g., clicking through different links, inferring the validity of sources from specific aspects of the web page). The second is more operational: Because actions take place in a technological environment, some of the observables can be evaluated automatically. Evidence rules for the observables—number of sources and time per source—are as straightforward as those for the GRE paper-and-pencil test. Other observables are better evaluated by people. For example, student performance on subtasks requiring information analysis would be scored by human raters using a rubric that evaluates students' discussion of coherence and discussion of credibility of the sites they visited.

The Statistical Submodel. In the icon for the statistical submodel in Figure 6.1, the observable are modeled as depending on some subset of the student-model variables. Item response theory, latent class models, and factor analysis are examples of models in which values of observed variables probably depend on unobservable variables. We can express them as special cases of Bayes nets and extend the ideas as appropriate to the nature of the student model and observable variables (Almond & Mislevy, 1999; Mislevy, 1994). In complex situations, statistical models from psychometrics can play crucial roles as building blocks. These models evolved to address certain recurring issues in reasoning about what students know and can do, given what we see them do in a limited number of circumscribed situations, often captured as judgments of different people who may not agree in their evaluations.

Figure 6.5 represents the components of the statistical model used in the evidence model of the GRE-CAT. An item response theory model is used. The key idea is that a given examinee can be administered different items from the item pool (represented on the right), and the items can be selected on the basis of the examinee's previous responses. When an item is administered, the statistical information for the item in the library is used to determine how the information in the response X_j is used to update the distribution that expresses current belief about that student's ability (represented on the left). Further discussion of the statistical aspects of this process can be found in Mislevy, Almond, Yan, and Steinberg (1999).

Figure 6.6 shows the Bayes net fragment that comprises the statistical submodel of one particular evidence model taken from the DISC example. It concerns gathering patient information when assessing a new patient's status. At the far left are student-model variables that we posit drive performance in these situations: *Assessment* of new patients and *Information Gathering/Usage*. The nodes on the right are generally defined observable variables. Two of them are *Adapting to situational constraints* and *Adequacy of examination proce-*

Figure 6.5. The Statistical Submodel of the Evidence
Model in the GRE-CAT

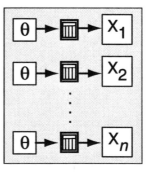

Sample Bayes net fragment
(IRT model and parameters for
this item)

Library of fragments

Figure 6.6. The Bayes Net Fragment in an Evidence Model in DISC

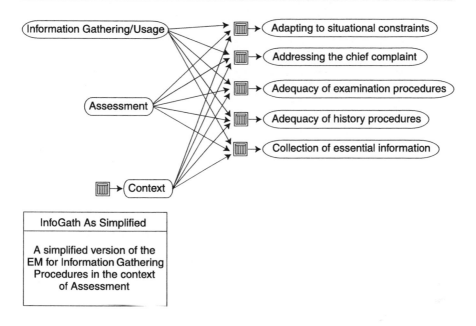

dures, in terms of how well their rationale is grounded. In a specific case, the values of the observable variables are the result of applying rubrics that have tailored the general rubric for this observable to the particulars of the case. Figure 6.7 shows how this evidence-model Bayes net fragment is "docked" with the student-model fragment when an examinee is working in a situation that has been constructed to conform with this evidence model.

Figure 6.8 depicts the statistical submodel of the evidence model related to student information analysis skills assessed in a hypothetical family of tasks like the MashpeeQuest task. The focus is on measuring student performance in the context of a problem that requires them to read, interpret, and use information on the web to solve a problem like those presented in the AmericaQuest program. At the left of the figure are two variables from the finer-grained student model introduced above, namely the *Ability to use multiple sources* and *Ability to evaluate sources* that are parts of information analysis skills (as shown in Figure 6.3). These parent variables drive the probabilities of the observable variables in the middle of the figure and the lower right. We see that *Ability to use multiple sources* is informed by the observable variables *Number of sources, Time per source*, and [quality of] *Comparison across links. Number of sources* could have as many values as there are links in the task. Because no prior information is given to students about

Figure 6.7. Docking Student-Model and Evidence-Model Bayes Net Fragments in DISC

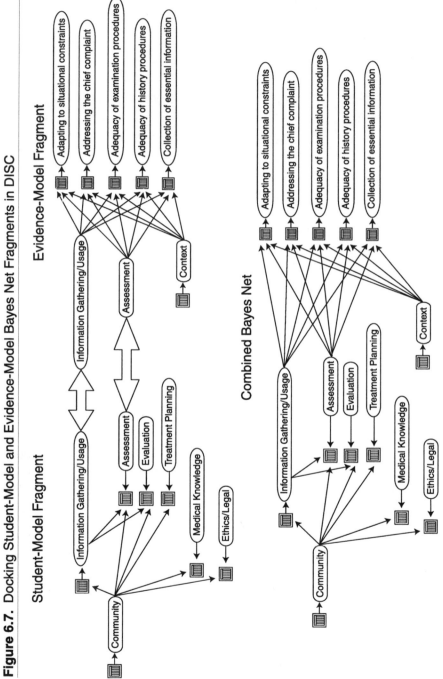

Figure 6.8. A MashpeeQuest Evidence Model

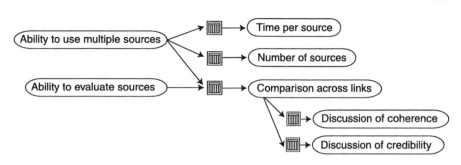

what sources are more likely to have useful information, more sources considered is taken as evidence of better information analysis skills.

Time per source could have any number of values from just a few seconds to several minutes. Here, one would see whether students were simply "clicking through" without reading a particular link. The time spent is an important counterbalance to the number of sources considered, since it is an (imperfect) indicator of whether students actually read the text on the links they used. [Quality of] *Comparison across links* is actually a composite of two ratings of the same student responses, namely evaluations of how well they participated in *Discussion of coherence* and *Discussion of credibility* of the sites they visited—key features of effective information analysis, according to experts in this domain (Wineburg, 1998).

We also see that the student-model variable *Ability to evaluate sources* is also informed by the *Comparison across links*. *Ability to evaluate sources* is *not* modeled as informed by *Number of sources or Time per source*, although students' inability to access sites would surely prevent them from providing evaluations. For this reason, the structure of the conditional probability distribution for this observable would indicate that at least some ability to gather information across sites would be required in addition to evaluative skill in order to have a high probability of good ratings on this observable. One could in principle get evidence about *Ability to evaluate sources* unconfounded by students' ability to find them and analyze the information they contained by presenting subtasks in which students were simply presented sites and synopses of them, and asked to evaluate their coherence and credibility.

The Task Model

"What tasks or situations should elicit those behaviors?" A task model provides a framework for constructing and describing the situations in which examinees act. A task model includes specifications for the environment in which the student will say, do, or produce something; for example, characteristics of stimulus material, instructions, help, tools, affordances. It also includes specifications for the work product, the form in which what the student says, does, or produces will be captured. Assigning specific values to task-model variables, and providing materials that suit the specifications there given, produces a particular task. A task thus describes particular circumstances meant to provide the examinee an opportunity to act in ways that produce information about what they know or can do more generally. Distinct, possibly quite different, evidence rules could be applied to the same work product from a given task. Distinct and possibly quite different student models, befitting different purposes or derived from different conceptualizations of proficiency, could be informed by data from the same task.

A task model in the GRE describes a class of test items. There is a correspondence between task models and GRE "item types" (e.g., sentence completion, passage comprehension, quantitative comparison). These item types require different task models, because different sets of variables are needed to describe their distinct kinds of stimulus materials and presentation formats, and different features may be important in modeling item parameters or controlling item selection.

Task-model variables for the DISC prototype specify information the simulator needs for the virtual patient and features that will evoke particular aspects of skill and knowledge. A test developer can create a case by first referring to a matrix that cross-references student-model variables, evidence models that can be used to get information about them, and task models around which tasks can be constructed to provide that evidence. Once a task model is selected, it is fleshed out with particulars to create a new virtual patient.

Task-model variables that describe the patient include, as examples, Age, Last Visit, Reason for Last Visit, Symptoms of Abuse/Neglect, Demeanor, and Risk for Medical Emergency. Some of these are also important in focusing on aspects of proficiency the CTA revealed. Risk for Medical Emergency, for example, should be set to "low" or "none" for cases in which evidence about Medical Knowledge is not sought, but values of "moderate" or "high" necessitate the use of evidence models that do include Medical Knowledge as one of the student-model variables.

Task models also include specifications for work products. The simulator records the sequence of actions an examinee makes, which can then be parsed by evaluation rules. Several of the performance features that emerged from the CTA concerned intermediate mental products such as identification of cues, generation of hypotheses, and selection of tests to explore conjectures—steps that are usually not manifest in practice but that directly involve central knowledge and skills for problem solving in dental hygiene. Work products that require the examinee to make such steps explicit will capture more direct evidence of the thinking behind a solution than the sequence of actions will. Following patient assessment, for example, the examinee will fill out a summary form that requires synthesized findings in a form similar to commonly used insurance forms.

In the assessment designed for AmericaQuest, a number of features of the task model are not content specific, but they are subject-matter specific. The kinds of problems should involve the consideration of historical and archaeological evidence, as AmericaQuest does, that does not necessitate a focus on the Mashpee or any other Native American tribe per se. The problem statement should ask students to formulate a hypothesis and back it with evidence gathered from information available to them in the web-based assessment environment, as they do in AmericaQuest and as specified in the student model of problem-solving skill. The task model would vary if students were asked to display analysis skills in ways other than stating a hypothesis and supplying web-based evidence, for then both the kinds of material made available to students and the kinds of work products they produced could differ.

There are important ways one could vary the task to isolate particular skills identified in the student model. At present, the different links on MashpeeQuest do not all contain evidence in support of one hypothesis or another about the Mashpee. Some links contain evidence suggesting the tribe disappeared, while others contain evidence suggesting the tribe has maintained its traditions and culture despite generations of acculturation to American ways of life. If one were interested solely in comparison of multiple sources of information—and not whether students could formulate ideas about the coherence of ideas across links or sources—one could vary the particular links so that students were simply accumulating different pieces of evidence in support of one particular hypothesis. All the links could, for example, support the idea that the Mashpee were in fact a tribe with a continuous historical existence, and the task for students would be to draw evidence to support that theory from as many different sources or links as possible. The task model could thus be defined to include variables about the number of sources available, the degree of ambiguity among them, and their variation in quality and credibility. By varying these features systematically in different contexts, the assessment designer could produce a family of web-based investigations that varied in predictable ways as to difficulty and skills emphasized.

LEVERAGE POINTS FOR IMPROVING ASSESSMENT

This has been a quick tour of a schema for the evidentiary-reasoning foundation of assessments. It gives us some language and concepts for talking about this central core of assessment, not only for familiar forms and uses of assessment but also for new forms and uses. We can use this framework to discuss ways in which we can take advantage of advances in psychology and technology.

Leverage Points for Psychology

While the familiar practices of assessment and test theory originated in trait and behaviorist psychology, contemporary views of learning and cognition fit more comfortably into the headings of cognitive and situative psychology (Greeno, Collins, & Resnick, 1997). The cognitive perspective includes both the constructivist tradition originated by Piaget and the information-processing tradition developed by Newell and Simon (1972), Chomsky, and others. The focus is on patterns and procedures individuals use to acquire knowledge and put it to work. The situative perspective focuses on the ways individuals interact with other people in social and technological systems, so that learning includes becoming attuned to the constraints and affordances of these systems (e.g., Rogoff, 1984). In this chapter, we use the term *cognitive psychology* broadly to encompass both of these perspectives.

As Messick (1994) has pointed out, in designing an assessment we start with the questions of what we want to make inferences about and what we need to see to ground those inferences. From the perspective of trait psychology (the approach that produced the GRE), the targets of inference were traits that presumably influenced performance over a wide range of circumstances, and samples of those circumstances were needed—the cheaper the better, since the specifics of domains and tools were noise rather than signal. From the perspective of cognitive psychology (which generated our other two examples), the targets of inference are cast in terms of the patterns, skills, and knowledge structures that characterize developing expertise. This perspective shapes design decisions at several points in the three models that comprise the conceptual assessment framework.

The Character and Substance of the Student Model. How we conceive of students' knowledge and how it is acquired helps us frame our targets of inference, that is, the ways in which we will characterize what students know and can do. Glaser, who has long advocated the value of a cognitive perspective in assessment, makes the following case:

> At various stages of learning, there exist different integrations of knowledge, different degrees of procedural skill, differences in rapid access to memory and in representations of the tasks one is to perform. The fundamental character, then, of achievement measurement is based upon the assessment of growing knowledge structures, and related cognitive processes and procedural skills that develop as a domain of proficiency is acquired. These different levels signal advancing expertise or passable blockages in the course of learning. (Glaser et al., 1987, p. 77)

The DISC project provides a first example of how this can be done. The CTA provided insights into the kinds of knowledge hygienists used—and thus the dimensions along which we might wish to characterize their levels and degrees of proficiency. Recall, though, that this information is necessary for defining the variables in a student model, but not sufficient. Equally important is the purpose the assessment is intended to serve. If DISC only wanted to make a single pass/fail decision on an overall index of proficiency, a student model with a single variable might still be used to characterize an examinee. They might even use the same task models that we outlined above for our "overall decision + supplementary feedback" purposes. If DISC wanted to build an intelligent tutoring system, they might need a far more detailed student model, again consistent with the same conception of expertise but now detailed enough to capture and manage belief about many more fine-grained aspects of knowledge structures and use. Only at that level would they be able to accumulate information across situations that required the targeted skills or knowledge in terms of a student-model variable, which could then be used to trigger feedback, scaffolding, or instruction.

MashpeeQuest provides a second example. A central issue in any technology-based assessment is that of contextualization of skills to the technology being used. It is often the case that exploiting the potential of technology—of any material or social system, for that matter—means learning about and taking advantage of its unique terminologies, conventions, and affordances. Indeed, from the point of view of situative psychology, this is of the essence in learning:

> Knowing, in [the situative] perspective, is both an attribute of groups that carry out cooperative activities and an attribute of individuals who participate in the communities of which they are members. . . . Learning by a group or individual involves becoming attuned to constraints and affordances of material and social systems with which they interact. (Greeno et al., 1997, p. 17)

These insights challenge the familiar strategy of assessing through standardization—"measuring the same thing" for all students by gathering the same data under the same conditions. For example, AmericaQuest is intended to develop student skill in analyzing information and problem solving specifically in the context of an Internet-based adventure learning experience. The adventure involves using inquiry tools and evidentiary-reasoning skills typically used by historians and archaeologists, but in an important sense the analysis and problem-solving skills students are learning are confounded with learning how to use the Internet to conduct inquiry. Observation data, however, suggest that teachers' offline instruction mediates students' learning these skills in significant ways (Penuel & Shear, 2000). If teachers' assignments to students are unrelated to the central historical dilemma posed by the quest and students are not directed to weigh evidence about particular hypotheses, students will fail to learn (at least through AmericaQuest) the information analysis and problem-solving skills identified in the student model.

To what extent are the skills confounded with the technological environment? This returns us to the issue of what we want to build into the student model—what we need to "tell stories about." In the Classroom Connect evaluation plan, it was determined that some of the skills of interest provide evidence to some degree outside the AmericaQuest technological environment, and other components of the evaluation plan are designed to provide evidence about them in ways that could be used as pretests or as comparisons with students who are not familiar with the AmericaQuest technological environment. But this would be an incomplete evaluation, for providing evidence about some of the skills of interest depends on giving students the environmental support and having had the students learn to exploit its affordances. MashpeeQuest provides an opportunity to get direct evidence, then, about these contextualized skills—but with different domain knowledge. We are thus attempting to define the skills in a way that is conditioned on the technological environment but generalizes across the specifics of subject matter. This is evidence that cannot, by its very nature, be obtained from students who have not "been acculturated" in the AmericaQuest environment. Rather than obtaining a measure of skills that can be quantitatively compared with students from outside the program, MashpeeQuest provides evidence about the degree to which the AmericaQuest students exhibit the skills they were meant to develop, in an environment in which their skills have been attuned. It provides evidence for a kind of "existence proof story" among the program students rather than a "horse race story" between these students and those from another program or even themselves before they experienced the program.

What We Can Observe to Give Us Evidence. Given the terms in which we want to characterize students' capabilities, what can we observe that will constitute evidence of those capabilities? That is, what do we need to see in what a student actually says or does (the work product) and how do we characterize it when we see it (the evaluation rules)? This is especially important in complex performances. Even when we rely on largely empirical tools such as neural networks to evaluate key characteristics of a performance, success will depend on identifying the right kinds of features. For example, Stevens, Lopo, and Wang (1996) produced neural nets that were better able to distinguish experts' diagnostic solutions from novices' solutions when the input data for the neural net analysis were ordered pairs of tests the examinees requested, as compared to when the input data were simply lists of the tests they requested. There was less information in the choice of any particular medical diagnostic test than in the choice of ordered pairs of diagnostic tests—one chosen after the other. This occurred because the experts' deeper understanding of the results of the first test would give them better hypotheses to investigate with an insightful choice of a follow-up test. The experts were better able than novices to understand the implications of the results of one diagnostic medical test to optimally select the next one.

Accumulating research in cognitive psychology again provides guideposts (e.g., Ericsson & Smith, 1991). What kinds of behaviors signal expert thinking? Similar patterns have been observed across many domains, as different as radiology is from volleyball or troubleshooting hydraulics systems is from solving middle school electrical circuit problems. In general terms, experts

> (a) provide coherent explanations based on underlying principles rather than descriptions of superficial features or single statements of fact, (b) generate a plan for solution that is guided by an adequate representation of the problem situation and possible procedures and outcomes, (c) implement solution strategies that reflect relevant goals and subgoals, and (d) monitor their actions and flexibly adjust their approach based on performance feedback. (Baxter, Elder, & Glaser, 1996, p. 133)

The trick is to understand the particular forms these general patterns take in different domains. In the DISC project, we encoded them as "performance features." We identified these features from similarities in behaviors and reasoning across many problems from many hygienists at different levels of expertise. We needed to specialize to the representational forms, the problem environments and tools, and the knowledge structures and procedural requirements of the domain in question but remain with statements sufficiently general to apply to many specific situations in that domain.

The kinds of historical-reasoning behaviors elicited in the MashpeeQuest example are behaviors that are parallel to the activities of professional historians. Expert historians spend much of their time analyzing historical texts, images, and artifacts (Wineburg, 1991), just as students in the MashpeeQuest task spend most of their time reading and interpreting the text on the various links to cities in the task. The MashpeeQuest scoring rubric would assign higher scores to student behaviors that suggested that students were not just spending time analyzing documents but were also analyzing them in ways that are similar to the ways expert historians analyze documents (Wineburg, 1998). Expert historians, for example, may consider how evidence in one document supports or contradicts evidence in another document, something that students are explicitly invited to consider in the MashpeeQuest task. Student skill in analyzing documents is made visible through the formulation of an argument backed by specific evidence from the documents, as well as a consideration of possible counterevidence from other links on the MashpeeQuest site.

Modeling which Aspects of Performance Depend on which Aspects of Knowledge. The objective in the statistical model is expressing the ways in which certain aspects of performance depend on particular aspects of knowledge. As discussed above, the purpose of an assessment drives the number and granularity of student-model variables. But a CTA can additionally show how the skills and knowledge that tasks require are called upon. An example from the HYDRIVE project illustrates the idea. HYDRIVE is a coached practice system for troubleshooting the hydraulics systems of the F-15 aircraft. The CTA (Steinberg & Gitomer, 1996) showed that not only are some elements of declarative, strategic, and procedural knowledge required for high probabilities of expert troubleshooting actions but that *all* are required; lack of any of the three components impairs performance. The building block in the statistical model that expresses the relationship between this knowledge and successful troubleshooting steps is therefore conjunctive.

Effective Ways to Elicit the Kinds of Behavior We Need to See. What characteristics of problems stimulate students to employ various aspects of their knowledge? We are beginning to hear phrases such as "principled task design" in assessment more often nowadays (e.g., Embretson, 1998). The idea is that by systematically manipulating the features of task settings—that is, controlling the constraints and the affordances—we create situations that encourage students to exercise targeted aspects of skill and knowledge. We describe these features in terms of task-model variables.

Work on systematic and theory-based task design dates back at least half a century. We may point to Guttman's (1959) facet design for tests, followed by Osburn's (1968) and Hively, Patterson, and Page's (1968) work in the 1960s with item forms, and Bormuth's (1970) linguistic transformations of texts to produce comprehension items. But now we can take advantage of concepts and methods from psychology to build tasks more efficiently and around cognitively relevant—and therefore construct-relevant—features. We have discussed ways we can manipulate the medical conditions of patients and the availability of information in the DISC simulator environment to either elicit evidence about hygienists' medical or information-gathering knowledge or to minimize the stress on this knowledge in order to highlight other aspects of their competence. We have also explored how a web-based environment can be used to determine student information analysis and problem-solving skills across a range of tasks; in particular, we have considered how the content available at different Internet links could be varied to isolate particular information analysis and problem-solving skills. A web-based environment is a particularly adaptable vehicle for presenting assessment tasks. The wealth of information available on the web makes it possible to vary the substance of the assessment task relatively easily, within an assessment schema under which task format and underlying targeted skills remain constant.

Leverage Points for Technology

Now let's look at some leverage points for using technology. We shall see that they can often be exploited to realize the possibilities that cognitive psychology offers.

Dynamic Assembly of the Student Model. First is the capability to use contextual or concurrent information to bring up or assemble a student model. In interactive contexts, we can think of shifting the focus of our inquiry or switching grain size of the student model as we learn about some parts of the model and update our options for action.

A simple example of this approach could be applied in the domain of document literacy (Kirsch & Jungeblut, 1986). An overall scale, from less proficient to more proficient, is useful when a student is referred to an adult literacy training program. It provides a quick idea of their general level of proficiency, perhaps on the 100–500 scale of the National Adult Literacy Survey, for the purposes of documentation and program accountability. Meredith comes out at 200 on the scale, say. But then a more diagnostic assessment, focused for students in this same neighborhood of overall proficiency, is more useful for determining what to work on, because Meredith, Jessica, Bob, and seven other people at 200 need different kinds of help to get to 250. Is Meredith familiar with the prototypical structures that documents are based on, such as lists, nested lists, and tables? What strategies does she have to work with? Does she recognize the kinds of situations that call for their use? Is vocabulary the stumbling block, making help with reading her best bet? What is key here is that the follow-up questions for students at 200 are different from the follow-up questions for students at 300 who want to get to 350. Tasks from the same pool as the initial assessment might be used for follow-up, but they would be hooked up with evidence models to inform more finely grained student models. The SM variables in these models would be tailored to feedback of different kinds for students at different levels of proficiency; they would be variables that answer a question such as "What is the nature of Meredith's proficiency, now that we know the level of her proficiency?"

Realistic Tasks to Produce Direct Evidence. Technology helps us create complex and realistic tasks that can produce direct evidence about knowledge used for production and interaction. In part this concerns the richness and complexity of the environment we can create for the student, and in part it concerns the richness and complexity of the responses we can capture. Video capture of a dance, for example, requires no new technology for presentation, but it makes it possible for the ephemeral performance to be viewed and evaluated many times and in many places—a wonderful mechanism for communicating evaluation standards (Wolf, Bixby, Glenn, & Gardner, 1991). This does not just help improve the consistency of evaluation; it helps students learn about the standards of good work in the domain. This is an application of ideas from situative psychology: Part of the social milieu of a student is participating in the assessment; the standards of evaluation are among the constraints of his or her environment; he or she must develop knowledge and skills to use the affordances of the settings to succeed in these socially required trials.

The MashpeeQuest performance assessment presents students with a realistic setting that they are likely to use on a regular basis in the 21st century to gather and evaluate information. MashpeeQuest requires that students be able to use the affordances of the web-based environment to analyze text from multiple sources using a browser and to use the Internet to communicate their ideas. It is not just the analysis skills that students learn, but the etiquette and protocol of communicating in the socially situated Internet community. Students' use of the web-based learning environment is of course mediated by their classroom teacher's support, their peer interactions and discussion, and their own skill in navigating the site. The MashpeeQuest assessment illustrates several of the ways in which technology can enhance the quality of assessment: It provides more possibilities in the content and formats that can be used to present materials and document students' competences, while at the same time providing task constraints to ensure that the assessment measures the construct intended.

Automated Extraction and Evaluation of Key Features of Complex Work. Some automated extraction and evaluation of key features of complex work make it possible to increase the efficiency of applying existing evaluation rules, and others make it possible to evaluate work products we could not routinely include in assessment at all. In an example mentioned above, Stevens and colleagues (1996) use neural networks to summarize the import of students' sequences of diagnostic tests. Examples from current projects at ETS include:

- Natural language-processing methods for scoring essays, with psycholinguistic and semantic theory to define features to extract and clustering algorithms to summarize them into scores
- Evaluation of constructed show-your-steps responses to algebra problems, with Goals, Operators, Methods, and Selection rules (GOMS) methodology to infer students' likely strategies
- Automatic scoring of features of architectural designs, such as whether a student's floor plan gives enough space for a person in a wheelchair to get from the door to behind the desk, with automated routines to evaluate clearances along the student's path

Examples from MashpeeQuest include:

- Counts of the number of Internet links checked and calculation of the amount of time spent examining each link
- Evaluation of student reasoning by identifying whether evidence from particular links is used to support particular hypotheses
- Comparison of students' own ratings of the relevance of particular links with experts' ratings.

Automated/Assisted Task Construction, Presentation, and Management. In a preceding section, we discussed how research in cognitive psychology reveals systematic relationships between the affordances and constraints of problem situations and the knowledge structures and procedures people can bring to bear on those problems. Understanding and systematically manipulating these features of tasks not only helps us produce tasks more efficiently; it strengthens the validity argument for them as well. Further benefits accrue if we can use technology to produce tasks as well. This is as true for producing familiar kinds of tasks as it is for ones that could not exist at all outside a technological setting (such as DISC's computer-based simulations). Likewise, the VideoDiscovery technology-based investigations and the SMART assessments developed by the Cognition and Technology Group at Vanderbilt illustrate the use of technology to assess phenomena that are too large, too small, too dynamic, too complex, or too dangerous (e.g., nuclear reactions) to be validly assessed using non-technology-based methods of assessment (Vye et al., 1998). The production side of assessment can exploit technology in several ways, including, for example, automated and semiautomated construction of items (e.g., Bennett, 1999) and tools to create tasks according to cognitively motivated schemas (e.g., Embretson, 1998).

A Further Comment on Technology-Based Assessment. Technology is as seductive as it is powerful. It is easy to spend all one's time and money designing realistic scenarios and gathering complex data, and only then ask "How do we score it?" When this happens, the chances are great that the technology is not being used to best effect. The affordances and constraints are not selected optimally to focus attention on the skills and knowledge we care about and to minimize the impact of incidental skills and knowledge. This is why we emphasize the evidentiary foundation that must be laid if we are to make sense of any complex assessment data. The central issues are construct definition, forms of evidence, and situations that can provide evidence, regardless of the means by which data are to be gathered and evaluated. Technology provides such possibilities as simulation-based scenarios, but evidentiary considerations should shape the thousands of implementation decisions that arise in designing a technology-based assessment. These are the issues that cause such an assessment to succeed or to fail in serving its intended purpose. Messick's (1994) discussion on designing performance assessments is mandatory reading for anyone who wants to design a complex assessment, including computer-based simulations, portfolio assessments, and performance tasks.

In the case of DISC, the simulator needs to be able to create the task situations described in the task model and to capture that behavior in a form we have determined we need to obtain evidence about targeted knowledge; that is, to produce the required work products. What possibilities, constraints, and affordances must be built into the simulator in order to provide the data we need? As to the kinds of situations that will evoke the behavior we want to see, the simulator must be able to:

- Present the distinct phases in the patient interaction cycle (assessment, treatment planning, treatment implementation, and evaluation)
- Present the forms of information that are typically used, and control their availability and accessibility, so we can learn about examinees' information-gathering skills
- Manage cross-time cases, not just single visits, so we can get evidence about examinees' capabilities to evaluate information over time
- Vary the virtual patient's state dynamically, so we can learn about examinees' ability to evaluate the outcomes of treatments that he or she chooses

As to the nature of affordances that must be provided, DISC has learned from the CTA that examinees should have the capacity to:

- Seek and gather data
- Indicate hypotheses
- Justify hypotheses with respect to cues
- Justify actions with respect to hypotheses

An important point is that DISC does not take the early version of the simulator as given and fixed. Ultimately, the simulator must be designed so the highest priority is providing evidence about the targeted skills and knowledge—not authenticity, not look and feel, not technology.

As for MashpeeQuest, the assessment task situations must parallel the kinds of situations faced by students as they analyze information and solve problems in the AmericaQuest program, so that the assessment tasks are more likely to be sensitive to the effects of the program itself. It should capture student performances on both skills that are specific to AmericaQuest and those that are valued by educators and policymakers who would look to the findings from a evaluation of AmericaQuest as the basis for decision making about purchasing or continuing to use the program.

As to the kinds of situations that will evoke the behavior we want to see, the assessment must be able to:

- Present students with a historical or archaeological dilemma with competing hypotheses to consider
- Present students with distinct phases of problem solving using historical documentation
- Vary the problem or dilemma, to provide evidence for generalizability of student skills across tasks
- Include multiple sources of pictorial and text-based evidence that can be used to support or to disconfirm different hypotheses
- Allow for students to enter a text-based argument regarding their own position about the dilemma
- Vary the outcomes of the search dynamically, so we can learn about students' ability to evaluate the outcomes of searches that he or she conducts

In turn, the students being tested in this environment should be able to:

- Seek and gather data on the Internet
- Carry out analyses of the evidence found on as many links as possible in the task

- Construct a coherent argument in support of one hypothesis using evidence from the links, with both confirming and disconfirming evidence that can be discovered and taken into account
- Enter text in an interactive web-based environment setting.

FINAL OBSERVATIONS

These developments will have the most impact when assessments are built for well-defined purposes and connected with a conception of knowledge in the targeted domain. They will have much less impact for drop-in-from-the-sky large-scale assessments like the National Assessment of Educational Progress. They are important in two ways for gauging students' progress and evaluating the effectiveness of educational programs.

First, these developments may be exploited to design assessments that better hone in on the most crucial questions in the application. But this requires resources—the time, the energy, the money, and the expertise to tailor an assessment to a purpose. Over time, we expect that technologies coming online will continue to make it easier and cheaper to create more ambitious assessments and to share and tailor assessment building blocks that have been provided by others. For now, however, resources remain a serious constraint.

Second, in recognition of the limitations resources inevitably impose, the new perspectives the developments offer may be used today to select assessments among available assessments—to do as well as possible at focusing on what matters. Knowing how we would proceed with unlimited resources to create assessments that suited our purposes to a tee, we are in a better position to evaluate the quality of existing assessments we may have to choose among. We can better say what they tell us and what they miss—and perhaps save enough money to gather some supplementary data on just those facets of competence that off-the-shelf instruments cannot address.

REFERENCES

Almond, R. G., & Mislevy, R. J. (1999). Graphical models and computerized adaptive testing. *Applied Psychological Measurement, 23*, 223–237.

Baxter, G. P., Elder, A. D., & Glaser, R., (1996). Knowledge-based cognition and performance assessment in the science classroom. *Educational Psychologist, 31*(2), 133–140.

Bennett, R. E. (1999). Using new technology to improve assessment. *Educational Measurement: Issues and Practice, 18*, 5–12.

Bormuth, J. R. (1970). *On the theory of achievement test items*. Chicago: University of Chicago Press.

Embretson, S.E. (1998). A cognitive design system approach to generating valid tests: Application to abstract reasoning. *Psychological Methods, 3,* 380–396.

Ericsson, K. A., & Smith, J. (1991). Prospects and limits of the empirical study of expertise: An introduction. In K. A. Ericsson & J. Smith (Eds.), *Toward a general theory of expertise: Prospects and limits* (pp. 1–38). Cambridge, UK: Cambridge University Press.

Glaser, R., Lesgold, A., & Lajoie, S. (1987). Toward a cognitive theory for the measurement of achievement. In R. Ronning, J. Glover, J. C. Conoley, & J. Witt (Eds.), *The influence of cognitive psychology on testing and measurement: The Buros-Nebraska Symposium on measurement and testing* (Vol. 3) (pp. 41–85). Hillsdale, NJ: Erlbaum.

Greeno, J. G., Collins, A. M., & Resnick, L. B. (1997). Cognition and learning. In D. Berliner & R. Calfee (Eds.), *Handbook of educational psychology* (pp. 15–47). New York: Macmillan.

Guttman, L. (1959). A structural theory for inter-group beliefs and action. *American Sociological Review, 24,* 318–328.

Hively, W., Patterson, H. L., & Page, S. H. (1968). A "universe-defined" system of arithmetic achievement tests. *Journal of Educational Measurement, 5,* 275–290.

Jensen, F. V. (1996). *An introduction to Bayesian networks.* New York: Springer-Verlag.

Johnson, L. A., Wohlgemuth, B., Cameron, C.A., Caughtman, F., Koertge, T., Barna, J., & Schultz, J. (1998). Dental Interactive Simulations Corporation (DISC): Simulations for education, continuing education, and assessment. *Journal of Dental Education, 62,* 919–928.

Kirsch, I. S., & Jungeblut, A. (1986). *Literacy: Profiles of America's young adults.* Princeton, NJ: National Assessment of Educational Progress/Educational Testing Service.

Linn, M. C., Bell, P., & Hsi, S. (1999). Lifelong science learning on the Internet: The knowledge integration environment. *Interactive Learning Environments, 6*(1–2), 4–38.

Messick, S. (1994). The interplay of evidence and consequences in the validation of performance assessments. *Educational Researcher, 23*(2), 13–23.

Mislevy, R. J. (1994). Evidence and inference in educational assessment. *Psychometrika, 59,* 439–483.

Mislevy, R. J., Almond, R. G., Yan, D., & Steinberg, L. S. (1999). Bayes nets in educational assessment: Where do the numbers come from? In K. B. Laskey & H. Prade (Eds.), *Proceedings of the Fifteenth Conference on Uncertainty in Artificial Intelligence* (pp. 437–446). San Francisco: Morgan Kaufmann.

Mislevy, R. J., & Gitomer, D. H. (1996). The role of probability-based inference in an intelligent tutoring system. *User-Modeling and User-Adapted Interaction, 5,* 253–282.

Mislevy, R. J., Steinberg, L. S., & Almond, R. G. (2003). On the structure of educational assessments. *Measurement: Interdisciplinary Research and Perspective, 1,* 3–67.

Mislevy, R. J., Steinberg, L. S., Breyer, F. J., Almond, R. G., & Johnson, L. (1999). A cognitive task analysis, with implications for designing a simulation-based assessment system. *Computers and Human Behavior, 15,* 335–374.

Mislevy, R. J., Steinberg, L. S., Breyer, F. J., Almond, R. G., & Johnson, L. (in press). Making sense of data from complex assessments. *Applied Measurement in Education, 15,* 363–378.

Newell, A., & Simon, H. A. (1972). *Human problem solving.* Englewood Cliffs, NJ: Prentice-Hall.

Osburn, H. G. (1968). Item sampling for achievement testing. *Educational and Psychological Measurement, 28,* 95–104.

Penuel, W., & Shear, L. (2000). Classroom Connect: Evaluation design. Menlo Park, CA: SRI International.

Quellmalz, E., & Haertel, G. D. (1999). *Breaking the mold: Technology-based science assessment in the 21st century.* Manuscript submitted for publication.

Rogoff, B. (1984). Introduction. In B. Rogoff & J. Lave (Eds.), *Everyday cognition: Its development in social context* (pp. 1–8). Cambridge, MA: Harvard University Press.

Schum, D. A. (1994). *The evidential foundations of probabilistic reasoning.* New York: Wiley.

Steinberg, L. S., & Gitomer, D. H. (1996). Intelligent tutoring and assessment built on an understanding of a technical problem-solving task. *Instructional Science, 24,* 223–258.

Stevens, R. H., Lopo, A. C., & Wang, P. (1996). Artificial neural networks can distinguish novice and expert strategies during complex problem solving. *Journal of the American Medical Informatics Association, 3,* 131–138.

Vye, N.J., Schwartz, D. L., Bransford, J. D., Barron, B. J., Zech, L., & the Cognition and Technology Group at Vanderbilt. (1998). SMART environments that support monitoring, reflection, and revision. In D. J. Hacker, J. Dunlosky, & A. C. Grasesser (Eds.), *Metacognition in educational theory and practice* (pp. 305–346). Hilldale, NJ: Erlbaum.

Wineburg, S. S. (1991). On the reading of historical texts: Notes on the breach between school and academy. *American Educational Research Journal, 28,* 495–519.

Wineburg, S. S. (1998). Reading Abraham Lincoln: An expert-expert study in the interpretation of historical texts. *Cognitive Science, 22,* 319–346.

Wolf, D., Bixby, J., Glenn, J., & Gardner, H. (1991). To use their minds well: Investigating new forms of student assessment. In G. Grant (Ed.), *Review of Educational Research* (Vol. 17) (pp. 31–74). Washington, DC: American Educational Research Association.

STUDYING LONG-TERM EFFECTS WITHIN A COMPLEX, MULTILEVEL SYSTEM

Barbara Means
Geneva D. Haertel

Newer forms of technology, many of which are used to support student-centered, open-ended activities such as design, model building and testing, and collaboration over the Internet, require not only teachers who are skilled users of the technology but also school and district infrastructures that support technology-based innovations through resource allocation and support for teacher learning (Blumenfeld, Fishman, Krajcik, Marx, & Soloway, 2000; Means, Penuel, & Padilla, 2001). Teachers' use of sound instructional practices incorporating technology may fail to have intended effects if the school or district technology infrastructure is too weak to support reliable technology access or the school fails to give teachers adequate time to learn how to implement the new technology-supported approach. Moreover, the effectiveness of a technology-supported innovation may vary with student characteristics, and these are likely to vary not just across schools but among classes within a school. Those students who receive the opportunity to use technology may be academically stronger—or weaker—than other students in the school, depending on school and district tracking and curriculum policies. Thus, research to evaluate the use and effects of educational technology must take into account variables at the district, school, classroom, and student levels.

Empirical investigations of educational innovations need to deal with the hierarchical nature of school systems and the multiple, overlapping contexts in which learning occurs. Students are nested within classrooms within schools within districts. As individuals, these same students are members of families, peer groups, and communities. Technology may be used and may exert an influence in one or more of these contexts. Especially when the student outcome of interest is a general ability—such as reading comprehension or technology proficiency—the multiple settings within which students may acquire knowledge and practice are all potential influences on outcome measures. This multiplicity of potential influences on the outcome measures produces requirements for the collection of data about each student's experiences in those multiple settings as well as for specialized analytic techniques capable of accounting for effects at multiple levels.

When general abilities or dispositions are the outcome measure of interest, there will be many potential explanations for observed differences across different groups of students. If students from one class or school receive more exposure to technology in school and also show higher reading comprehension scores, it may be tempting to assert that their experiences using technology in class fostered literacy skills. But it may be (and, in fact, is quite often the case) that those with more in-school technology exposure come from homes with more highly educated parents and more reading resources. They may also have better or more demanding teachers. Such competing explanations for observed effects are the impetus for advocating research designs in which students (or classes or schools) are randomly assigned to treatment and control conditions (see discussion in Part I).

But random assignment may not be feasible in addressing some fundamental questions around the effects of in-school use of technology. In Chapter 9, Means and colleagues argue that policymakers confronting decisions about investments in a technology infrastructure are concerned not with the short-term impact of particular pieces of software but rather with the cumulative, long-term effects of exposure to technology. Moreover, research tells us that there is a substantial period of time needed for a technology innovation to become well enough integrated into a school setting to be used to its greatest advantage (Sandholtz, Ringstaff, & Dwyer, 1997) and result in the desired effects. Thus, we want to evaluate technology-based innovations when they are mature and to continue data collection for several years to determine whether the outcomes they generate are sustained (Lipsey & Cordray, 2000). Random assignment to different technology exposure conditions over long periods of time is difficult within the political climate of American school districts.

Longitudinal designs, examining effects at multiple levels within the school system, are an alternative approach discussed in Chapters 7, 8, and 9. Although the longitudinal elements of the designs do not confer all of the benefits of random assignment to treatment and control conditions, the use of a longitudinal design where each student serves as his or her own control does rule out many alternative explanations for the superiority of the treatment group at the end of the study. Such designs allow researchers to measure gains rather than just postintervention performance and to check the equivalence of treatment and comparison groups before the intervention began. Differences in student growth over time, when based on large samples, can be related to the influence of the intervention and contextual variables at multiple levels of the educational system.

The value of the longitudinal approach with a rich data set can perhaps best be understood by examining a nonlongitudinal study. Wenglinsky (1998) related fourth- and eighth-grade students' mathematics scores on the National Assessment of Educational Progress (NAEP) to the responses the students and their teachers gave to survey items concerning use of technology and teacher training in technology use. A widely cited finding from this study is that fourth-grade students who spent more time using mathematics drill-and-practice software had lower NAEP scores. Those who spent more time on mathematics games had higher scores. Many readers of the study interpret the results to suggest that drill-and-practice software *causes* lower mathematics achievement and that more cognitively challenging experience with game software *causes* higher achievement. However, we do not know anything about the students' mathematics achievement prior to their differential technology experiences. Although Wenglinsky attempted to use school-level data to control for prior achievement, he did not have scores on individual students at two points in time. Many observational studies of classroom use of technology suggest that students who are struggling with mathematics are often directed to use drill-and-practice software in the hope that it will help them catch up, while those who are ahead of grade-level expectations may be given time using computer games as a "reward" for their achievement. With retrospective reports of technology use and measurement of achievement at only one point in time, there is little basis for giving greater credence to one interpretation over the other.

The kinds of longitudinal studies of the influence of school technology use envisioned by the authors in this section have not been done. Perhaps the closest available approximation is the widely disseminated retrospective longitudinal study of the results associated with a statewide technology implementation effort in West Virginia. That research examined the strength of association between gains in students' achievement test scores and amount of use of basic skills practice software, attitude toward computers, and teacher training in computer use (Mann, Shakeshaft, Becker, & Kottkamp, 1999).

What the retrospective longitudinal study could not do, which the authors in this section advocate, is to also measure contextual and implementation variables at various levels of the education system at multiple points in time to seek greater understanding of the mechanisms through which the technology experience exerts its effects. Such prospective longitudinal designs would incorporate much more information about individual students' characteristics and experiences (as described in Chapter 9). This richer data set could support analyses that would help policymakers and practitioners understand the conditions that must be in place for a technology-supported intervention to be successful (for example, teacher belief that technology is a tool that can improve students' learning in content areas) and to raise flags concerning spurious effects (for example, negative correlations between use of drill-and-practice software and scores on tests of the basic skills the software is designed to teach).

To guide the design and interpretation of a multilevel, longitudinal study, it is considered good practice to develop a comprehensive, conceptual framework. Such a framework describes the multiple levels and contexts of the educational system. It also articulates the inputs, processes, and outcomes that comprise the innovation's theory of change. Context variables, implementation milestones, and interim and outcomes measures should be specified as well. Presumed causal and temporal relationships among the influences, processes, and outcomes can also be depicted.

The three chapters in this part describe longitudinal, multilevel designs that specify the relationships among influences, contextual variables, implementation, and outcomes in different ways. The framework proposed in Chapter 8 by Russell W. Rumberger of the University of California, Santa Barbara, is similar to those used in economics and studies of educational productivity. In such studies, relationships are drawn among the system's inputs, processes, and outcomes. Rumberger's framework is depicted graphically in a way that demonstrates the many interconnections among the levels and outcomes of the system. In Chapter 9, Barbara Means and her colleagues from SRI propose a conceptual framework that identifies several contexts, the variables that would be measured in those contexts, and a comprehensive list of outcomes to be measured, as well. The authors agree that the technology innovation itself should be carefully defined as part of the framework. Beyond providing a complete description of the innovation, the relationship of the innovation to other instructional activities and materials that are part of the instructional package must be specified. These concerns are similar to those stressed in the highly contextualized evaluations discussed in Part I of this book. There are differences in emphasis between the two lines of thought, however. Those concerned with performing multilevel analyses need to have quantifiable data across an adequate number of cases to perform their analyses. While the value of an implementation variable (e.g., teacher support for technology integration) might be determined on the basis of observations or in-depth interviews, the use of survey data is more typical. In contrast, those who have performed highly contextualized evaluations, perhaps best represented by Culp and colleagues (Chapter 3, this volume), have made greater use of the kind of qualitative data obtained through observations and interviews. While the contextualized evaluation advocates—both Culp and colleagues and Baker and Herman (Chapter 4, this volume)—are pushing now for ways to get comparable data across different projects, many of those who have been doing multilevel analyses—notably Rumberger and, in Chapter 7, Larry V. Hedges and his colleagues at the University of Chicago—are seeing a need for greater richness in the data sets they can incorporate into their analyses.

Conceptual frameworks also specify the short- and long-term outcomes that are expected to occur as a result of the innovation. If there are interim outcomes that must occur, they are also identified. This is especially important if those interim outcomes are related to the technology intervention's implementation at several levels of the educational system. The presence or absence of interim outcomes can be detected before the long-term outcomes can be measured, and these outcomes provide a preliminary test of whether the theory holds water and is being implemented according to design (either problem, singly or in combination, could result in a failure to obtain the desired interim outcomes).

The framework should also incorporate key steps in the implementation of the innovation. Measures of implementation should go beyond simple checklists. In particular, the amount, nature, and quality of professional development provided to teachers should be documented, using both qualitative and quantitative methods. Amount of hands-on training, availability of just-in-time support, and the technology infrastructure available in practice to support the implementation should be described.

Analyzing the data collected in these complex, longitudinal designs requires special statistical techniques. Sophisticated modeling approaches, such as hierarchical linear modeling (HLM), were designed for this purpose. Such techniques require large sample sizes, however, and, like other analytic techniques, are more difficult to apply where students have membership in multiple classrooms (i.e., middle or high school) and are reassigned to classes each year or each term.

If probability samples are used in multilevel longitudinal studies, then the results of a longitudinal, multilevel design can be generalized to the populations from which the samples were drawn, an important advantage over the typical random-assignment experiment. (See Chapters 7, 8, and 9 for discussion of this issue.)

While considerable progress has been made in the development and application of statistical models for dealing with the kinds of complex data sets proposed in this section, technical challenges remain. One of these involves disentangling of multiple influences over time. While recent work in Tennessee (Finn & Achilles, 1990) and elsewhere has demonstrated an approach for estimating the "value added" by a year with a particular teacher, this approach has yet to be extended to the upper grades, where each student has not one but perhaps eight or more teachers in a single year. Given the likely differences in the amount and nature of technology experience in different teachers' classrooms, this analytic challenge is highly germane to longitudinal studies of technology effects.

Another issue, briefly mentioned in this last section, is the need for measures of the kinds of complex performances technology innovators try to foster that have the psychometric quality that would permit estimations of growth over time. Most research using techniques to estimate growth curves have used standardized test scores for this purpose. Performance assessments and attitudinal measures developed to date have lacked sufficient reliability to permit application of these techniques. Many groups are working on the problem of developing more reliable assessments of conceptual understanding and complex performance (Pellegrino, Chudowsky, & Glaser, 2001; Chapter 6, this volume). The implementation of the designs proposed in this section will depend on progress being made in that area as well.

REFERENCES

Blumenfeld, P., Fishman, B. J., Krajcik, J., Marx, R. W., & Soloway, E. (2000). Creating useable innovations in systemic reform: Scaling-up technology-embedded project-based science in urban schools. *Educational Psychologist, 35*(3), 149–164.

Finn, J. D., & Achilles, C. M. (1990). Answers about questions about class size: A statewide experiment. *American Educational Research Journal, 27*(3), 557–577.

Lipsey, M. W., & Cordray, D. S. (2000). Evaluation methods for social intervention. *Annual Review of Psychology, 51*, 345–375

Mann, D., Shakeshaft, C., Becker, J., & Kottkamp, R. (1999). *West Virginia story: Achievement gains from a statewide comprehensive instructional technology program.* Santa Monica, CA: Milken Family Foundation.

Means, B., Penuel, B., & Padilla, C. (2001). *The connected school: Technology and learning in urban schools.* San Francisco: Jossey-Bass.

Pellegrino, J., Chudowsky, N., & Glaser, R. (2001). *Knowing what students know: The science and design of educational assessment.* Washington, DC: National Academy Press.

Sandholtz, J., Ringstaff, C., & Dwyer, D. (1997). *Teaching with technology: Creating student-centered classrooms.* New York: Teachers College Press.

Wenglinsky, H. (1998). *Does it compute? The relationship between educational technology and student achievement in mathematics.* Princeton, New Jersey: Policy Information Center, Educational Testing Service.

Chapter 7

Studies of Technology Implementation and Effects

Larry V. Hedges
Spyros Konstantopoulos
Amy Thoreson

In commerce and manufacturing, in multinational corporations and individual households, computer technology has fundamentally altered how
business is conducted and how people communicate. In the field of education, computers have become a common fixture in this country's schools. In
1980, less than 20% of elementary, junior high, and senior high schools in
the United States were equipped with microcomputers. Less than a decade
later, virtually all public schools had some computing capability (U.S. Bureau of the Census, 1989). Similarly, student access to computers has increased dramatically, from more than 60 students per computer in 1984 to
approximately 6 students per computer in 1998 (U.S. Bureau of the Census,
1998). Important questions for educators and policymakers concern the
availability, use, and impact of computers in American schools.

The results from a number of published studies on the relationship between computer use and academic achievement indicate this technology can
bolster student outcomes (Becker, 1994; Christmann & Badgett, 1999;
Hativa, 1994; Kozma, 1991; Kulik & Kulik, 1987; Liao, 1992; Niemiec &
Walberg, 1987, 1992; Ryan, 1991; Van Dusen & Worthen, 1994). In their
research synthesis on computer-based instruction (CBI), for example, Niemiec
and Walberg (1992) calculated a positive average CBI effect on achievement
of 0.42 standard deviation. Ryan (1991) computed a mean effect size of 0.31
in a meta-analysis of 40 published and unpublished studies on computer use

and achievement in elementary schools. Most of the subject-specific research on computer use and achievement has examined performance in science and mathematics.

There is some evidence, however, that access to computers and the academic benefits that can be derived from computer use are not the same for all students. Although money from federally funded programs, such as Title 1, that are targeted to assist disadvantaged students is often used to purchase computers (Scott, Cole, & Engel, 1992), high-income and White students tend to have greater access than low-income and Black students, and non-English-speaking students tend to have the least access (Cuban, 1993; Neuman, 1991; Sutton, 1991). Moreover, even with high and low socioeconomic status (SES) have comparable student-to-computer ratios, students in low-SES schools are likelier to use computers for drill-and-practice exercises while their more affluent counterparts engage in more challenging activities (Cole & Griffin, 1987; Kozma & Croninger, 1992; Watt, 1982). A number of quasi-experimental studies of the computer-achievement relationship for students of different abilities have also been conducted. The results from these designs are mixed. Some studies show that even under the same treatment conditions, high-ability students receive greater benefits from learning by computer than their lower-ability classmates (Hativa, 1994; Hativa & Becker, 1994; Hativa & Shorer, 1989; Munger & Loyd, 1989; Osin, Nesher, & Ram, 1994), while others indicate that high- and low-ability students attain similar gains (Becker, 1992; Clariana & Schultz, 1993). However, the results from longitudinal studies of computer-assisted instruction prompted some researchers to conclude that computerized learning contributes to the increasing achievement gaps between high- and low-SES students and between high- and low-ability students (Hativa, 1994; Hativa & Becker, 1994; Hativa & Shorer, 1989).

Considerable evidence indicates that even though teachers have had increasing access to computers for instruction, very few actually use them. In 1996, for example, the National Education Association reported that although 84% of all public school teachers said personal computers were available to them, only around 60% indicated that they ever used them (U.S. Bureau of the Census, 1998). Analysis of teacher data from National Education Longitudinal Study (NELS) showed that about half of eighth-grade math teachers have students who spend less than 10% of class time working on computers (Owens, 1993), while across subject matter, teachers average only about 4% of all instructional time with computers (Cuban, 1993). A survey of middle school math and science teachers in South Carolina (Dickey & Kherlopian, 1987) also showed that although 70% of these teachers had access to computers, almost half of those with access did not use them. Thus, even though computer technology may be widely available, in general, it is poorly integrated into the classroom curriculum and is underused (Becker, 1991; Maddox, Johnson, & Harlow, 1993; Ognibene & Skeele, 1990).

Most of the research on technology in schools indicates that computers have had little effect on teaching practices or classroom activities. Some authors (Cuban, 1993; Scott, Cole, & Engel, 1992) have argued that computer use in schools simply follows the pattern of any new technology, such as radio and television when they were introduced. According to this view, the educational system's conservatism resists innovation, seeking to retain current goals and social organization. As a result, new technology is incorporated in old ways. Moreover, the sharp increase in the number of computers in schools is due to the efforts of those who profit from this expansion, such as hardware and software makers, not educators. These profiteers have been particularly successful in supplying goods and services for federally funded programs for low-achieving minority students. These programs often feature computer systems with drill-and-kill software and are designed to replace teachers and control student behavior (Scott, Cole, & Engel, 1992).

A SYSTEM OF STUDIES TO PROVIDE INFORMATION ON THE IMPLEMENTATION AND IMPACT OF TECHNOLOGY IN AMERICAN SCHOOLS

The purpose of this chapter is to consider the kinds of studies that are necessary to obtain the information needed to measure the implementation and impact of technology in American schools. We will argue that no single study or even genre of studies is adequate for the task of understanding and monitoring the uses and impact of technology. Instead, a system of data collection, including studies of different types for different purposes, is necessary. Little of what is recommended here is revolutionary. Indeed, much of it is rather straightforward, even simple minded. However, many of the things suggested here are not part of current practice. Therefore, they may have particular utility precisely because they are feasible but not currently done.

A comprehensive program of assessment of technology must include a program of interrelated studies. The individual component studies would focus on different aspects of technology, use different methods, and have different purposes and time horizons. Some of the components (such as the National Assessment of Educational Progress as a large-scale survey component) are either already in place or studies that are already in place could be modified slightly to accomplish the purposes of a component of a technology information system. Other components would have to be created as wholly new systems. However, regarding them all as components of a unified system could bring certain efficiencies and improve the overall quality of information about technology in education.

The system of assessment we envision should include as components four kinds of studies. The first component consists of large-scale surveys of technology availability and use based on probability samples of schools and students. Such surveys provide the broad base of information about technology that is necessary to understand the extent of technology availability and use in American schools. They also provide information about the availability and use of technology in the homes of schoolchildren. They can also provide useful, albeit limited, information about the ways technology is used in classrooms in particular subject matters. Such studies are absolutely essential in providing the framework for designing more detailed studies of technology use. They are also essential for monitoring the inequality of access to technology and its use, the so-called digital divide that threatens to expand societal inequality.

It is important to realize, however, that large-scale surveys cannot provide all the information that is needed to understand the impact of technology in American education and inform national policy formation in this area. Large-scale surveys cannot, with plausible cost constraints, provide detailed information on the detailed use of technology in American classrooms and the meaning of that technology use to teachers, students, and parents. Large-scale cross-sectional surveys cannot provide adequate information on cause and effect. In particular, they cannot provide convincing information about the effects of technology use on student achievement. Moreover, while large-scale surveys with probability samples are the best tools available for understanding the current status of schools and their students, they are complex and therefore time consuming. In a rapidly changing environment like that of computer and information technology, large-scale surveys may not be able to provide timely information about important trends; the information provided may be obsolete by the time it is available. The other three components of the system are designed to address the information needs that surveys are ill suited to address.

The second component of the system we envision is a program of intensive studies of technology use in actual schools and classrooms. Such intensive surveys could be coordinated with a large-scale survey but would not have as extensive a sample of schools and would not necessarily be based on a probability sample. Such studies would be designed to provide detailed information about how technology was actually used in classrooms, who uses it, its relation to the broader curriculum, how it affects teacher and student roles, and the general level of satisfaction of students and teachers. Such studies would almost certainly involve interviews or classroom observations as well as conventional survey methods. Coordinating such intensive studies with large-scale surveys would provide an opportunity to situate the intensive information provided within the broader national context.

The third component of the system would be studies designed to assess cause and effect. It is critical to assess not just that technology is used, but that it has effects on student achievement, attitudes, and behavior. Cross-sectional surveys alone simply cannot be used to make persuasive causal arguments in this area. Consequently it is necessary to do studies with designs that can provide evidence with higher internal validity. Such studies would include both longitudinal studies and randomized experiments. Longitudinal studies measuring many process variables can provide much less ambiguous evidence about cause than cross-sectional studies. The measurement of intervening variables can also be an important benefit of such studies. However, even longitudinal studies without random assignment do not rule out all rival hypotheses about cause. Randomized experiments provide the least ambiguous information about causal effects. Randomized experiments are both desirable and feasible in education, and they should be seriously considered as part of a system of work to understand the effects of technology in American education.

The fourth component of the system we envision involves new methods of assessment and new research designs constructed to provide very timely information about trends in the rapidly changing technology environment. It would involve a system of teacher-researchers in a network of schools distributed across the country. The purpose of the network would be to provide ongoing feedback about technology issues. In principle, the system could alert us to emerging trends that were not anticipated. Moreover, it could be adaptive in the sense that it could be used not only to identify new data needs but also to collect preliminary data about issues that were not previously identified. Moreover, such a network of teacher-researchers could provide useful formative information for the design of surveys or more intensive data collections at a later time.

The next four sections expand somewhat on each of the components outlined above, providing examples where available and relating the work to existing data-collection efforts. In each case we argue that the component is feasible in terms of cost and the current state of technical competence in educational research.

LARGE-SCALE SURVEYS

Much of our insight about cross-sectional surveys of technology use is based on recent analyses of the National Assessment of Educational Progress

(NAEP), including the 1996 main assessment in mathematics and the 1998 main assessments in reading and writing (Hedges, Konstantopoulos, & Thoreson, 1999). NAEP is an important component of the nation's educational data-collection system, and its regular data collections based on cross-sectional probability samples will likely remain so for the foreseeable future. NAEP already asks questions about technology availability and use in its student, teacher, and school questionnaires as part of the general background information collected. Therefore, it is reasonable to assume that the cross-sectional studies component of a technology information system would rely on NAEP for all or part of this component of the system.

NAEP is well funded and superbly executed with respect to sampling design and execution. It is the most extensive and valid source of data on what fourth-, eighth-, and twelfth-grade students in the United States know and are able to do. Therefore NAEP is well suited to its primary purpose of describing the patterns of academic achievement in America. Other cross-sectional surveys will share its weaknesses, but it is difficult to conceive of any that would provide superior measurement of academic achievement.

However well designed NAEP may be for its primary purpose of collecting achievement data, it is less adequate for its secondary purpose of collecting data about technology availability and use in American schools. A major shortcoming in NAEP for the purposes of providing information about technology is that the subject-matter-specific surveys in NAEP are not always seen as part of a coordinated system. The background information collected by NAEP (such as information about technology) is sometimes varied across subject matters and changes from year to year. However, what is background for some purposes is foreground in others, and such practices can limit the usefulness of the data provided.

Question Design Should be Principled, Considering All NAEP Surveys as Components of a Single Data-Collection System

The strategy for designing the computer-use questions in NAEP is unclear. For example, the subject-matter content (e.g., assessed subject matter or not), location (e.g., at-home or at-school computer use), and amount of time spent using the computer (time-on-task) could be used to provide one logical design framework around which computer use might be measured. No doubt there are wiser design frameworks; this one is intended as a simple-minded example to illustrate the point. Questions designed around a more specific framework would yield more useful information about computer use and its relationship to achievement. In any event, more specific and consistent questions would be a valuable forward step. Note that there might be good reason to vary question wording across subject-matter assessments (for example, in a matrix-sampled design). The argument here is that such variation should be thoughtfully designed to yield maximum information.

For example, the 1996 mathematics assessment and the 1998 writing assessment student questionnaires ask how often students use a computer at home for schoolwork and how often they use a computer when they do mathematics at school. The intent of each question is unclear. The first question may have been intended to elicit general information about computer use for all schoolwork in all subjects, not just mathematics. Such a question may well yield valuable information. However, we believe it would be useful to also ask (or to ask instead) how often students use a computer at home for schoolwork in mathematics (or some other construction that specifically targets at-home use of computers for mathematics or writing schoolwork). Such a question, in addition to the question about using computers for mathematics at school, would provide a more complete picture of how computers are being applied in mathematics learning.

Similarly, the 1998 reading assessment student questionnaire asks how often the student uses a computer for schoolwork but does not specifically mention at-home use. Thus, this question does not explicitly distinguish home computer use for schoolwork from school computer use. We believe that it would be desirable to do so. Moreover, it does not specify whether the computer use is for reading or some other subject matter. Again, the intent of the question is unclear. Was it intended to measure general computer use in any subject matter? If so, it would be desirable in a reading assessment to have a question that focused entirely on computer use in reading or language arts.

One advantage of a question about computer use that is not specific to subject matter is that it might provide a basis for comparing computer usage in different years. However, we noted that the 1996 mathematics and 1998 reading assessment student questionnaires did not ask the same general questions about computer use. The 1996 questionnaire asked how often students use a computer at home for schoolwork, but the 1998 reading assessment asked how often students use a computer for schoolwork. Thus, a comparison between the rates of computer use in 1996 and 1998 is not possible from these data. We did note that the 1998 writing assessment used the same question for home computer use as did the 1996 mathematics assessment, so a comparison of these data is possible, but it is unclear if this was a deliberate design feature or a mere coincidence.

Principled design of questions about technology use should include questions that are more specific about the use of technology and the purposes of that use. While the question about the primary purpose of computer use in the 1996 mathematics assessment is a good start, the categories of use chosen are more ambiguous than would be desirable. For example, one of the categories of use that the survey respondent could choose to that question was mathematical learning games. We found that category of use difficult to interpret. Did it refer to higher-order thinking involving mathematically rich learning activities or relatively lower-order game playing? None of the questions gave much insight about what the technology actually did or how it related to the standard curriculum. While we realize that it is difficult to create good questions of this type, such questions are highly desirable.

Questions Should Be Carefully Validated

We do not know the extent to which questions about computer use were validated prior to their use in the NAEP assessments, but some of the data we examined raised validity concerns. First, the ambiguity of some of the questions raises validity concerns because the intent of the questions may be unclear to respondents. For example, do questions in a mathematics assessment that refer to schoolwork intend to mean schoolwork in just mathematics or do they refer to all schoolwork? Similarly, when a question about using a computer appears among various questions about the home and family, will it be interpreted to mean computer use at home or both at home and at school? Our initial readings of these questions did not reveal the nuances in the actual text of the questions, and it seems plausible that students (particularly fourth and eighth graders) might also fail to grasp the intended meaning of the questions.

The rather low level of agreement between student reports of computer use and teacher reports of computer use also raises validity concerns. For example, we noted several surveys in which teachers reported never or almost never using computers in the classroom when their students reported frequent use of computers in the classroom. While the disagreements observed might not be logically impossible if both variables are perfectly valid, they do seem implausible. A serious effort to validate the questions about computer use is warranted.

Note that in other NAEP student background questions querying students on frequency of events, the validity of "every day" as a response has been questioned. For example, when fourth graders were questioned on the frequency of writing assignments of three or more pages, their answers of "every day" seem unlikely to be valid. Students—particularly minority and low-SES students—reported a surprisingly high frequency of computer use every day. This may reflect a real phenomenon, but it also might reflect a validity problem that is exaggerated among these groups.

Surveys Can Collect Open-Ended Information That Is Valuable but Not Immediately Analyzed

One of the problems in interpreting the results of NAEP data on computer use is that we have very few details on how the computer is being used. Previous research (and common sense) indicates that computer software is a critical component in determining whether computer use is a tool that enhances achievement. Without knowing which software is being used, it is difficult to determine the quality of the instructional experience. One possible solution is to develop a more detailed set of questions about the capabilities of the software. Another strategy is to ask teachers to provide the name (and edition) of computer software they are using. This could permit NAEP or secondary analysts to do their own coding of software capabilities.

Similarly, it is difficult to interpret data on computer use without knowing what computer hardware is available to teachers and students. Hardware not only imposes limitations on the software that can be used; it may determine whether teachers attempt to use computers at all. They may not do so if the hardware is too antiquated to effectively run desirable software. Pertinent to these concerns is the availability of Internet access and networking capability, since access to the Internet is an increasingly important educational tool. As when suggesting questions about software usage, one might develop a more detailed set of questions about hardware capabilities. Another (not necessarily alternative) possibility is to ask teachers for the name (and edition) of computer hardware and networking applications they are using.

We believe that NAEP could collect open-ended information about hardware and software that is available to teachers, including the frequency and purposes of their use. Such data collections can be made whether or not there is an explicit plan to analyze it as part of the core NAEP program. The analysis of that data need not be on the critical path of NAEP production (and thus need not interfere with the core NAEP mission of providing timely achievement data). In fact analysis plans need not be developed by the time that the data are collected. It could be relegated to special NAEP studies or even left to externally funded studies conducted by other researchers.

There are ample precedents for collection of such information. Within NAEP the transcript studies provide an instructive example. Other U.S. Department of Education data collections provide different examples. The information about textbooks collected in the Third International Mathematics and Science Study (TIMSS) is a good example, since a considerable amount of subsequent research was carried out that involved the analysis of textbook content that was not part of the production of the core TIMSS analytic data set. Another example from TIMSS is the collection of classroom videotapes. The collection of these videotapes in conjunction with the survey provided a valuable data source, which is still undergoing analysis.

Cross-Sectional Surveys Are Weak Sources of Data for Studying the Effects of Technology on Achievement

One-point-in-time, cross-sectional surveys have major weaknesses as instruments for studying the effects of technology on academic achievement (or any other variable). While cross-sectional surveys are appropriate and efficient for assessing achievement status (the major purpose of NAEP), technology availability, or broad patterns of technology use (secondary purposes of NAEP), they pose problems for the inference of cause about relations between variables measured at the same point in time. In particular, it is difficult to determine the direction of cause (e.g., do differences in computer use cause achievement differences or do achievement differences cause differences in computer use?). To put it another way, there is a very plausible rival hypothesis that could explain any relation found between computer use and achievement. While it might be that computer use influences achievement, it is also plausible that students are selected to have certain patterns of computer use because of their achievement. This could take the form of assigning low-achieving students to more frequent computer use than other student populations as a compensatory strategy. In such a case, one might find a spurious relation between computer use and achievement, much as one finds that elementary school students who spend more time doing homework do less well in school.

A longitudinal study design that permits the examination of changes in achievement over time as a function of explanatory variables such as computer use would provide information about causality that would be much less ambiguous (albeit much less efficient for the purposes of assessment of current status, which is the primary mission of NAEP). Probability sampling can provide good evidence for generalizing findings in longitudinal surveys. However, the data from longitudinal surveys are not completely unambiguous regarding causal factors associated with change. They do not rule out the possibility that relations are confounded by other factors, such as another factor correlated both with change and a potential explanatory variable. For example, if differences in achievement gains are actually caused by differences in school resources or social capital, and the latter is related to computer use, there would be an apparent relation between computer use and achievement gains—a spurious relation that would not necessarily be discovered from analyses of a longitudinal survey.

Of course, if the mechanisms underlying the creation of academic achievement were understood completely, and if each of the variables was measured well, then a longitudinal survey (or even a cross-sectional one) could provide adequate information on causal effects. Analyses of NAEP, or any other cross-sectional survey that attempts to determine causal relations, must make assumptions about such a mechanism. While it is clear that some aspects of mechanizing academic achievement are elusive, educational researchers have made considerable progress in identifying key aspects of these mechanisms, and there is considerable consensus about many of them. Thus it is not completely unreasonable to imagine that some progress might be made in identifying causal relations from cross-sectional surveys. We turn to the adequacy of measurement in the next section.

Randomized experiments would provide much less ambiguous data about causality than longitudinal surveys. Well-implemented experiments have the great virtue of providing valid causal inferences in the absence of knowledge of the mechanism that generates achievement. Randomized experiments with multiple waves of data collection (longitudinal experiments) can provide even more compelling evidence. However, randomized experiments (unless they are conducted on probability samples) do not necessarily provide results that can be generalized to a well-defined universe of settings other than those in which they were conducted. That is, randomized experiments may provide locally valid causal inferences, but they do not necessarily generalize elsewhere. Randomized experiments on probability samples or on a large enough scale to make (nonprobability based) claims of representativeness reasonable are possible—but they are difficult, expensive, and time consuming. However, when they are conducted, the evidence is often extremely compelling, as for example, in the case of the Tennessee class-size experiment (e.g., Nye, Hedges, & Konstantopoulos, 1999).

INTENSIVE STUDIES OF TECHNOLOGY USE IN ACTUAL CLASSROOMS

It is difficult to obtain a detailed picture of computer use in schools from the data now collected in NAEP. Any feasible improvements in the NAEP teacher and student questionnaires will yield only marginal improvements. Indeed, any feasible cross-sectional survey will be limited in the richness of information that it can provide. However, rich information about the use of technology is needed to develop insights about the meaning of the survey data and to develop intuition about technology use in schools.

Detailed evidence might be obtained by studying actual computer use in a small sample of schools. The actual design of such a study would have to be carefully planned, but it could involve detailed interviews, teacher logs, or observations of computer use over a period of at least several days. Such a study could greatly enhance knowledge about how computers are actually being used and how those uses might relate to achievement. One might even imagine some detailed ethnographic studies of sites selected on the basis of outstanding characteristics that make them particularly attractive for various reasons (e.g., particularly distinctive, apparently effective, or apparently ineffective patterns of technology use). The Technology Rich Environment Study, currently underway as a special study in connection with NAEP, is a prototype from which much may be learned about this kind of study.

Such an intensive study of actual classrooms would be more valuable if it were coordinated with a large-scale representative survey. Such coordination would permit the situation of the students' studies in the national population. It might also permit tenuous extrapolation of some evidence to a national sample of demographically similar classrooms. Note, however, that such a study need not be conducted before the assessment (which might prompt fears that it would compromise the validity of the NAEP cognitive data). Detailed data on computer use could be collected for a short period after the cognitive data collection, which would make it just as useful for descriptive purposes and only marginally less useful for association with NAEP cognitive results.

RANDOMIZED EXPERIMENTS OR LONGITUDINAL STUDIES TO ASSESS THE EFFECTS OF TECHNOLOGY

Surveys such as NAEP have substantial limitations as sources of information about cause and effect. NAEP is ideally suited to assess the frequency of computer use and the level of academic achievement of various groups of students. However, it cannot provide definitive evidence about the relation between computer use and achievement. A randomized experiment would be a much more persuasive source of such information. While large-scale experiments in education are difficult to carry out, they are not impossible; when they have been conducted, they have had extraordinary influence (as in the case of the Tennessee class-size experiment).

We propose that the U.S. Department of Education consider a carefully designed, randomized experiment to determine how computers are being used in schools and what effects they produce on student achievement. Because the effects are likely to be subtle and may vary across school contexts, we recommend inclusion of a diverse set of schools in the sample. The schools should ideally represent the spectrum of schools in America with respect to social class, racial and ethnic composition, and community contexts. The sample should also be geographically diverse, including urban, suburban, and rural areas.

The design of such an experiment would have to be carefully chosen to ensure that it provided causal information about the variables of greatest interest. For example, if the most significant questions are how availability of computers and the preparation of teachers to use computers in instruction impact achievement, then an experiment could be designed that randomly assigned teachers and students to different conditions of computer availability and preparation. Ideally, the design of experiments to answer multiple questions would incorporate the possibility of assessing both the main effects and at least some of the interactions among effects. For example, it is likely that preparation of teachers to use computers has a much larger effect when there is high availability of computers (i.e., there is an interaction between computer availability and preparation of teachers). Experimental designs need to be planned so that they can estimate plausible interactions and have sufficient statistical power to detect interactions of the size that can reasonably be expected.

Such a randomized experiment might involve other design factors beyond computer use. It would also be possible to vary other factors explicitly connected to technology use in schools, such as the density of technology in a school, the amount of in-service training for teachers, the degree of ongoing support teachers receive in technology use, the type of software provided, and so on. Note that factors related to technology use outside the school might also be varied, such as the availability of computers, software, or Internet connections at home, parental training in support for technology use, extracurricular programs in technology use, and so on.

Because it takes time to change patterns of instruction and student learning, we recommend that such an experiment be longitudinal, examining patterns of computer use and student achievement over a period of several years. Such a longitudinal experiment could provide insight about how educational technology changes schools as well as how technology's effects on students may change over time. Whenever possible, we recommend a modest follow-up study be conducted after the experiment concludes to examine the long-term benefits of technology use. Analyses of long-term effects can be important evidence for policy decisions and were particularly persuasive in the case of the Tennessee class-size experiment.

While there are many advantages to large-scale multisite experiments, it is wise to remember that experiments need not be long-term enterprises with durations of several years. For some purposes, relatively short-term experiments of a semester or a year may provide answers to relevant questions in a timely fashion. Once an organizational and technical infrastructure (such as that provided by research organizations such as the Manpower Development Research Corporation or Mathematica Research Corporation have provided for job training experiments) is in place, there is no reason to assume that experiments in educational technology could not be mounted rapidly. Because the analysis of experiments is relatively easy (compared to many quasi-experiments that require complicated statistical modeling to attempt to control for selection effects), there is no reason that reports from experiments could not be produced relatively rapidly.

NEW METHODS OF ASSESSMENT AND NEW RESEARCH DESIGNS TO PROVIDE TIMELY INDICATIONS OF TRENDS

It is clear that the field of educational technology has evolved very quickly. Moreover, much of the effort in the field is devoted to making the technology evolve even more rapidly. However, large-scale assessments such as NAEP operate in cycles of development and analysis that span years. The questions may be written a year before the field test, which is a year before the actual data collection, and it may take a year or two after data collection for results to be finally reported. This makes it very difficult to anticipate which questions will be of the greatest interest by the time the data obtained are finally analyzed—usually years after questions were written. Large-scale surveys will therefore be relatively poor instruments for identifying new developments in technology use in schools or the abandonment of old uses or technologies.

We believe that new assessment methods and new study designs will be necessary to provide rapid and adaptable information about trends in technology use. Such designs may involve trade-offs between internal validity and timeliness. Modern information technology will provide us with an increasing number of alternatives for such research designs, but we sketch one of them here to be concrete.

In epidemiology it is often useful to track trends in public health by monitoring a few indicators in locations throughout the country. For example, tracking the use of drugs used to treat epidemic diseases is often a way to obtain early indication of an impending public health problem. For example, one of the earliest indications of the impending AIDS epidemic was the identification by Centers for Disease Control researchers of an unusually high number of orders for pentamidine, a drug usually used to treat patients with Pneumocystis carinii pneumonia, a very rare kind of pneumonia (Shilts, 1988).

Sentinel surveillance systems are used in epidemiology to monitor health by enrolling specific sentinel sites (often hospitals or clinics) in providing key information on a continuing basis. For example, information about patients diagnosed as having certain specified infectious diseases in sentinel hospitals is reported to a central site (such as the Centers for Disease Control) and used to monitor trends that might presage new epidemics or changes in the course of existing ones. We propose a similar idea for monitoring technology use in American schools.

We propose the continuous monitoring of a set of sentinel schools throughout the country. The schools would be selected to be reasonably representative (though not necessarily a probability sampling basis)—representing the variation in contexts, student population composition, and teaching staff that is present in American education. Arrangements could be made to obtain both structured quantitative sort data (e.g., responses to questionnaires or structured interviews) and more qualitative, open-ended data (e.g., conversations about what is happening with technology in your classroom) on a regular basis. Much of this information would not be particularly useful, although it would provide a continuous portrait of technology use in a set of American schools that could be useful in itself. However, it could provide valuable early warning of trends that would otherwise be invisible for a considerable time (possibly years) in large-scale surveys. Although such a system would probably not provide data that are as valid or statistically precise as those collected in a large-scale survey with a probability sample, it could provide timely early warning about potential trends.

Such a system would provide important input to policymakers by enhancing their general knowledge about emerging trends. This would permit the assessment of potential policy issues rapidly enough to permit a more reasoned and informed response. By helping to identify emerging issues about which information was needed, it would also enhance our capacity to design more valid and precise data collections to better understand these emerging issues. That is, it would improve the quality and timeliness of the other components of the technology information system.

Such a network of sentinel schools would need to be developed as a research community that involves the schools as partners in a joint research enterprise. School personnel would have to be recruited as practitioner-researchers, probably as a (externally funded) part of their professional responsibilities (e.g., 25% time). Presumably the practitioner-researcher would relay data from the school site to the central monitoring center via the Internet and would regularly be available by e-mail to the central site and perhaps would also be able to communicate with practitioner-researchers at other sites. Note that there is a tension between the additional contextual information that might result from communication among the sites and the possibility that such intercommunication might contaminate the information developed by transmitting expectations and prejudices among sites. The question of how much communication among sentinel sites would be encouraged or even allowed would need to be decided.

This kind of surveillance system has the advantage that it can be adaptive. That is, if a potential trend was spotted in a few sites, the other sites might be asked to gather information specifically to investigate that potential trend. Moreover, response time could, in principle, be very rapid. This would permit detection of trends, refinement of measurement, and tracking of trends in a very efficient and timely manner.

The network of practitioner-researchers can also be a valuable resource for the development of instrumentation for other technology-related data collections. They might prove to be excellent sources of item writers and certainly an insightful group for pilot testing of technology use items developed by others.

There are, of course, precedents for this kind of data collection. Apple Computer sponsored a group of schools from which the collected data were used to refine educational software. Other such user groups have emerged as a consequence of common use of curriculum materials or evaluation technologies. The difference here is the national scope and the focus on collection of data about technology use strictly for purposes of policy research.

REFERENCES

Becker, H. J. (1991). Mathematics and science uses of computers in American schools. *Journal of Computers in Mathematics and Science Teaching, 10,* 19–25.

Becker, H. J. (1992). Computer-based integrated learning systems in the elementary and middle grades: A critical review and synthesis of evaluation reports. *Journal of Educational Computing Research, 8,* 1–41.

Becker, H. J. (1994). Mindless or mindful use of integrated learning systems. *International Journal of Educational Research, 21,* 65–79.

Christmann, E., & Badgett, J. (1999). A comparative analysis of the effects of computer-assisted instruction on student achievement in differing science and demographic areas. *Journal of Computers in Mathematics and Science Teaching, 18,* 135–143.

Clariana, R. B., & Schultz, C. W. (1993). Gender by content achievement differences in computer-based instruction. *Journal of Computers in Mathematics and Science Teaching, 12,* 277–288.

Cole, M., & Griffin, P. (Eds.). (1987). *Improving science and mathematics education for minorities and women.* Madison: University of Wisconsin, Wisconsin Center for Educational Research.

Cuban, L. (1993). Computers meet classroom: Classroom wins. *Teachers College Record, 95,* 185–210.

Dickey, E., & Kherlopian, R. (1987). A survey of teachers of mathematics, science, and computers on the uses of computers in grades 5–9 classrooms. *Educational Technology, 27*(6), 10–14.

Hativa, N. (1994). What you design is not what you get (WYDINWYG): Cognitive, affective, and social impacts of learning with ILSC: An integration of findings from six-years of qualitative and quantitative studies. *International Journal of Educational Research, 21,* 81–111.

Hativa, N., & Becker, H. J. (1994). Integrated learning systems: Problems and potential benefits. *International Journal of Educational Research, 21,* 113–119.

Hativa, N., & Shorer, D. (1989). Socio-economic status, aptitude, and gender differences in CAI gains of arithmetic. *The Journal of Educational Research, 83,* 11–21.

Hedges, L. V., Konstantopoulos, S., & Thoreson, A. (1999). *Computer use and its relation to academic achievement in mathematics, reading, and writing.* Unpublished manuscript.

Kozma, R. B., (1991). Learning with media. *Review of Educational Research, 61,* 179–211.

Kozma, R. B., & Croninger, R. G. (1992). Technology and the fate of at-risk students. *Education and Urban Society, 24,* 440–453.

Kulik, J. A., & Kulik, C.-L. C. (1987). Review of recent literature on computer-based instruction. *Contemporary Education Review, 12,* 222–230.

Liao, Y. K. (1992). Effects of computer-assisted instruction on cognitive outcomes: A meta-analysis. *Journal of Research on Computing and Education, 24,* 367–380.

Maddox, C. D., Johnson, L., & Harlow, S. (1993). The state of the art in computer education: Issues for discussion with teachers-in-training. *Journal of Technology and Teacher Education, 1,* 219–228.

Munger, G. F., & Loyd, B. H. (1989). Gender and attitudes toward computers and calculators: Their relationship to math performance. *Journal of Educational Computing Research, 5,* 167–177.

Neuman, D. (1991). *Technology and equity.* College Park, MD: University of Maryland. (ERIC Document Reproduction Service No. EDO IR 91 8)

Niemiec, R. P., & Walberg, H. J. (1987). Comparative effects of computer-assisted instruction: A synthesis of reviews. *Journal of Educational Computing Research, 3,* 19–37.

Niemiec, R. P., & Walberg, H. J. (1992). The effect of computers on learning. *International Journal of Education, 17,* 99–108.

Nye, B., Hedges, L. V., & Konstantopoulos, S. (1999). The long term effects of small classes: A five year follow-up of the Tennessee class size experiment. *Educational Evaluation and Policy Analysis, 21,* 127–142.

Ognibene, R., & Skeele, R. (1990). Computers and the schools: Unused and misused. *Action in Teacher Education, 12,* 99–108.

Osin, L., Nesher, P., & Ram, J. (1994). Do the rich become richer and the poor poorer? A longitudinal analysis of pupil achievement and progress in elementary schools using computer-assisted instruction. *International Journal of Educational Research, 21,* 53–64.

Owens, E. W. (1993, March). Technology access and use in urban, suburban, and rural eighth grade mathematics classrooms. In D. Carey, R. Carey, D. A. Willis, & J. Willis (Eds.), *Technology and teacher education annual 1993* (pp. 528–

530). Charlottesville, VA: Association for Advancement of Computing in Education.

Ryan, A. W. (1991). Meta-analysis of achievement effects of microcomputer applications in elementary schools. *Educational Administration Quarterly, 27,* 161–184.

Scott, T., Cole, M., & Engel, M. (1992). Computers and education: A cultural constructivist perspective. *Review of Research in Education, 18,* 191–251.

Shilts, R. (1988). *And the band played on: Politics, people, and the AIDS epidemic.* New York: Penguin.

Sutton, R. E. (1991). Equity and computers in the schools: A decade of research. *Review of Educational Research, 61,* 475–503.

U.S. Bureau of the Census. (1989). *Statistical abstract of the United States: 1989* (109th ed.). Washington, DC: U.S. Government Printing Office.

U.S. Bureau of the Census. (1998). *Statistical abstract of the United States: 1998* (118th ed.). Washington, DC: U.S. Government Printing Office.

Van Dusen, L. M., & Worthen, B. R. (1994). The impact of integrated learning system implementation on student outcomes: Implications for research and evaluation. *International Journal of Educational Research, 21,* 13–24.

Watt, D. (1982). Education for citizenship in a computer-based society. In R. Seidel, R. Anderson, & B. Hunter (Eds.), *Computer literacy* (pp. 53–68). New York: Academic Press.

Chapter 8

The Advantages
of Longitudinal Design

Russell W. Rumberger

Investment in computer-related forms of educational technology in American schools has increased rapidly in recent years. The most common indicator of this growth is the number of students per computer, or computer density. According to the most recent data, the number of students per computer declined from 13.7 in 1992 to 6 by 1998 (Teaching, Learning, and Computing [TLC], 1999). By 1998 there were more than 8.6 million computers in American classrooms (TLC, 1999). An even more rapid change has occurred in access to the Internet. In 1994, only 35% of all schools in the United States had access to the Internet; by 1999 the figure had climbed to 95% (National Center for Education Statistics, 2000, table 1).

This large investment is based on the belief that educational technology can radically transform teaching and learning. Earlier forms of computer-based educational technologies, such as desktop or stand-alone computers, were used primarily to teach students about technology or to provide self-contained drill-and-practice programs to enhance basic skills. But newer and more powerful desktop computers, along with the development of computer networks and the Internet, provide the opportunity for educational technology to transform teaching and learning in more fundamental ways across the curriculum and throughout the educational system. Yet such a transformation presents a more formidable challenge to the educational system. As the President's Committee of Advisors on Science and Technology (PCAST) points out in its 1997 report:

> While the widespread availability of modern computing and networking hardware will indeed be necessary if technology is to realize its promise, the devel-

opment and utilization of useful educational software and information resources, and the adaptation of curricula to make effective use of technology, are likely to represent more formidable challenges.

Particular attention should be given to the potential role of technology in achieving the goals of current educational reform efforts through the user of new pedagogic methods focusing on the development of higher-order reasoning and problem-solving skills. (p. 7)

Of course, the promise of technologies to transform education is not new. Earlier technologies, such as tape recorders, movies, and television, were also heralded for their potential to improve teaching and learning in schools. In 1922 Thomas Edison said, "I believe that the motion picture is destined to revolutionize our educational system, and that in a few years it will supplant largely, if not entirely, the use of textbooks" (quoted in Cuban, 1986, p. 9). And many schools adopted these "new" and promising technologies. But according to educational historians David Tyack and Larry Cuban (1995), not all technologies were widely adopted by teachers. Those that were, such as chalkboards, overhead projectors, and hand-held calculators, were familiar to teachers and fit into classroom routines and procedures, enabling teachers to be more efficient and effective in the things they were already doing. But other technologies, such as movies, television, and computers, have not been widely adopted by teachers because they require significant changes in classroom practices and teacher training, activities that the technologies themselves cannot change.

Will newer, computer-based technologies fundamentally alter teaching and learning in ways that past technology has not? It is probably too early to tell because the widespread adoption and use of these newer technologies is still in its infancy (for one study, see Wenglinsky, 1998). Nonetheless, in order to ascertain the potential of these technologies, it is important to design studies to evaluate their effectiveness. But designing such studies presents a host of methodological problems. Some of these problems are common to the design of intervention studies in general, while others are unique to the problem of evaluating the effectiveness of educational technologies.

This chapter begins with a conceptual framework that provides background for designing evaluations of educational technology based on a multilevel, longitudinal approach. This approach can help address some of the challenges that evaluators face when trying to document the effects of educational technologies on student outcomes. I then discuss the types of samples, data, and analysis that are needed to apply this conceptual framework to conduct evaluations of educational technology. Next I consider some of the difficulties in designing evaluations of educational technology and the extent to which existing national data sets are appropriate for evaluating the effectiveness of educational technologies.

A MULTILEVEL CONCEPTUAL FRAMEWORK
FOR EVALUATING EDUCATIONAL TECHNOLOGY

Research designs should be based on a conceptual framework that characterizes the nature of the phenomena being studied. In this section I introduce a framework that can be used to design evaluations of educational technologies. The framework is not new. It is based on frameworks that have been used previously to study and monitor the effectiveness of educational institutions, such as classrooms and schools (e.g., Rumberger & Thomas, 2000; Shavelson, McDonnell, Oakes, & Carey, 1987; Willms, 1992). But I have adapted these frameworks and discuss how such a framework can be useful in studying educational technologies. After introducing the framework, I also talk about how this framework can be used to evaluate the effectiveness of educational technology.

Educational Technology as a Multilevel Phenomenon

The framework is based on the concept of educational technology as a multilevel phenomenon. As noted earlier, one of the challenges in designing evaluations of educational technology is that educational technology can take on many different forms. In reality, educational technology represents a vast array of specific technologies that encompass a range of hardware and software that can be used for a variety of educational purposes, from the very specific to the very general. Moreover, these technologies can be located in different levels of the educational system and used by different people. This variation and complexity in educational technologies make it difficult to develop an overall conceptual framework that can capture this variation.

Table 8.1 illustrates some of this variation at three different levels of the educational system—the school level, the classroom level, and the student level. Several specific technologies and their designated uses are described at each of the three levels. For example, schools may establish local area networks (LANs) to facilitate sharing of hardware and software as well as communication among desktop computers connected to the network. Many schools also have computer laboratories with groups of desktop computers, where a classroom of students may come to receive instruction or where individual students may do their own work. Educational technologies at the school level serve the entire community of teaches, staff, and students in a school, although the extent to which these technologies are used—and thus their impact—can vary widely.

Educational technologies can also be used at the classroom level, primarily by teachers. Teachers can use desktop computers to plan lessons and track student progress. They can also use dedicated technologies, such as televi-

Table 8.1. Examples of Educational Technologies and Their Use at Different Levels of the Educational System

Level	Technology	Use
School	Local Area Networks (LANs)	Facilitate communication and sharing of school resources
	Website	Promote communication with students, parents, and teachers
	Computer laboratories	Provide access to computers for students during and after school
	Internet connection	Support student and teacher access to World Wide Web
Classroom	Multimedia hardware and software	Facilitate presentation of material to students
	Teacher workstation and software	Provide access to Internet, LAN
Student	Stand-alone drill-and-practice software	Improve learning of facts and skills
	Tutorial software	Improve learning of concepts and reasoning skills
	Application software (word processors, spreadsheets, etc.)	Facilitate problem solving and reporting
	Web browser software	Assist in searching and retrieving information

sions, to present material to students. Technologies used by teachers can have an impact on the learning and achievement of all students in the class.

Finally, individual students can use a number of educational technologies to benefit their own learning, both in school and out of school. They can use desktop computers and software to do class work, including general word-processing programs and Internet search engines. They can also use specific software, such as tutorial programs, that can teach specific skills.

This framework illustrates several difficulties of designing evaluations of educational technologies. First, educational technologies comprise a wide range of specific technologies with applications from the very narrow to the very broad. Second, these technologies can be applied at different levels of the educational system. Third, different individuals at these different levels can use these technologies for various activities and for varying amounts of time. What this framework suggests is that to properly evaluate the impact of educational technology, it is important to correctly specify the nature of the technology that one wishes to evaluate and at the appropriate level. And one way to do this is to conceptualize educational technology as a multi-level phenomenon.

Schooling as a Multilevel Phenomenon

Educational technology is not the only aspect of schooling that can be characterized as a multilevel phenomenon. The entire enterprise of school-ing has been conceptualized as a multilevel phenomenon in which different aspects of the educational system operate at different levels (Barr & Dreeben, 1983; Willms, 1992). More specifically, there are aspects of schools that can impact student learning and achievement throughout the school, there are other aspects of schools that can impact student learning and achievement only in specific classrooms, and there are aspects of the schooling process that operate only on individual students.

In addition, the process of schooling can be divided into three distinct components, based on a economic model of schooling (e.g., Hanushek, 1986; Levin, 1994): The first component consists of the inputs of schooling—stu-dents, teachers, and other resources (including technology); the second com-ponent consists of the educational process itself, that determines how those inputs or resources are actually utilized in the educational process (Levin, 1997; Miles & Darling-Hammond, 1998); the third component is the out-puts of schooling—student learning and achievement.

This conceptual framework is illustrated in Figure 8.1. The framework shows the three components of the educational process operating at the three levels of schooling—schools, classrooms, and students. The frame-work also shows how educational technologies may be evaluated within this framework. For example, the framework distinguishes the mere exist-ence of computers and other technologies as educational inputs or resources from their actual use within the educational process. In other words, schools can have elaborate computer laboratories stocked with fancy computers and sophisticated software, but if those machines are not used or used in specific ways, they may have little impact on student learning. Similarly, teachers can have desktop computers in their classrooms but not have the interest or ability to use the machine to enhance their teaching. At the stu-dent level, the impact of computers may again depend on how much and in what ways students actually use computers in pursuing their educational activities.

Figure 8.1. Conceptual Framework for Analyzing Education as a Multilevel Phenomenon

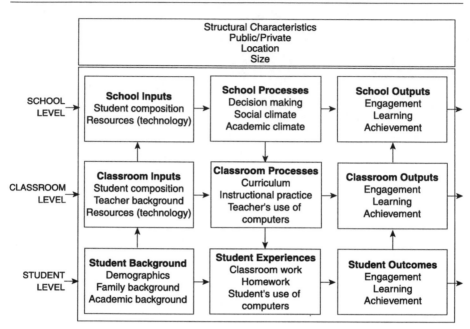

The framework also suggests that the impacts of educational technologies can be evaluated at different levels, depending on which level of the system the educational technologies are used within. For example, the impact of LANs and computer laboratories should be evaluated at the school level, since that is where they operate. Such an evaluation would examine the impact of those technologies on the average performance of students in the school and may involve comparisons with other schools that do not have those technologies or use them in different ways. Similarly, the impact of classroom-level technologies, such as teacher desktop computers, would be at the classroom level and would involve looking at average student performance in classrooms and comparisons with other classrooms. Finally, the impact of technologies at the student level would involve comparisons among students who differ in their use of educational technologies.

Learning as a Longitudinal Process

The framework is also useful for examining the impact of educational technologies over both the short and the long term. The concepts and measures specified in the framework are not tied to any particular time frame. But the framework does suggest that to evaluate the impact of educational technologies on student learning and achievement over time would require that one measure change in the inputs and processes over the same period of time. Of course, the longer the time frame, the more difficult it becomes to collect and analyze data because of the high student turnover in many schools (Meyer & Fienberg, 1992).

DESIGN FEATURES FOR MULTILEVEL, LONGITUDINAL STUDIES

This section discusses some of the features of multilevel longitudinal research designs based on the framework presented in the previous section. These features include type of research design, sampling, data requirements, and methods of analysis.

The section also considers the extent to which these design features are addressed in existing national longitudinal studies being carried out by the U.S. Department of Education (DOE). Over the last three decades, the DOE has carried out several national longitudinal studies "to study the educational, vocational, and personal development of students at various grade levels, and the personal, familial, social, institutional, and cultural factors that may affect that development" (Ingles, Scott, Lindmark, Frankel, & Myers, 1992, p. 1). These longitudinal studies, which are based on surveys of students, teachers, and parents as well as test scores and student records, have been used by countless researchers throughout the United States to study a variety of fundamental issues about schooling and student performance, such as academic achievement, parental involvement, and school dropouts. For the most part, they have not been used to study the impact of educational technologies on student achievement. But these designs could be adapted to do so, which I discuss below.

Research Designs

The proposed framework is compatible with several research designs that could be used to study and evaluate educational technology.

Experimental Designs. The framework could be used to study the impact of educational technologies using experimental research designs that compared student achievement or achievement growth among a relatively small number of classrooms that differ in their use of educational technology. The major advantage of experimental methods, especially those employing random assignment, is that they provide the most effective controls for other, student-level factors that could influence student achievement by creating equivalent comparison groups at the beginning of the experiment. However, it is often difficult to carry out random assignment in actual schools, where teachers and parents wish to exercise the right to place students in particular classrooms for personal or educational reasons.

In addition, because educational technologies are so widespread and pervasive, it may be hard to create an experimental condition where one group of students is provided access to a particular educational technology and another group is not. It may be relatively easy to do so in the case of classroom- or school-based technologies, such as the use of technology by teachers in teaching or the access and use of computers by students in school. But it may be hard to control differences among students in their access to computers and technologies outside of school. This would make it hard to clearly determine the nature of the "treatment" that one group of students is getting and another group is not.

Finally, experimental designs are normally used to study treatments affecting one experimental group as compared to another group. In the proposed framework, this would be akin to studying the impact of educational technology at a single level rather than as a multilevel phenomenon, as illustrated below.

Longitudinal Studies of Students, Classrooms, and Schools. Although this framework could be used to design any study of educational technology, it is particularly useful for designing large-scale studies of students, classrooms, and schools, which vary widely in their use of educational technology. Because technology is already so pervasive in the educational enterprise, it is important to design studies that can evaluate its impact on different aspects of the educational system. It is also important to identify not only the existence of the technologies but also the specific ways they are being used by teachers, students, and staff.

This framework could also be used to study differences in achievement growth among a much larger sample of students based on survey research designs. Survey research designs are typically based on some sort of probability sampling of a large population so that the results of the study can be generalized back to that larger population. The National Center for Education Statistics (NCES) uses such sampling techniques to design its national longitudinal studies of students and schools (e.g., Carroll, 1996). These studies employ stratified, clustered sampling that first involves selecting a sample of schools among different types and regions of the country, and then selecting samples of students within schools. Questionnaire data are collected from students, teachers, school officials, and parents, along with test data and data from school records (e.g., transcripts). Because of the form of sampling and the types of data collected, these studies are particularly useful in carrying out multilevel analysis, most typically of students and schools (e.g., Gamoran, 1996; Lee & Bryk, 1989; McNeal, 1997; Rumberger, 1995).

Sampling

The choice of samples and sampling technique is one of the critical features in designing evaluations of educational technology. One reason is that educational technologies operate at several different levels of the educational system, as illustrated in the conceptual framework. Therefore, the sampling technique should be tied to the conceptual level where the study will focus. For example, if a study were designed to study the impact of educational technology at the classroom level, a sampling framework would have to identify an appropriate sample of classrooms. If a study were designed to study the impact of educational technology at the school level, a sampling framework would have to identify an appropriate sample of schools. Because educational technology can operate at multiple levels, a more comprehensive design would be to select samples of schools and classrooms.

Another consideration would be the age group of the students. The value and impact of educational technology could vary widely among students of different ages and abilities. That is, different types of educational technologies may be more appropriate for teaching different subjects and concepts at different age or ability levels. So the choice of samples might also consider the ages of the students. A comparative design might select samples of students at different ages.

Table 8.2 and Figure 8.2 present a multilevel, multiage sampling design. This design could be used to study the impact of educational technology at three levels—the school level, the classroom level, and the individual level. The primary sampling unit would be the school. Within each school, all the classrooms and all the students at a given grade level would be included in the study. The sampling framework could provide appropriate samples to study the impact of educational technologies at the school, classroom, and individual level.

This sampling framework differs from the one typically used in the NCES studies described earlier. Those studies are designed to focus on student outcomes over time and on school effectiveness, but not on classroom or teacher effectiveness. That is, students are sampled within schools, not classrooms, with within-school samples of about 25 or 30 students. While such samples are sufficient to make inferences about school effects, they are not sufficient to make inferences about classroom or teacher effects. This above framework would select entire classrooms within schools in order to make inferences about

Table 8.2. Illustration of Sampling Framework for Multilevel, Longitudinal Cohort Study

	Schools	Teachers	Students
Elementary (3 teachers/grade level)	12		
Grade K (20 students/teacher)		36	720
Grade 3 (20 students/teacher)		36	720
Middle (2 teachers/grade level)	12		
Grade 6 (30 students/teacher)		24	720
High (2 teachers/grade level)	12		
Grade 9 (30 students/teacher)		24	720
Total	*36*	*120*	*2,880*

classroom and teacher effects. One use of such a design, for example, would be to select at least two classrooms per grade level, with one classroom implementing a specific educational technology and the other serving as a comparison group. Achieving a true experimental design would require randomly assigning students to classrooms. If random assignment was not possible, then a quasi-experimental design could be used that would require extensive pre-intervention measures to provide statistical controls. Having a number of schools in the study would permit examination of how the impact of the intervention varied across sites that might differ in student composition, school characteristics, and implementation of the intervention (e.g., Seltzer, 1994).

Data Requirements

There are a number of important data requirements to consider in designing multilevel longitudinal studies. The most important requirement is to have suitable outcome measures that provide valid and reliable assessments of growth over time. Since educational technologies are designed to impact student learning, suitable measures of learning outcomes are required. Existing national surveys of older children have measured learning outcomes based on standardized tests that readily lend themselves to scaling achievement growth over time. The most recent national educational studies, which focus on a birth cohort and a kindergarten cohort, are focusing on a broader range of developmental outcomes in cognitive, social, and psychological domains (see Early Childhood Longitudinal Study [ECLS], National Center for Education Statistics, n.d.).

Figure 8.2. Illustration of Longitudinal Cohort Study

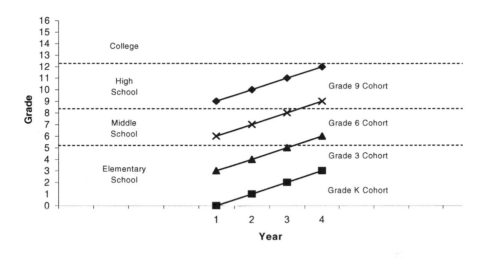

As pointed out earlier, educational technologies are thought to improve constructivist learning outcomes. Such outcomes are better assessed through less traditional means, such as student portfolios and open-ended assessments. Such approaches are more difficult to score, especially if the intent is to provide valid and reliable measures of change in learning outcomes over time (Shavelson, Baxter, & Gao, 1993; Shavelson, Solano-Flores, & Ruiz-Primo, 1998).

Another important measurement issue concerns how to assess the use of educational technology. One of the long-standing criticisms about school effectiveness research is that it typically focuses on the inputs to the educational process—such as the characteristics of teachers—and not how those inputs or resources are being used. Consequently, reviews of this research have found little systematic relationship between educational inputs and educational outcomes (e.g., Hanushek, 1997). Yet studies that have examined how resources are used, especially at the student level, have found them to have important impacts on student outcomes (e.g., Brown & Saks, 1987; Summers & Wolfe, 1977).

Methods of Analysis

This same problem exists when trying to study the impact of educational technology. Educational technologies—computers, specific software programs, and so on—simply represent new resources available to students, teachers, and schools. In order to determine whether these resources impact learning, it is necessary to determine the extent to which (amount of time) and specific ways those resources are being used by students, teachers, and schools.

At the classroom level, this requires examining how teachers utilize educational technologies in their teaching practice, particularly in the instructional strategies they use. There are several ways to measure teaching practice: (1) observation, (2) teacher logs, (3) classroom assignments, and (4) surveys. Each of these methods has been used to conduct research on teaching. Observational methods are most often used in small-scale studies, while survey methods are most often used in large-scale studies. Teacher logs and classroom assignments have not been widely used by themselves, but they have been used to help validate other methods (e.g., Burstein et al., 1995; Mullens & Gayler, 1999).

Although survey methods have been widely used in large-scale studies, questions have been raised about the validity of the information reported by teachers regarding their educational practice. Burstein and colleagues (1995) validated survey responses from 70 secondary mathematics teachers with course textbooks, teacher logs, and classroom assignments in the areas of instructional content, instructional strategies, and instructional goals. They found that instructional goals were not validly measured by surveys but that instructional content and instructional strategies were, although there was little variation in instructional strategies among the teachers they studied. Mayer (1999a) also found that the amount of time teachers reported spending on innovative mathematics practices was highly correlated with the amount of time ascertained from classroom observations. Nonetheless, he also found that "the survey did not adequately capture *quality* of the interaction between teacher and student" (Mayer, 1999a, p. 43, emphasis in original). The results of these validity studies are being used by NCES to design better measures of classroom practice in future national surveys (Mayer, 1999b; Mullens & Gayler, 1999). Thus, future surveys might provide a useful means of gathering information on how teachers are using educational technologies to improve classroom practice and student learning outcomes.

Multilevel Modeling

One of the advantages of conceptualized educational technology as a multilevel phenomenon is to evaluate the impact of educational technologies at multiple levels. Although the problem of modeling educational outcomes at multiple levels has been acknowledged for some time (e.g., Burstein, 1984), techniques for estimating such models are relatively recent (Bryk & Raudenbush, 1992). These techniques are now routinely used to study a wide range of social science phenomenon (Draper, 1995; Lee, 2000).

Figure 8.3 provides an illustration of how multilevel modeling might be used to evaluate the effectiveness of educational technologies operating at two levels of the educational system—the classroom level and the student level. The top panel shows two hypothetical classrooms of students and changes in mean achievement of the two classrooms over time. This situation might characterize a quasi-experimental design that compares two existing classrooms in which the students have different achievement levels at the beginning of the experiment (in contrast, a true experimental design with random assignment would ensure that the two mean achievement levels would be statistically identical). A typical evaluation might simply compare the two classrooms on changes in mean achievement or achievement growth over some time period. The classroom with the largest achievement growth would be deemed the most effective—in this example, it would be classroom 2. If the teacher in classroom 2 were using a particular type of educational technology to augment his or her instruction that otherwise was identical to the instruction provided to students in classroom 1, then this might support a finding that the educational technology improved student achievement.

But comparing changes in mean achievement does not reveal differences in the growth rates of individual students and what accounted for those differences. The bottom panel shows the individual growth rates of four students in each classroom. As the figure reveals, students in classroom 1 showed more variability in growth rates compared to students in classroom 2. Multilevel modeling would allow one not only to identify factors that predicted differences in mean growth rates between the two classrooms but also to identify factors that predict differences in individual growth rates. Based on the conceptual framework of educational technologies presented earlier, the model could investigate both the impact of educational technologies at the classroom level and the impact of educational technologies at the student level. In other words, the model could help determine whether students who used educational technologies to perform their schoolwork showed larger gains in achievement, after controlling for other factors (such as socioeconomic status and ability) that could also effect achievement growth.

Multilevel modeling can also be used to examine variability among classrooms in large-scale, multisite studies and to explain that variability. Even though an evaluation may find that, on average, a particular intervention is effective over a large sample of classrooms or sites, it is also likely that there is considerable variation in the effectiveness. Multilevel modeling can be used to measure that variability and model it as a function of predictor variables, such as the extent to which the program was fully implemented at each site (Seltzer, 1994).

Not only are multilevel modeling techniques useful to evaluate the impacts of educational technologies at different levels, they also provide other

Figure 8.3. Multilevel Growth Modeling Research Design with Students from Two Classrooms

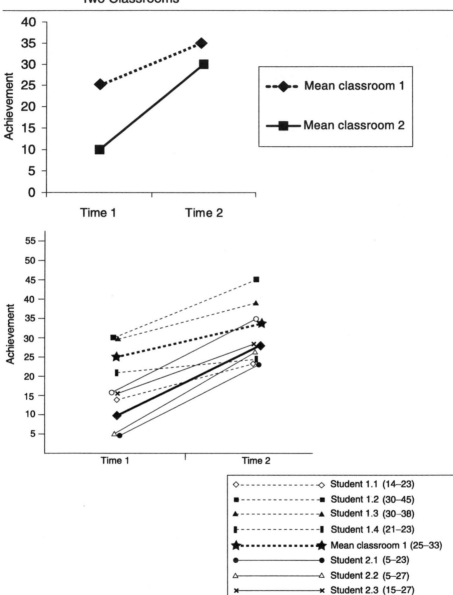

advantages to the researcher. First, they can be used with different research designs, including experimental and survey designs. Second, the types of statistical techniques that are used to estimate multilevel models address a number of problems with nested or hierarchical data: unbalanced designs in which there are different numbers of respondents in groups, missing data, and data collected at different times (Bryk & Raudenbush, 1992).

SOME DIFFICULTIES IN DESIGNING EVALUATIONS OF EDUCATIONAL TECHNOLOGY

This section describes several difficulties in designing evaluations of educational technology, including conceptualizing, specifying, and measuring the educational technology intervention or treatment that is to be implemented. Finding or developing adequate measures of educational technology is challenging, as is selecting appropriate outcome measures. In addition, there are problems with the various designs that have guided past evaluations.

Conceptualizing and Measuring Educational Technology

Probably the most fundamental problem in designing evaluations of educational technology is to properly conceptualize and measure educational technology. Although the singular term *educational technology* tends to suggest that technology used in educational settings is somehow homogeneous, in reality there are a wide range of distinct technologies that have been used in the educational process for many years. These technologies have included very basic devices, such as chalkboards and pencils, as well as very sophisticated devices, such as desktop computers. Much of the recent interest in educational technology has focused on the rapid emergence of sophisticated, digital, electronic technologies such as computers, local networks, and, most recently, the Internet. Accompanying this growth of sophisticated hardware has been a wide range of both general-purpose (e.g., word processors, web browsers) and dedicated software (e.g., stand-alone tutorial programs).

The wide range of educational technologies that have been developed over the last decade, and will likely be developed in the future, can be used for many different purposes and by different people throughout the educational system. Students can use general-purpose word processors to write papers and reports; they can also use stand-alone, dedicated software programs to learn either basic skills through drill and practice—commonly referred to as computer-assisted instruction (CAI)—or more advanced conceptual and problem-solving skills through tutorial and exploratory computer environments (Cognition and Technology Group at Vanderbilt [CTGV],

1996). Teachers can use a variety of multimedia tools to make audio and video presentations to students; they can also use desktop computers and the Internet to locate and retrieve information for lesson planning and communicating with other teachers and educators. School administrators and staff can use local area networks and the Internet to share data and information both with teachers and students within the school and with parents and others outside the school.

The many forms and uses of educational technology present a major challenge to designing studies to assess the impact of educational technology—to develop a clear concept and measure of the educational technology that is to be evaluated. With some forms of technology, this may not be particularly problematic. For example, the most common use of early-generation computers was for computer-assisted instruction to teach basic skills through drill and practice. In this application, the form and use of the educational technology was fairly well defined, making it relatively easy to develop outcome measures and estimate costs for this type of educational technology (e.g., Kulik & Kulik, 1991; Levin, Glass, & Meister, 1987).

But these older forms and uses of educational technology, which were designed to transmit basic facts and skills, are giving way to new forms of technology that are designed to teach higher-order thinking and problem-solving skills by supporting student-initiated inquiries and group activities (PCAST, 1997). These new applications are based on a student-centered, constructivist paradigm derived from recent research on intelligence and motivation (for a review, see CTGV, 1996). Examples of these applications are tutorial and exploratory computer environments, enhanced application tools that support the learning process, and communication programs that promote collaboration (CTGV, 1996).

Although these newer forms and uses of educational technology appear to hold great promise for promoting student learning, they also present a major methodological difficulty in how to develop appropriate measures and indicators of such technologies. Increasingly, these technologies become an integral part of the instructional process itself and, as such, make it difficult to assess its impact. As PCAST (1997) put it:

> Technology has in recent years been increasingly seen not as an isolated addition to the conventional K–12 curriculum, but as one of a number of tools that might be used to support a process of comprehensive curricular (and in some cases, systemic) reform. In such an environment, attempts to isolate the effects of technology as a distinct independent variable may be both difficult and unproductive. The Panel believes the kinds of findings that might actually prove more useful in practice are more likely to arise from research aimed at assessing the effectiveness and cost-effectiveness of specific educational approaches and techniques that make use of technology. (p. 94)

The CTGV (1996), which has been involved in researching educational technology for many years, reached a similar conclusion when it argued for "the need to investigate the effects of different instructional designs rather than effectiveness of various technologies as the means to deliver or transmit content to learners" (p. 814). This same concern has been raised by critics of earlier CAI evaluations because, they argue, such evaluations failed to identify whether observed differences in student outcomes between CAI and regular instruction was due to the technology (e.g., computers) itself or the exact nature of the instruction provided (Clark, 1983).

Appropriate Outcome Measures

A related problem concerns the use of appropriate outcome measures. Because different educational technologies have been used for different educational purposes, it is important to have different and appropriate measures of student-learning outcomes to assess the effectiveness of these technologies. But some outcomes are easier to assess than others.

Earlier applications of educational technologies were not only easier to identify and measure; their use in the transmission of basic skills and knowledge made it easier to develop appropriate measures of student-learning outcomes. Basic skills and factual knowledge can be easily and accurately assessed through standardized tests that are widely available for assessing learning outcomes in a number of content areas across grade levels.

But newer, constructivist applications of educational technology are designed to develop higher-order thinking and problem-solving skills that are not readily assessed through standardized tests. Rather, such skills are best assessed through performance-based assessments carried out over extended periods of time (Lesgold, Lajorie, Brunzo, & Eggan, 1992). But establishing the reliability and validity of such assessments is problematic (Shavelson et al., 1993, 1998). And even performance-based assessments may not provide an appropriate measure of the lifelong learning that may result from these newer forms and uses of educational technology (Brown, Bransford, Ferrara, & Campione, 1983).

The fact that newer, constructivist forms of educational technology may foster higher-order skills but not necessarily lower-level basic skills can present a political as well as a technical problem. Because an investment in new technologies involves changes in instructional practice as well as outcome measures, they require the full support of students and parents. Yet with all the increased emphasis in raising scores on standardized tests through statewide accountability systems in places like California and Texas, it may be more difficult to garner the political support for such changes. Such was the case in a California school that invested in new technologies oriented to constructivist learning but also saw a drop in standardized test scores, prompting parents to demand a "back-to-basics" agenda (PCAST, 1997).

Laboratory Versus School Settings

One issue concerns whether to conduct the research in a laboratory versus schooling setting. Laboratory settings offer a number of advantages: The researchers have considerable control over all the parameters, including the selection of participants and an equivalent control group through random assignment and the fidelity with which the technology is being used, as well as the opportunity to carry out multifaceted and in-depth assessments. Although laboratory settings may be particularly useful in the initial development of a particular technology, such as a self-contained tutoring or simulation program, they will not provide any information on how effective the technology will be in the real world of everyday classrooms with regular classroom teachers.

Consequently, the evaluation of any educational technology must ultimately include school- or field-based settings. But moving from the laboratory to the school presents a number of difficulties. One is that the designer or researcher has much less control on how the technology will be used, particularly whether it will get used in the manner intended. That is, the issue of fidelity of implementation becomes very important (CTGV, 1996). One way to ensure a high degree of fidelity is to provide adequate training to the teachers or students who are going to use the technology, at least for those forms of educational technology that are meant to have specific uses (CTGV, 1996). But even generic forms of educational technology that can have many uses, such as desktop computers, require sufficient staff development to help ensure their use (PCAST, 1997).

Small-Scale Versus Large-Scale Studies

A related problem concerns the scale of study; that is, whether the research study is small-scale, involving a relatively small number of research sites, or large-scale, involving a large number research sites. Small-scale studies will obviously be cheaper to undertake and can minimize variation in the fidelity of implementation. But small-scale studies cannot be easily generalized to the larger population of students, teachers, and schools that might also benefit from the technology. In addition, the results of small-scale studies will be highly dependent on the methods for selecting the participating students, teachers, and schools. In general, teachers and schools that have embraced the use of new, computer-based technologies, largely on their own initiative, are unlikely to be representative of the larger populations of teachers and schools, so the results of small-scale studies that have found improved student outcomes from such teachers and schools may tell us very little about what the average teacher or school may expect. Moreover, as pointed out earlier, to the extent that other aspects of schooling, such as instructional practice, changed along with the use of new educational technologies (which may, in fact, be necessary), it is hard to judge the effectiveness of educational technology alone.

Large-scale studies can provide a much stronger base with which to judge the effectiveness of educational technology across a wide range of students, teachers, and schools. But large-scale studies are more expensive, and they will likely result in greater differences in the fidelity of implementation.

Choice of Research Design

One of the most important issues in designing the evaluation of any educational research design is the choice of research designs. Historically, most evaluations have been based on some sort of quantitative research design. But more recently, some evaluators have pointed out the value of using qualitative as well as quantitative research designs in conducting educational evaluations (Fetterman, 1988; Firestone, 1987; Rossman & Wilson, 1985).

The most rigorous research design for evaluating any educational intervention is a controlled experiment in which students are randomly assigned to a treatment group that receives the intervention and a control or comparison group that does not. Randomized experiments are the only research design that can definitely establish a causal relationship between the intervention and any observed differences in outcomes between treatment and control groups.

But randomized experiments are not easy to conduct, especially in school settings. Students are generally not assigned to classrooms randomly. Rather, assignment decisions are based on student and parent preferences, teacher preferences, and the fit between student needs and teacher qualifications. It is hard to convince parents and teachers to engage in randomized experiments, especially over a long period of time. In one of the largest randomized experiments in recent history—the Tennessee class-size reduction study—it was hard to maintain the random assignment of students (Finn & Archilles, 1999).

Even if random assignment can be achieved initially, experiments can suffer from the problem of student attrition. Many urban and high-poverty schools can experience annual student turnover of 30% per year or more, which can greatly reduce the useful samples in experimental studies. And the small number of students in many classrooms means that attrition can impact treatment and control classrooms differently, introducing potential biases in the samples.

Because of the difficulty in carrying out random assignment in school settings, many educational evaluations rely on quasi-experimental designs where treatment and control groups are not created through random assignment. Often, experiments are based on some sort of voluntary participation and statistical controls are used to create equivalency between treatment and control groups. But voluntary participation can create selection biases in the samples that commonly used statistical controls do not adequately account for (Maddala, 1983).

Another research design that has been used in evaluations of educational interventions, including educational technologies, is large-scale surveys. These studies typically involve large probability samples of schools, which can be generalized to a larger population, and statistical models of student achievement that include a wide range of predictor variables. But such studies may not include adequate controls for prior achievement and other factors that may be associated with computer use, particularly attitudes and motivation. Thus, it is difficult to make strong causal inferences about the impact of technology from such studies. Yet with appropriate methods, including the use of longitudinal growth models described below, such designs can be used to develop useful predictive models of the relationship between the use of educational technology and student outcomes.

Another research design that could be used with this framework is mixed-methods research that employs both quantitative and qualitative techniques. Such designs are being used increasingly in large-scale studies of schools and education (e.g., Bryk, Lee, & Holland 1993). Mixed-methods designs can be used to (1) *corroborate* findings from different methods, (2) *elaborate* findings from one method to another, such as providing descriptions and real-life examples for descriptive statistics and quantitative predictions, and (3) *initiate* new directions or research questions because findings from one method are inconsistent with those of other methods (Rossman & Wilson, 1985). While experimental methods are most appropriate for making strong causal inferences, and survey methods are most appropriate for making inferences to the larger population of students and schools, observational techniques and other qualitative methods allow investigators to address questions of "how" and "why" specific programs or techniques (including technology) produce the impacts they do. Combining qualitative and quantitative methods in a single study can harness the strengths of each approach, while simultaneously mitigating the weaknesses inherent in single-methods research.

Suitable Comparison Groups

An issue related to that of research designs is the choice of suitable comparison groups. All experimental designs involve comparisons between two groups of students—one group that receives the intervention and one group that does not. But this requires that one can clearly specify what is and what is not part of the intervention. Everything that is not part of the intervention should be similar between the two groups so that any differences that are detected at the end of the experiment can be attributed to the effects of the intervention.

Many evaluations of earlier educational technologies, such as computer-assisted instruction, utilized this experimental approach because the educational technology was used to deliver the same educational content to the treatment group as to the comparison group—but through a different media. Yet even these studies have been criticized because they could not demonstrate whether the generally positive effects of CAI were due to the media itself or to differences in the nature of the instruction that was provided (Clark, 1983). This problem is likely to persist and become an even larger issue in designing evaluations of newer educational technologies that are supposed to support a more student-oriented, constructivist form of instruction. In other words, if newer educational technologies are supposed to improve student learning exactly because they do alter the instructional process, including the way teachers interact with students and the way students interact with each other (e.g., promoting cooperative learning groups), then evaluations will have to measure these critical features of classroom practice along with the specific uses of educational technologies in order for evaluators to understand exactly what is being changed. And it again raises the question of what the appropriate comparison group is.

Another issue that makes evaluations of instructional interventions difficult is the role of teacher effects. Early adopters of new forms of educational technologies have been characterized as technological leaders and may have other attributes that make them effective teachers independent of whether or not they utilize technologies. Comparisons with other teachers, who may differ in important ways from technology-oriented teachers, also make it difficult to disentangle the effects of educational technologies themselves and other qualities of teachers that can also impact student achievement.

Short-Term Versus Long-Term Studies

A final issue concerns whether the focus of the study is short term or long term. Short-term studies may be useful in examining the impact of a more narrowly focused form of educational technology, such as a software program to teach typing. Long-term studies may be more useful in looking at the cumulative impacts of a more general form of technology, such as the Internet, that could be used for many different educational activities and whose benefits could be observed over a long period of time.

Short-term studies generally lend themselves to experimental designs that can be more carefully controlled, while long-term studies may be more suitable for survey designs that can track students over longer periods of time.

SUMMARY AND CONCLUSIONS

Educational technologies hold great promise to transform the schooling process and improve student-learning outcomes. Yet past technologies were also thought to hold great promise, and, for the most part, that promise never produced much change in the traditional process of schooling (e.g., Tyack & Cuban, 1995). Whether the new, computer-based technologies will produce more profound and lasting changes remains to be seen.

But in order to determine whether educational technologies are changing the educational process and improving student learning, well-designed evaluations will be required. This has proven to be a difficult task for a number of reasons. First, educational technology consists of a wide variety of specific technologies that can impact the educational process in many different ways and at many different parts of the process, making it hard to clearly identify the nature of the intervention that is to be studied. Second, in the area of teaching it is hard to disentangle the effects of teaching itself from the effects of the educational technology that the teacher may employ. Third, many proponents believe educational technologies have the greatest impact on student-centered, constructivist learning, yet such learning is hard to measure with traditional standardized tests.

To address some of these concerns, this chapter presented a conceptual framework for designed evaluations of technology. The framework views educational technology as a multilevel phenomenon that can impact student learning at the school, classroom, and student level. It is based on similar frameworks that have been used to study inputs, processes, and outcomes of schooling. The framework could be used to design more comprehensive, multilevel evaluations of educational technology.

Evaluations based on this framework would have several features: (1) They would investigate technology within multiple contexts of family, school, and classroom; (2) they would employ a sampling framework to ensure substantial variability in learning contexts; (3) they would focus on learning, or the growth in achievement, over time; (4) they would collect data at multiple levels of the learning process; and (5) they would employ suitable multilevel modeling techniques in order to correctly identify the impact of technology at different levels. Evaluations based on this framework could be done using experimental or survey research designs.

At a time when the nation is making a huge investment in educational technology, it is more important than ever to evaluate its impact in a comprehensive and scientifically rigorous fashion. Only then will it be possible to determine whether this investment lives up to its promise.

REFERENCES

Barr, R., & Dreeben, R. (1983). *How schools work*. Chicago: University of Chicago Press.

Brown, A. L., Bransford, J. D., Ferrara, R., & Campione, J. (1983). Learning, remembering, and understanding. In J. Flavel & E. Markman (Eds.), *Mussen handbook of child psychology* (2nd ed., Vol. 1, pp. 77–166). New York: Wiley.

Brown, B. W., & Saks, D. H. (1987). The microeconomics of the allocation of teachers' time and student learning. *Economics of Education Review, 6*, 319–332.

Bryk, A. S., Lee, V. E., & Holland, P. B. (1993). *Catholic schools and the common good*. Cambridge, MA: Harvard University Press.

Bryk, A., & Raudenbush, S. (1992). *Hierarchical linear models: Applications and data analysis methods*. Newbury Park, CA: Sage.

Burstein, L. (1984). The use of existing data bases in program evaluation and school improvement. *Educational Evaluation and Policy Analysis, 6*, 307–318.

Burstein, L., McDonnell, L. M., Van Winkle, J., Ormseth, T. H., Mirocha, J., & Guiton, G. (1995). *Validating national curriculum indicators*. Santa Monica, CA: RAND.

Carroll, D. (1996). *National Education Longitudinal Study (NELS:88/94): Methodology Report*. Washington, DC: U.S. Government Printing Office.

Clark, R. E. (1983). Reconsidering research on learning from media. *Review of Educational Research, 53*, 445–459.

Cognition and Technology Group at Vanderbilt (CTGV). (1996). Looking at technology in context: A framework for understanding technology and education research. In R. C. Calfee & D. C. Berliner (Eds.), *Handbook of educational psychology* (pp. 807–839). New York: Macmillan.

Cuban, L. (1986). *Teachers and machines: The classroom use of technology since 1920*. New York: Teachers College Press.

Draper, D. (1995). Inference and hierarchical modeling in the social sciences. *Journal of Educational Statistics, 20*, 115–148.

Fetterman, D. M. (1988). Qualitative approaches to evaluating education. *Educational Researcher, 17*, 17–23.

Finn, J., & Achilles, C. (1999). Tennessee's class size study: Findings, implications, misconceptions. *Educational Evaluation and Policy Analysis, 21*, 97–109.

Firestone, W. (1987). Meaning in method: The rhetoric of quantitative and qualitative research. *Educational Researcher, 16*, 16–21.

Gamoran, A. (1996). Student achievement in public magnet, public comprehensive, and private city high schools. *Educational Evaluation and Policy Analysis, 18*, 1–18.

Hanushek, E. A. (1986). The economics of schooling: Production and efficiency in public schools. *Journal of Economic Literature, 24,* 1141–1177.

Hanushek, E. A. (1997). Assessing the effects of school resources on student performance: An update. *Educational Evaluation and Policy Analysis, 19,* 141–164.

Ingles, S. J., Scott, L. A., Lindmark, J. T., Frankel, M. R., & Myers, S. L. (1992). *National education longitudinal study of 1988, first follow-up: student component data file user's manual.* Washington, DC: U.S. Department of Education.

Kulik, C. C., & Kulik, J. A. (1991). Effectiveness of computer-based instruction: An updated analysis. *Computers in Human Behavior, 7,* 75–94.

Lee, V. E. (2000). Using hierarchical linear modeling to study social contexts: The case of school effects. *Educational Psychologist, 35,* 125–141.

Lee, V. E., & Bryk, A. S. (1989). A multilevel model of the social distribution of high school achievement. *Sociology of Education, 62,* 172–192.

Lesgold, A., Lajorie, S. P., Brunzo, M., & Eggan, G. (1992). Possibilities for assessment using computer-based apprenticeship environments. In J. S. Regian & V. J. Shute (Eds.), *Cognitive approaches to automated instruction* (pp. 49–80). Hillsdale, NJ: Erlbaum.

Levin, H. M. (1994). Production functions in education. In T. Husen & T. N. Postlethwaite (Eds.), *International encyclopedia of education* (pp. 4059–4069). New York: Pergamon.

Levin, H. M. (1997). Raising school productivity: An x-efficiency approach. *Economics of Education Review, 16,* 303–311.

Levin, H. M., Glass, G., & Meister, G. R. (1987). Cost-effectiveness of computer-assisted instruction. *Evaluation Review, 11,* 50–72.

Maddala, G. S. (1983). *Limited-dependent and qualitative variables in econometrics.* Cambridge: Cambridge University Press.

Mayer, D. (1999a). Measuring instructional practice: Can policy makers trust survey data? *Educational Evaluation and Policy Analysis, 21,* 29–45.

Mayer, D. (1999b). Moving toward better instructional practice data. *Education Statistics Quarterly, 21.* (Retrieved September 14, 1999, from http://nces.ed.gov/pubs99/quarterlyjul/index.html)

McNeal, R. B., Jr. (1997). High school dropouts: A closer examination of school effects. *Social Science Quarterly, 78,* 209–222.

Meyer, M. M., & Fienberg, S. E. (1992). *Assessing evaluation studies: The case of bilingual educational strategies.* Washington, DC: National Academy Press.

Miles, K. H., & Darling-Hammond, L. (1998). Rethinking the allocation of teaching resources: Some lessons from high-performing schools. *Educational Evaluation and Policy Analysis, 20,* 9–29.

Mullens, J., & Gayler, K. (1999). *Measuring classroom instructional processes: Using survey and case study field test results to improve item construction* (NCES 1999–08). Washington, DC: NCES Working Paper.

National Center for Education Statistics (NCES). (2000). *Internet access in U.S. public schools and classrooms, 1994–99* (Statistics in Brief #NCES 2000–086). Washington, DC: Author.

National Center for Education Statistics (n.d.). U.S. Department of Education, Washington, DC. (Available: http://uces.ed.gov/ecls)

President's Committee of Advisors on Science and Technology (PCAST), Panel on Educational Technology. (1997). *Report to the president on the use of technology to strengthen K–12 education in the United States.* Washington, DC: Author.

Rossman, G., & Wilson, B. (1985). Numbers and words: Combining quantitative and qualitative methods in a single large-scale evaluation study. *Evaluation Review, 9,* 627–643.

Rumberger, R. W. (1995). Dropping out of middle school: A multilevel analysis of students and schools. *American Educational Research Journal, 32,* 583–625.

Rumberger, R. W., & Thomas, S. L. (2000). The distribution of dropout and turnover rates among urban and suburban high schools. *Sociology of Education, 73,* 39–67.

Seltzer, M. H. (1994). Studying variation in program success: A multilevel modeling approach. *Evaluation Review, 18,* 342–361.

Shavelson, R.J., Baxter, G. P., & Gao, X. H. (1993). Sampling variability of performance assessments. *Journal of Educational Measurement, 30,* 215–232.

Shavelson, R., McDonnell, L., Oakes, J., & Carey, N. (1987). *Indicator systems for monitoring mathematics and science education.* Santa Monica, CA: RAND.

Shavelson, R. J., Solano-Flores, G., & Ruiz-Primo, M. A. (1998). Toward a science performance assessment technology. *Evaluation and Program Planning, 21,* 171–184.

Summers, A. A., & Wolfe, B. L. (1977). Do schools make a difference? *American Economic Review, 67,* 639–652.

Teaching, Learning, and Computing (TLC). (1999). *Computer presence in U.S. schools.* Irvine, CA: Department of Education.

Tyack, D., & Cuban, L. (1995). *Tinkering toward utopia.* Cambridge, MA: Harvard University Press.

Wenglinsky, H. (1998). *Does it compute? The relationship between educational technology and student achievement in mathematics.* Princeton, NJ: Policy Information Center, Educational Testing Service.

Willms, J. D. (1992). *Monitoring school performance: A guide for educators.* Washington, DC: Falmer.

Chapter 9

Studying the Cumulative Impacts of Educational Technology

Barbara Means
Mary Wagner
Geneva D. Haertel
Harold S. Javitz

Although small-scale implementations of specific learning technology applications can produce impressive gains in student learning (SimCalc, ThinkerTools, PUMP Algebra Tutor, etc.), there is a pressing need for a more comprehensive picture of students' broader experiences with technology and of the cumulative impact of technology use. Policymakers and the general public want to know not just whether a particular piece of software or web resource teaches something, but whether the cumulative effects of exposure to technology will have long-lasting value for children. Technology infrastructure and the training of teachers to use technology effectively are significant expenses; the estimated cost for technology in U.S. schools is more than $7 billion annually. Schools, districts, states, and the federal government do not make such major investments because they believe any one piece of software or experience with technology will have profound benefits. Rather, they seek to provide students with technology experiences that will accrue over time and result in an accumulation of academic, motivational, and economic benefits. Some view access to modern technology in schools as an entitlement issue and do not require research evidence to support the investment, but others—both policymakers and researchers—are questioning the evidentiary basis for spending so much on technology rather than on other interventions (e.g., Cuban & Kirkpatrick, 1998; Oppenheimer, 1997). The evidence these skeptics seek is that of long-term, widespread benefits stemming from sustained use of technology.

Existing survey data (Anderson & Ronnkvist, 1999; Milken Exchange on Education Technology, 1999; National Center for Education Statistics, 1999) provide a portrait of the distribution of technology resources in U.S. schools and, to a lesser extent, the distribution of different general categories of technology use (e.g., drill and practice on basic skills, games, CD-ROM reference materials, Internet search). What the data cannot tell us is whether involvement with one or multiple kinds of technology is having a long-term impact on the students who use them. Wenglinsky's (1998) well-publicized attempt to relate technology uses to student outcomes was problematic because measures of both technology use (teacher survey responses) and mathematics performance (National Assessment of Educational Progress [NAEP] mathematics scores) were taken at a single point in time. Although it may be true, as Wenglinsky suggests, that eighth graders who work with simulations acquire better math skills, the same relationship will appear in the data if being allowed to use simulations in mathematics class is a *consequence* of having mastered assigned mathematics skills, rather than a contributor to their development. This example illustrates the need to measure student skills and knowledge at multiple points in time, ideally with administration of the outcome measure preceding the technology intervention.

Admittedly, the complexity of the education system and the indeterminacy and rapid evolution of technology use pose formidable challenges for research design. The research challenge is heightened by the facts that (1) technology is only one component, and often not the most influential, in a learning activity; (2) students in middle and secondary schools experience different instructional approaches and technology uses in different classes and over time; (3) the tremendous variability in students and in their family, educational, and community contexts may well produce varied outcomes in response to a given technology experience; (4) students may be exposed to technology use in school, at home, and in community organizations, making it difficult to specify exposure to the intervention; and (5) the impacts of broad exposure to multiple technology-based or technology-enhanced learning experiences are likely to be multidimensional, affecting students' academic performance, motivation, courses taken, social interactions, and aspirations.

Yet similar complexities and loosely specified "treatments" characterize other areas of education as well. In the case of both compensatory education and special education, Congress has directed the U.S. Department of Education to conduct national longitudinal studies of the impacts of these programs. Such studies have been viewed as critical to guiding reauthorizations and setting policies for program implementation. Now that large numbers of students do in fact use technology in their academic subject areas, there is the potential to design and implement research of a comparable scale on the impacts of using technology supports for learning.

We argue that meta-analyses of multiple studies of specific technology uses, although valuable, are no substitute for a major longitudinal study of cumulative impacts. Few previous research studies on learning technology have followed a student sample of any size for multiple years. Most of the available studies were designed to measure the short-term impact of a particular technology-supported intervention on specific learning outcomes. The desired learning outcomes in these extant studies vary widely, and transforming different measures of learning into a common metric is fraught with technical difficulties (National Research Council, 1999). Further, the developers and implementers of many technology-supported interventions do not regard standardized test scores as appropriate outcome measures for their programs (Frederiksen & White, 1998; Roschelle, Pea, Hoadley, Gordin, & Means, 2000), despite the salience of such measures in the minds of the public.

We are unlikely to answer policymakers' basic question about the long-term student impacts resulting from the use of technology by piecing together findings from previous research studies of very different types of interventions, using diverse outcome measures, implemented in very different settings, often with atypical student populations and levels of support from university research teams. Rather than a patchwork of individual studies of varying quality and design, we need a coherent design that is woven of whole cloth. We call for a major new national study whose coherent research design addresses a broad set of policy-oriented research questions with a nationally representative sample that includes diverse groups and contexts. For federal and state educational technology policies to have broad support and broad impact, they must be informed by research that is national in scope, comprehensive in its conceptualization, and sensitive to the range of students, contexts, and impacts that characterize this arena.

OVERVIEW OF A LONGITUDINAL STUDY
OF EDUCATIONAL TECHNOLOGY

In this chapter, we outline a design for an ambitious national longitudinal study of the impact of using technology to support students' learning. The study would be both descriptive and explanatory in nature, providing for focused studies of the impact of technology use in specific classrooms within the context of a broader longitudinal study of students' use of technology in and out of school. Both the focused classroom studies and the broader longitudinal study would incorporate a common core of data elements. Following a nationally representative cohort of students from middle school through the end of secondary school, this Longitudinal Study of Educational Technology (LSET) would collect data on the nature and quantity of students' technology use and on student outcomes, such as school attendance and engagement, self-concept as a learner, technology skills, career/ college plans, achievement test performance, and scores on performance tests that target advanced information synthesis and communication skills.

With the student as the primary unit of analysis, LSET would employ a large enough sample to enable examination of a wide variety of experiences for key subgroups of students. LSET is likely to be most informative if it includes both a large, national probability sample and a special sample of students clustered in classrooms whose technology use practices are studied intensively and in some cases manipulated through carefully designed experiments. This approach would ensure inclusion of students with extensive technology experiences of different types, permit the investigation of causal questions, and support extrapolations of trends in a world where the amount and nature of technology access and use are changing rapidly. Repeated measurements would assess changes in students' in-school and out-of-school uses of technology and changes in student outcomes in a variety of domains as students move from ninth grade through high school graduation. Clearly, a study of the scope and magnitude we envision for LSET would require a comprehensive conceptual framework and a set of research questions derived from a process that includes representatives of key stakeholder groups.

DESIGN PROCESS

Although some of the major parameters of an LSET design are identified in this chapter, only options are identified for others, and all aspects of the design require further refinement and elaboration. Here, we outline several issues to consider in choosing a strategy for developing the LSET design, including the advisability of a design contract and the importance of opening the design process to input from outside the design team.

Many major research studies incorporate both a study design phase and implementation of the design into a single contract or grant. However, a separate design contract is likely to serve the needs of LSET better than a combined design/implementation contract. With so many parameters of the LSET design still undefined, it would be extremely difficult for contractors to specify or budget for its implementation or even to know the optimal mix of skills to include on their teams. Further, the skills needed for study design and study implementation are different; the procurement process for a design contract could target teams that incorporate design strength, rather than the combination of strengths needed for both design and implementation.

We recommend that the LSET design process request input from technical experts in sampling, research design, measurement development, and data analysis. In addition, input should be solicited from the multiple audiences and stakeholder groups that will be interested in LSET results (e.g., federal, state, and local policymakers; teachers; parents). It is appropriate to view the database that will result from LSET as an asset to the field, and, as such, its designers will want to maximize its value to as many users and consumers as possible. Sponsors of LSET also will want the "buy-in" of key stakeholder groups and leading researchers so that their investment in LSET will have ongoing support.

We recommend that the LSET design contract specify that a stakeholder group be convened to help the designers refine and elaborate on the conceptual framework for the study. This framework will identify the key domains (e.g. technology infrastructure, classroom experience, school characteristics) within which LSET will collect data and the key relationships that it will illuminate in analyses. The group can also suggest the specific research questions that should have priority when making study design trade-offs. A priority-setting process could order the questions so that LSET can address the most important issues with the resources assigned to it. It will be important that the stakeholder group represent the multiple perspectives and audiences that will be interested in LSET results.

In addition to this substantively focused stakeholder group, LSET will want to form a Technical Work Group (TWG) of expert researchers who are familiar with design, sampling, measurement, logistical, analytic, and dissemination issues to advise the LSET designers. The TWG should include individuals familiar with other major federal data-collection efforts, so that the group can consider whether it would be appropriate and cost-efficient to conduct LSET in conjunction with another large-scale national study. In addition to helping to set the initial direction for the design, the TWG could provide input at key stages in the design implementation, for example, by reviewing draft instruments to ensure that they address the research questions adequately. Researchers who have participated in Developing a Foundation for a Decade of Rigorous Educational Technology Research, a project funded by the U.S. Department of Education, would be one pool from which TWG members could be drawn, although others are likely to be identified who have expertise in particular aspects of the LSET design.

In advance of the kind of extended, collaborative design effort that a design contract could provide, we set forth here a very preliminary conceptual framework to illustrate the types of variables and outcomes—as well as the trade-offs and issues—that we believe would be central to LSET's design. Following the description of the conceptual framework and the parameters for a centralized data-collection effort, we describe how LSET might incorporate a set of testbed sites within which different research groups could pursue their own investigations, capitalizing on the LSET infrastructure and data collections.

CONCEPTUAL FRAMEWORK

Figure 9.1 provides a preliminary conceptual framework for the LSET design parameters. The framework illustrates the influences of the educational system, the technology infrastructure, the home environment, and the students' individual abilities, prior achievement, and interests on near- and long-term student outcomes. Although recognizing the hierarchically layered nature of the education system shown in the upper-left-hand corner of the framework, LSET would focus on studying individual students and their experiences at the classroom and school levels as specified in the center of the framework. The framework specifies studying both near-term (i.e., between fall and spring of ninth grade and between ninth and eleventh grades) and longer-term (end of secondary school) outcomes and views those outcomes as multiply determined.

Many of the outcomes of interest are known to vary with demographic variables related to students, their homes, and their communities. Given the interest in relating technology uses to effects on students' academic achievement, LSET would need to measure and control statistically for prior academic achievement and other student variables such as age, gender, out-of-school technology exposure, interests, self-concept, English fluency, and ethnicity. In addition, LSET should collect information on parental involvement in and expectations for their children's education, on access to a home computer and the Internet, and on whether parents use computer technology in their work. This latter variable (parental use of computers in their jobs) has been found to mitigate the differential home technology use associated with lower socioeconomic status (Becker, 2000).

The technology infrastructure of the school, which includes not just hardware and Internet access but also software and technical support, is just one kind of educational influence in this framework. School characteristics and programs—including the extent to which the school promotes and supports teachers' use of technology; student body characteristics, such as student mobility and enrollment; program type (i.e., college prep, vocational, or general); and schoolwide reform efforts—are potential influences on student outcomes.

In addition to these school-level variables, LSET could collect fairly detailed information on student activities in class and more general information about their overall academic programs.

Figure 9.1. Preliminary Conceptual Framework

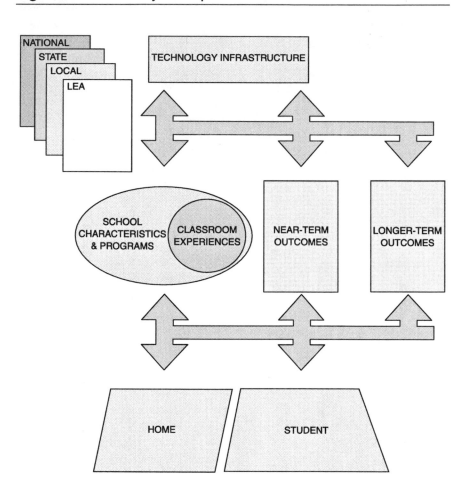

Types of outcome measures LSET would track on the participating students as they moved from the ninth to the twelfth grades would include both standardized tests of reading, language arts, and mathematics skills and more performance-oriented measures of advanced inquiry and communication achieved with technology supports. In addition, LSET should measure students' skills in using common technology tools, self-concept as a learner, engagement in school, metacognitive and reflective skills, and aspirations and preparations for life after secondary school. Each of these outcomes raises design and measurement issues, several of which are discussed later in this chapter.

RESEARCH QUESTIONS

Major categories of questions that would drive the study design include:

- To what extent are the different dimensions of technology use associated with different student outcomes (e.g., standardized achievement tests, performance-oriented tests, metacognitive and reflective skills, engagement in school) nationally?
- To what extent are different technology activities (e.g., drill and practice, Internet research, word processing, model building) integrated into the academic instruction experienced by students nationally? How do technology experiences vary for subgroups of students (e.g., defined on the basis of urbanization, income level, prior academic achievement, ethnicity, and gender)?
- What dimensions of technology use are associated with greater gains? Do the dimensions associated with significant gains differ across different types of schools or for different subgroups?
- Are significantly different outcomes obtained for students selected from Local Education Agencies (LEAs) that make a concerted effort to implement technology on a broad basis?
- What patterns of technology use over time are associated with sustained gains in student outcomes? For example, does early introduction of technology or some minimum cumulative exposure predict desired outcomes?

Below we briefly discuss several of the major components of a potential LSET design, including key constructs, sample parameters, data-collection components and time line, and analysis issues.

SELECTION OF KEY CONSTRUCTS

Key constructs to be included in LSET and how those constructs could be measured are discussed below. Providing input on measurement issues would be a key function of the TWG.

Conceptualizing Technology Use

Unlike a study designed as a program evaluation, LSET would describe the range of technology uses and modes of implementation across U.S. schools. After exploring the option of categorizing technology use within a school or even a given classroom in terms of some manageable set of technology use "models," we came to the conclusion that technology use in U.S. schools is so variable that we are unlikely to be able to classify large numbers of students into any idealized set of models. Instead, we would expect LSET to collect data on multiple features of technology use, including the way students are typically grouped for using technology (one per computer, pairs or small groups per computer, watching a single teacher-controlled computer, etc.), the intended learning goals for technology use (e.g., technology skills, basic skills, acquisition of knowledge in a subject area, advanced inquiry and communication skills), frequency and duration of technology exposure, degree of student control, and so on. LSET then would identify how these dimensions are distributed for different kinds of students and how they covary with student outcomes.

Rationale for Academic and Technology Skill Measures

Although there is widespread agreement on the importance of measuring technology's effects on student learning, there are strongly debated competing views concerning appropriate student-learning measures. The content knowledge for which students are held responsible varies from subject area to subject area, grade to grade, and state to state, making tests of academic knowledge in particular subject areas problematic for research. Rather than try to measure learning of a small piece of academic content in one or a few subject areas, LSET should focus on measures of widely applicable skills that support competent performance both in and out of school. We recommend a balance between more traditional, "basic" skills measures and more experimental assessments of the kinds of advanced skills promoted by many education groups.

Basic Skills Measures. Many technology implementations, particularly with low-achieving students and in schools serving low-income students, are explicitly designed to boost basic reading and mathematics skills. For this reason, we would expect LSET to include a widely used, nationally normed standardized test of reading and mathematics. Scores on such tests, like the California-mandated SAT-9, are indicators valued by policymakers and the general public and will provide a measure of the relationship of technology experiences to basic literacy and mathematics performance. The use of normal curve equivalents could support comparisons across different tests, but no statistical approach can compensate for the large amount of missing data likely since some districts will not assess students at one or more of the grade levels in the LSET design. Thus, it is quite likely that LSET will need to administer subtests of a standardized achievement test to participating students.

Advanced Inquiry and Communication Skills Measures. We would not want to limit measures of student learning to multiple-choice basic skills tests, however. The uses of technology most often advocated by education reformers involve having students use technology tools to advance their learning, problem solving, analysis, and communication. Designers of such innovations assert that they are trying to support kinds of learning and performances that would not be possible without technology, rather than merely to do more efficiently what education has always done (Frederiksen & White, 1997; Roschelle et al., 2000; Thornburg, 1999). An investigation of the outcomes associated with such approaches to technology integration needs to incorporate measures of the kinds of advanced skills targeted by these innovations.

The specific academic content dealt with in various technology-based projects and learning environments varies, yet there is a great deal of agreement about the need for certain generalizable inquiry, analysis, and communication skills that are not tapped by multiple-choice exams. The National Council of Teachers of Mathematics (NCTM, 1989) calls for important problem-solving skills to be developed, and the American Association for the Advancement of Science's benchmarks for science literacy (AAAS, 1993) call for critical response skills. These skill sets overlap with technology skills the International Society for Technology in Education (ISTE, 1998) says are required to become "capable information technology users." In addition, six standards proposed by the National Educational Technology Standards for Students (NETS, 2000) have a similar thrust, as do the Applied Learning Skills promoted by the New Standards project (National Center on Education and the Economy, New Standards Project, 1997) and the new basics promoted by the Secretary's Commission on Achieving Necessary Skills (SCANS, 1991).

LSET could incorporate assessments of the process-oriented skills involved in searching for, evaluating, analyzing, synthesizing, and communicating information. Moreover, although these advanced inquiry and communication skills will be exercised to an increasing extent in online environments, they are equally applicable and measurable as students do research, analysis, and composition without network or computer resources.

Assessments of these advanced skills require a task or problem context. Examples of the types of problems that might be used in such assessments are illustrated in the ThinkerTools Inquiry Curriculum (Frederiksen & White, 1998), the Jasper Woodbury Problem Solving Series (Barron et al., 1998; Cognition and Technology Group at Vanderbilt, 1997), and the MashpeeQuest (Shear & Penuel, 2000). These tasks are sufficiently rich and complex that students can articulate a reasoned argument about a line of inquiry and use their inquiry and communication skills to analyze information and solve a problem.

Integrating Metacognitive and Reflective Skills. Increasingly, educators recognize that many of the problems that individuals face in their lifetime are ill structured and open to multiple approaches. Solving these problems requires acquiring and developing "not only technical knowledge of concepts and methods of practice, but also a knowledge of one's knowledge and how it can be employed in solving problems" (Frederiksen & White, 1997, p. 1). Many technologies help students solve problems by acting as scaffolds and tools that prompt higher-order thinking and reflection about what one knows and can do. For example, some technology applications have students make their conceptual models and inquiry processes explicit, and others provide an interpretive framework that students use to reflect on their progress and to evaluate project work. To determine whether students are using metacognitive processes and reflection, LSET could evaluate the written rationales students provide in the context of the inquiry and communication skills assessments. If students have developed a clear understanding of the process concepts, then their written rationales should incorporate those concepts and the language of reflection. These rationales can be scored by using the principles of concept mapping or using a rubric describing levels of performance.

Technology Skills

LSET also could assess students' technology skills, such as keyboarding, Internet use, e-mail use, word processing, database/spreadsheet use, art/graphics use, learning games/simulations/modeling applications, reference use, multimedia and presentation applications, and so on. A number of instruments for self-reporting technology skills have been developed for use in state and local evaluations, and LSET could review available tools as a basis for adapting or developing its own. In addition, if the problem-based assessment of inquiry and communication skills is done online, measures of demonstrated (as opposed to self-reported) technology proficiency could be embedded in the same tasks.

Student Assessment Modality

A key design question is whether to measure student inquiry and communication skills online (which either limits the sample to students with access to technology or requires the research team to provide computing and perhaps network facilities) or offline (which precludes measuring these skills as they unfold with technology supports). The online option presents logistical challenges and is likely to increase the expense of the study. Using an offline assessment, however, reduces the likelihood of finding what can be regarded as legitimate contributions of technology experience to students' ability to function in a technology-supported context. (See also the discussion of this issue by Becker and Lovitts, Chapter 5, this volume.) For the purposes of this design, we would use the online option in order to gather more information about technology's affordances.

Rationale for Motivational Measures

Student Engagement. Many technology-supported school innovations report dramatic effects on students' engagement and willingness to expend sustained effort on school tasks. Student engagement is a near-term outcome of technology use to the extent that such use engages the imagination of students and increases the time they spend on learning. Student engagement can also contribute directly to student learning (Wiley & Harnischfeger, 1974); that is, with more time and creative attention spent on learning activities, students can be expected to learn more, which, in turn, may encourage them to include continued learning in their plans for the future. LSET could define and measure student engagement by using a variety of indicators, attitudinal measures, student self-assessments, and teacher ratings.

Classroom teachers are able to observe the changes that occur in students as their understanding and skill levels increase. They are particularly well positioned to judge the way students participate in classroom activities and changes in participation patterns with the passage of time and exposure to technology. Parent surveys could also indicate perceived changes in their child as a student, their child's interest in school, and motivation levels.

Self-concept as a Learner. Technology may provide experiences that have enduring effects on the way students view their own capabilities and prospects for success. If technology does indeed have a positive influence on students' concepts of themselves as learners, it may affect subsequent behaviors both in school and out of school. The student interview or a written survey administered in conjunction with the assessments could examine how a student's self-concept as a learner has been influenced by the use of technology in his or her classrooms, at school, and at home.

LSET SAMPLE

Initiating the study during the ninth grade would provide for a longer-term picture of students' technology use and inclusion during what may well be highly formative years. The influence of technology on students' lives after high school can be anticipated only as students move toward the end of secondary school, however; and the longer the study term, the greater the complexity and expense of keeping track of and repeatedly measuring sample members. Some students make the transition from junior high to high school after ninth grade, but many are in the same school from ninth through twelfth grades. Although it would not necessarily encompass all of their years of intensive school technology use, a 4-year data-collection period would follow students through critical years in which they engage seriously in complex subject matter, refine their educational aspirations, and make and act on their plans for their postsecondary careers. Retrospective reports from ninth graders regarding their previous technology experiences in and out of school would provide some level of information concerning earlier technology exposure.

Sample Parameters

The study sample must meet the following requirements in order to serve its multiple purposes:

Focus on students. The student is the unit of analysis. The study must produce accurate estimates about the characteristics, programs, and outcomes of students who have different kinds and levels of experience with educational technology.

Stratified sample. The first-stage sample of LEAs should be drawn to represent variation on key factors that influence the experiences of students.

Longitudinal design. Study data would be collected repeatedly over a 4-year period or longer.

Multiple data sources. Multiple data sources (e.g., students, teachers, principals, parents, school records, transcripts) will be needed to obtain the breadth of information specified in the study's conceptual framework.

Multiple analytic purposes. The richness of the LSET database will support a variety of analyses that have implications for the sample design. For example, subgroup analyses will examine experiences and outcomes of students who are differentiated by particular characteristics (e.g., dimensions of technology use, gender, ethnicity, or initial level of school achievement). We envision LSET as consisting of two samples of students: (1) a large, nationally representative sample of the general population of ninth graders and (2) a smaller clustered sample of ninth graders in classes within schools selected for the LSET testbed. The first sample would be used primarily to characterize the experiences and outcomes of students nationwide, while also allowing for subgroup analyses. The second sample, the LSET testbed, would permit the more detailed exploration of classroom-level activities and outcomes. Whereas the students in the first sample are intended to be nationally representative, the students in the testbed sample would be selected purposively and involved in specific types of technology use.

Representative Sample Selection

LSET's samples could be generated through a two-stage sample design that involves randomly selecting students from rosters of LEAs that serve ninth-grade students. Clustering within LEAs is necessary for three reasons: (1) The student rosters cannot be obtained at any higher aggregation level; (2) when the LEA consents to participate in the study, schools within the LEA typically consent as well; and (3) there is significant expense associated with recruiting LEAs.

Stage 1: LEAs. A stratified random sample of LEAs will ensure representation of major dimensions of variation. Stratification (1) increases the precision of estimates by eliminating between-strata variance, (2) ensures that low-frequency types of LEAs (e.g., large urban districts) are adequately represented in the sample, and (3) makes the study responsive to concerns voiced in policy debates (e.g., differential effects of federal policies in particular types of communities or LEAs of different sizes).

Specific stratifying variables should be determined as part of a comprehensive study design task. The following are suggestive of those that might be considered:

District size (student enrollment). LEAs vary considerably in size, the most useful available measure of which is pupil enrollment. A host of organizational and contextual variables are associated with size and exert considerable potential influence over how technology is implemented and what effects it has. These include the extent of district administrative/supportive capacity, the degree of specialization in administrative structure, the nature of citizen and interest-group activity in education, and the characteristics of relationships with state and federal governance systems.

Region. This variable captures essential political differences as well as subtle differences in the organization of schools, the economic conditions under which they operate, and the character of public concerns.

District/community wealth. LEAs differ greatly in the resources they have available and in the demands placed on those resources by virtue of their students' needs. Policies and programs may differ in LEAs that face these differential demands. As a measure of district wealth, the Orshansky index (the proportion of the student population living below the federal definition of poverty) is a well-accepted measure.

Technology infrastructure. Quality Education Data provides a database
with a "technology presence index" of the infrastructure within
schools and districts. Although it would be desirable to stratify LEAs
by a surrogate measure of the level of technology integration into
the curriculum and the intensity of technology use rather than simply
infrastructure presence, we are unaware of any satisfactory measure
of technology use that is available for large numbers of LEAs.

The levels for each stratification variable can be defined so that they
contain approximately equal numbers of students. (For example, four tech-
nology-presence strata could be defined so that each stratum contains approximately 25% of all students.) Because the number of LEAs will be quite
small in the strata containing the largest LEAs, to obtain an adequate number of large LEAs in the sample, it will be necessary to use different sampling fractions in the different strata.

Stage 2: Representative Student Sample. A random sample of ninth-grade
students would be selected in each sampled LEA, with all ninth-grade students within an LEA having an equal probability of selection. This approach
would ensure variability in key student factors—such as gender, ethnicity,
and other demographics, as well as family factors such as parent involvement in and support of educational activities—that are important influences
on student achievement. Student sampling fractions would vary as a function of LEA size. Sampling fractions would be lower for larger LEAs and
therefore would tend to "counterbalance" the discrepancy in LEA sampling
percentages. As a result of these different sampling fractions, students in the
nationally representative sample would need to be weighted to be nationally
representative. If the budget permits a sufficient number of LEAs to be selected, the resulting student weights would be approximately equal and the
number of students in each LEA would be modest; consequently, the design
effects would be relatively small and the sample would be efficient. On the
basis of previous studies, a sampling efficiency of 75% could be expected.
That is, the sample would yield standard errors that are the same magnitude
as those that could be obtained from a simple random sample (selected from
a hypothetical roster of all ninth-grade students) that was 75% of the size of
the actual sample selected with the proposed two-stage sampling approach.

Sample Size for Nationally Representative Sample

Sample size calculations optimally begin with consideration of the hypotheses that will be tested (e.g., that a certain student outcome will be
enhanced as a function of the degree of technology exposure), the expected
effect size (e.g., that each 100 hours of exposure will enhance student per-

formance by 1%), and the desired power (e.g., 95% confidence in detecting a difference of 3% or more between two groups of students). Because the LSET research questions are not yet fully specified, it is premature to implement this approach.

Alternatively, the sample size can be derived from consideration of the desired standard errors of measurements for selected subpopulations. Because a sample size that is sufficient to yield an acceptable standard error for a "yes/no" question is generally sufficient for other variables, we suggest a total sample size that is sufficiently large so that any subgroup containing 20% or more of the total sample would achieve a standard error of estimate of no more than 2% for any binary variable for which the true "yes" percentage in the universe is 50%.

For a simple random sample, the number of respondents in a subgroup necessary to achieve the level of precision specified above would be 625 students. To achieve this level of precision for a subsample of 20% of the students, the total number of respondents in a simple random design would need to be 3,125. However, clustering students in LEAs is less efficient than a simple random design, so the expected design effects (a sample efficiency of 75%) would increase the LSET sample size to 4,165 students. SRI's experience with previous national longitudinal studies suggests that the annual attrition rate is likely to be in the 8% range. With that attrition per year (after the first year), the fourth-year sample would be only 75% of its original size. To have 4,165 respondents in the fourth year, the study would need 5,340 students in the first year. Finally, if for every 1,000 students selected in the first year, data were actually collected for approximately 70% of sample members for any given measure, achieving 5,340 respondents would require sampling 7,629 students. To the extent that key analyses require that data be available from more than one instrument administered at different times, the number would need to be higher (to obtain the desired number of cases with data on both instruments).

DATA-COLLECTION PLAN

Because the recommended study is intended to be far-reaching in terms of the conceptual domains that it will address, data would be collected from multiple sources with different data-collection methods. Below, we describe the major potential data-collection components.

School Background Survey

A survey focusing on schoolwide characteristics and resources, including technology, would provide data for the school characteristics domain of the conceptual framework. The principal of each school attended by one or more sample students could be asked to complete a mail questionnaire that describes the general characteristics of the school and school district, including, for example, the demographics of the school, student enrollment, grade levels served, and technology and other resources that support student learning.

As a measure of each school's success in engaging its students to participate fully and persist in their academic careers, a number of school-level indicators could be collected through the school background survey, including:

Average daily attendance
Percentage of students who complete coursework at a particular grade level
Percentage of students who attain a high school diploma
Percentages of students who engage in particular course-taking patterns
Percentage of students accepted to colleges

Student Survey

Students bring a perspective to their own experience that cannot be obtained by interviewing others. Learning about both the in-school and out-of-school technology uses of students will be critical to answering many of the key research questions posed for the study. Only students can accurately describe the range of technology activities in which they engage outside the classroom, the purposes of those activities, and the time invested in them.

Data collection from students should go beyond describing technology-related activities, however, to include students' feelings about and perceptions of the value of those experiences. The student survey should also contain motivational measures that explore the extent to which students perceive technology as a means of pursuing their own goals, accomplishing challenging academic and real-world tasks, and participating more fully in work groups and in the life of the school.

Self-administered written surveys have been used successfully with middle and high school students and are usually less costly to administer than telephone interviews. However, such surveys are generally used when whole classrooms of students are involved in a study. Phone interviews would be likely to yield a considerably better response rate from students in the nationally representative sample given that students will not be surveyed as part of an intact classroom. The use of a telephone interview would also prevent differences in response patterns stemming from differences in reading level. Finally, using a telephone rather than a mail survey would provide access to parents, who are an important source of information for some research questions (see discussion below).

Parent Survey

The LSET conceptual framework holds that characteristics of a student's household environment (such as the technology and other educational resources in it), a family's level and type of involvement in school-related activities, and their expectations for a student's educational achievement influence student outcomes. These kinds of influences vary considerably by such parent characteristics as education level, economic status, and whether their work includes the use of technology. Parents or guardians are the most knowledgeable about these factors.

Given the response rate problems associated with household mail surveys, telephone interviews are likely to be the preferred method for collecting data from parents. The student interview could then complete the telephone contact with the household. Aggressive efforts would need to be made to minimize any potential bias resulting from the telephone interview approach by developing alternative methods for obtaining information for families without telephones.

Student Assessment

The ultimate outcomes of interest in the study are the academic performance and technology skills of students. To accurately assess performance, a multifaceted direct assessment of a student's skills by a trained on-site professional would need to be included in the study design. The potential contents of this assessment were discussed at length in this chapter's section, Rationale for Academic and Technology Skill Measures, and included components addressing academic, communication, metacognitive, motivational, and technology skill outcomes.

Teacher Survey

LSET's initial conceptual framework suggests the importance of the classroom experience in the lives of students, as well as the importance of behaviors and performance in the classroom setting. Teachers would be asked to complete a mailed, self-administered questionnaire that would focus on the technology, instructional techniques, and curriculum that the teacher uses with the student and on the teacher's training and perceived competence in using technology in instruction. The same instrument could include questions regarding the student's classroom performance, thus contributing to the set of student outcomes available for analysis.

Given the assessment approach outlined above, with its emphasis on inquiry and the fact that technology is used more often in English and language arts than in other high school classes (Becker, Ravitz, & Wong, 1999), English or language arts and science teachers might be appropriate respondents for the teacher survey, at least in the early years of the study. The important point here is to select one or two subject areas to rule out subject-matter effects. Later waves, when students would be in higher grades, could expand the teacher survey to include a broader cross section of subject areas. This would provide more information about the way technology is used across the board in academic instruction.

Student Transcripts

The kinds of academic courses students take (e.g., basic or advanced math) and students' choices of or exposure to technology-oriented courses (e.g., an elective in Web page design) are important contexts for interpreting the pattern of students' technology exposure over time. Transcripts are the chief source of information on course-taking; they are also good sources for key outcome measures, such as grades and attendance. Transcripts could be collected in any study year or, alternatively, in the last study year to capture each student's course-taking and grades over his or her high school career.

DATA-COLLECTION CONSIDERATIONS

Determining the appropriate frequency and timing of various components of data collection entails balancing the data requirements of key research questions with resource constraints and the practicalities of study administration.

Key Research Questions

Some important research questions may have specific implications for the timing of data collection. In the case of LSET, the desire to assess the relationship between a student's experiences with educational technology and educational performance has such implications. To address this issue most effectively requires repeated measures of student achievement over a period of time during which technology exposure and use are also measured, that is, a single school year. This analysis would also require holding students' starting point regarding achievement and technology exposure statistically constant. Other questions, however, would not require repeated measurement with such frequency (e.g., students' plans for postsecondary education). Some questions imply a particular temporal sequence (i.e., some factors must be measured before others to serve as predictors), whereas others cannot be measured at all until students are older (e.g., high school completion status).

Practical Considerations

A fundamental concern in longitudinal research is maintaining the sample. Experience demonstrates that long gaps between data collections increase sample attrition because location information becomes out of date and interest in the study on the part of sample members declines. On the other hand, very frequent data collection can be perceived as unduly burdensome by sample members. Cost considerations can also drive choices regarding frequent data collection. If cost were not a limitation, we would collect pre-test data at the beginning of grade 9 and post-test data at the end of grades 9, 11, and 12. Collecting data at four points in time allows us to use the pre-test in grade 9 as a covariate and to use the subsequent three data collections to compute growth curves for individual students and groups of students.

DATA ANALYSIS APPROACHES

A study as complex as LSET would encounter a variety of analysis issues, as illustrated by those discussed below.

The challenge for LSET analysts would be in defining an analysis agenda that identifies key policy-relevant hypotheses and that selects carefully from among analysis purposes (e.g., description, comparison, correlation, and explanation) and approaches. The policy focus of LSET needs to be kept clearly in mind, with critical questions being addressed through analyses that use methods that produce findings that can be communicated in a straight-forward way.

At the same time, a research investment as significant as LSET would provide data to address a wider array of questions than are likely ever to be included in the funder's agenda. Making LSET data available for public use as soon as possible would enable researchers with wide-ranging interests to investigate their questions, thereby maximizing the value of the LSET investment to the field.

Analysis of Growth

The power of longitudinal research is that repeated measurement of the same individuals over time allows for an assessment of change that is not possible with other designs. Two types of individual change analyses would be possible at different points during the study. At the end of wave 2 (i.e., spring of ninth grade), differences in student performance and other variables in wave 1 and wave 2 could be calculated to produce difference scores. These difference scores would be compelling information in and of themselves. They, in turn, become an important dependent variable to identify factors that correlate with positive growth. The testbed sample should provide instances where independent variables have been manipulated for classes randomly assigned to conditions.

In further waves of data collection, additional data points would be available, which would allow for the computation of growth curves and growth curve analysis. Growth curves could be fitted for individual students and groups of students, and submitted for modeling. It is likely that profiles of growth would emerge differently for different groups of students.

Although it would be valuable to look at the change or growth in any single dimension of technology use or student outcomes, the real challenge to analysts would be to integrate the multidimensionality of both technology use and student outcomes into a coherent picture of change over time. Analyses would undoubtedly observe change in different degrees or even in different directions across the multiple dimensions of technology use and/or the multiple student outcomes of interest.

Multiple Levels of Data

The LSET conceptual framework depicts the multiple levels of factors that are thought to influence student outcomes, including those at the individual and household, classroom, school, and LEA levels. Multilevel data can be analyzed effectively to explain social phenomena with hierarchical linear modeling (HLM), which improves specification and estimation of multilevel models of dynamic processes, such as academic growth. This approach has been used successfully to examine a variety of factors related to student development (Bailey, Burchinal, & McWilliam, 1993; Burchinal, Bailey, & Snyder, 1994; Raudenbush & Bryk, 1988). HLM is appropriate for LSET because it is especially good for estimating and modeling change. HLM can estimate growth curves, composed of a mean level and rate of growth, for individual students, even when some data points are missing. HLM is also a useful analysis tool for comparing growth by different groups of students. Thus, it is possible to understand differences in growth with respect to important school, classroom, and background factors. The LSET analysis plan should include exploration of the applicability of HLM to the LSET analysis context.

THE LSET TESTBED SAMPLE

Although a nationally representative sample such as that proposed for LSET can reveal much concerning both the nature of school technology use as experienced by different types of students and the outcomes associated with those dimensions of technology, it would not be suited to providing a detailed description of classroom interactions around technology. The latter type of study would require different sampling and data-collection approaches (e.g., looking at a small set of intact classrooms rather than a few students each from many schools). Intact classrooms could also be used in experimental tests of the outcome of different kinds of technology-based instruction (e.g., Internet research assignments). We recommend LSET include a national testbed of classrooms willing and able to participate in educational technology research. (We wish to acknowledge the inspiration from Alan Lesgold's notion of a network of testbed classrooms in Chapter 2. Our testbed concept can also be compared to the system of "sentinel" schools proposed by Hedges, Konstantopoulos, and Thoreson in Chapter 7.)

The major advantages of coupling a nationally representative sample and a set of testbed sites are threefold. First, the time-consuming effort of obtaining a sample with known characteristics, including characteristics related to technology infrastructure and support, could support multiple projects. Second, the measures developed for LSET through a rigorous process of synthesizing expert advice, screening existing measures, and developing or adapting and validating instruments could be available to all the studies using the testbed. In this way, a de facto "standard" for measuring contextual and moderator variables as well as some important outcomes emerge, greatly facilitating the synthesis of research and accumulation of knowledge in the field. Finally, investigations using the LSET testbed could arrange to have the same longitudinal follow-up for their subjects as that performed for students in the nationally representative sample. Both comparisons with a nationally representative sample and longitudinal follow-up would be supported by LSET.

The testbed sample could be obtained in conjunction with the selection and negotiations for the national sample. Districts that agree to participate in LSET's nationally representative sample also could be asked to nominate up to 10 of their schools that include ninth grade to participate in the LSET testbed. Districts could be encouraged to nominate schools with a variety of demographic characteristics and levels of educational attainment. Schools chosen to participate in classroom experiments should receive an incentive. The incentive might be cash, material resources, or access to state-of-the-art technology and technology support. For each nominated school, LSET staff could obtain basic information concerning the number of teachers in each subject area, the number and types of courses that they teach, and the types of technology used in their classrooms.

Concurrent with the nomination of testbed schools, researchers who are interested in performing classroom experiments could prepare a statement of their classroom requirements. Such requirements would include the number of classrooms needed, whether control classrooms are needed (and, if so, whether they are needed within the same schools), whether the same teacher can administer the treatment and control conditions (to different classes) or whether treatment and control groups must have different teachers, the desired geographic location of the schools, and so on. LSET staff could coordinate requirements of the various researchers and allocate the schools to researchers that satisfy the researcher's requirements, while assuring that schools are not overwhelmed by requests from multiple researchers.

Integrating Analyses of the Two LSET Samples

To take full advantage of the two samples envisioned for LSET, planning for the nationally representative sample data collection and for the various testbed studies need to be carefully coordinated. Testbed researchers are likely to be seeking very specific characteristics for the teachers and classrooms that participate in their experiments, and relatively few classrooms will participate in any given experiment. Thus, it should not be expected that the classrooms that participate in an experiment will be nationally representative. Even so, if the experiment contains control groups and teachers or classrooms are assigned randomly to treatment and control groups, it should be possible to conduct experiments that are statistically as valid as classical clinical trials. However, it is likely that there will be cases where control groups are not used or the control sample size is relatively small or made suspect because of differential attrition.

In such cases, it should be possible to match respondents from the nationally representative sample with the treated groups. Such comparisons require that the experimental and nationally representative samples have equivalent outcome measures and that adequate information exists on which to conduct the matching. Experimenters who desire to use the nationally representative sample in this manner will need to contact LSET staff at an early date to determine whether any modifications to the survey instruments for the nationally representative sample need to be implemented to provide the desired outcome and matching items. Once the national representative sample has been done, experimenters will be able to compare the change in outcomes for the experimental group with the change in outcomes for the matching subset of the nationally representative group, while also controlling for variables on which matching was less than perfect and examining the influence of other variables on individual student outcomes. Cases in which specification of the requirements for school or classroom participation results in both experimental and control groups that are very nonrepresentative in terms of demographics, technology infrastructure, or any of a host of other potentially modulating variables could be used to compare the experiment's sample characteristics with those of a nationally representative sample to make judgments about the likely external validity of the experimental findings.

CONCLUSION

The study outlined in this chapter is ambitious in scope and duration but well within the tradition of longitudinal studies conducted to inform policy in education and other areas. For example, the original National Longitudinal Survey of Youth (NLSY) began in 1979 and continues to collect new data on participants. SRI is currently designing the National Longitudinal Transition Study-2, which will involve five waves of data collection on 13,000 students over 9 years, and is conducting the Special Education Elementary Longitudinal Study, whose 5-year data-collection time frame is similar to the one LSET might adopt. Prospects, the national longitudinal study of 28,000 Chapter 1 participants (1991 through 1997), was also similar in duration to recommendations made here for LSET, as is the Early Childhood Longitudinal Study, Kindergarten Cohort (1998 through 2004), with its sample of 22,000 kindergartners.

Given the tremendous increase in the investment in computer technology and telecommunications for schools over the past 5 years, the United States has arrived at a point where there is both the degree of technology use to warrant looking for its impacts and an imperative to conduct the research that can guide investment decisions in the future. At a time when the digital divide has become a commonly used reference (as exemplified in former president Clinton's State of the Union address in 2000) and schools are spending billions of dollars to take advantage of still more billions in Universal Service Fund for Schools and Libraries (E-rate) telecommunications discounts, information concerning differences in the way technology is used in schools is sorely needed, as is an understanding of how that use varies for different kinds of students and schools.

The proposed study is unusual in its student focus and in its attempt to characterize the totality of a student's technology use experiences and the cumulative effects of those experiences over time. Careful measurement of school and student characteristics and a multifaceted approach to characterizing student outcomes would support a more comprehensive, balanced view of technology's contribution or lack thereof than can be provided by studies that look at small slices of time and a narrow range of student outcomes and experiences. We anticipate that different intensities of and approaches to technology use will prove most effective for different outcomes and that the pattern of findings may vary for different types of schools and for different student groups.

Going one step further, it may well be time to envision a study such as LSET within a more long-range program of longitudinal research. Technology use is developing rapidly. Although LSET would enable us to watch that development play out for a single cohort of students over the study period, the picture of technology use surely will change markedly within 5 or 10 years. By studying subsequent cohorts of students in periodic implementations of LSET— perhaps under the aegis of a larger data-collection program, such as the National Assessment of Educational Progress (see Hedges, Konstantopoulos, & Thoreson, Chapter 7, this volume)—policymakers would have a continuing stream of up-to-date, policy-relevant information on the state of technology use for and by students and the impacts of that use on student outcomes. This repeated implementation of longitudinal studies is not without precedent. The NLSY, mentioned above, is in its second implementation, as are Monitoring the Future, a national study of middle and high school students and their educational experiences, and the National Longitudinal Transition Study, which examines the secondary school experiences and postschool outcomes of youth with disabilities. These second-wave studies allow us to compare the experiences of schooling today with those of a decade or more ago so that policy can reflect the realities of our changing world.

The very nature of technology development pushes us to look to the future to envision new forms of technology and new applications to support learning. Looking to the future in defining a research agenda suggests the importance of having a foundation of solid understanding of current technology use and its impacts, and of the commitment to building on that foundation with an ongoing program of research that can keep pace with the change in its subject of study. Teachers, principals, superintendents, and legislatures are making decisions about educational technology that involve millions of students and billions of dollars. It is none too soon to develop a solid research base to support those decisions.

REFERENCES

American Association for the Advancement of Science (AAAS). (1993). *Benchmarks for science literacy: Project 2061.* New York: Oxford University Press.

Anderson, R., & Ronnkvist, A. (1999). *The presence of computers in American schools* (Teaching, Learning, and Computing Report No. 2). Irvine, CA: University of California, Irvine, Center for Research on Information Technology and Organizations.

Bailey, D. B., Burchinal, M. D., & McWilliam, R. A. (1993). Age of peers and early childhood development. *Child Development, 64,* 848–862.

Barron, B. J., Schwartz, D. L., Vye, N. J., Moore, A., Petrosino, A., Zech, L., Bransford, J. D., & Cognition and Technology Group at Vanderbilt. (1998). Doing with understanding: Lessons from research on problem- and project-based learning. *Journal of the Learning Sciences, 7*(3&4), 271–312.

Becker, H. J. (2000). Who's wired and who's not: Children's access to and use of computer technology. *The Future of Children, 10*(2), 44–75.

Becker, H. J., Ravitz, J. L., & Wong, Y. T. (1999). *Teacher and teacher-directed student use of computers and software.* Irvine, CA: Center for Research on Information Technology and Organizations.

Burchinal, M. D., Bailey, D. B., & Snyder, P. (1994). Using growth curve analysis to evaluate child change in longitudinal investigations. *Journal of Early Intervention, 18*(3), 342–361.

Cognition and Technology Group at Vanderbilt. (1997). *The Jasper Project: Lessons in curriculum, instruction, assessment, and professional development.* Mahwah, NJ: Erlbaum.

Cuban, L., & Kirkpatrick, H. (1998). Computers make kids smarter—Right? *Technos, 7*(2), 26–31.

Frederiksen, J. R., & White, B. Y. (1997). Metacognitive facilitation: A method for promoting reflective collaboration. *CSCL 97, Proceedings of the Second International Conference on Computer Support for Collaborative Learning.* Mahwah, NJ: Erlbaum.

Frederiksen, J. R., & White, B. Y. (1998, April). *Assessing students' scientific inquiry: Enhancing validity by creating multiple warrants for performance standards.* Paper presented at the annual meeting of the American Educational Research Association, San Diego, CA.

International Society for Technology in Education (ISTE). (1998). *National educational technology standards for students.* Eugene, OR: Author.

Milken Exchange on Education Technology. (1999). *Will new teachers be prepared to teach in a digital age?: A national study on technology in teacher education.* Santa Monica, CA: Author.

National Center on Education and the Economy, New Standards Project. (1997). *Performance standards: English language arts, mathematics, science, and applied learning: Vol. 3. High school.* Pittsburgh: New Standards, Learning Research and Development Center, University of Pittsburgh.

National Center for Education Statistics. (1999). Internet access in public schools and classrooms, 1994–98 (Issue Brief No. NCES 199-017). Washington, DC: Author.

National Council of Teachers of Mathematics (NCTM). (1989). *Curriculum and evaluation standards for school mathematics.* Reston, VA: Author.

National Educational Technology Standards for Students (NETS). (2003, March 13). (Available: http://www.alpine.k12.ut.us/training/nets.html)

National Research Council. (1999). *Uncommon measures: Equivalence and linkage among educational tests.* Washington, DC: National Academy Press.

Oppenheimer, T. (1997, July). The computer delusion. *The Atlantic Monthly*, pp. 45–62.

Raudenbush, S. W., & Bryk, A. A. (1988). Methodological advances in analyzing the effects of schools and classrooms on student learning. *Review of Research in Education, 15*, 423–475.

Roschelle, J., Pea, R., Hoadley, C., Gordin, D., & Means, B. (2000). Changing how and what children learn in school with computer-based technologies. *The Future of Children, 10*(2), 76–101.

Secretary's Commission on Achieving Necessary Skills (SCANS). (1991). *What work requires for school: A SCANS report for America 2000*. Washington, DC: U.S. Department of Labor.

Shear, L., & Penuel, W. (2000, January). *QUEST and CT in the classroom: Summary of preliminary observations*. Menlo Park, CA: SRI International.

Thornburg, D. (1999, December). *Technology in K–12 education: Envisioning a new future*. Paper presented at the Forum on Technology in Education—Envisioning the Future. Washington, DC: U.S. Department of Education.

Wenglinsky, H. (1998). *Does it compute? The relationship between educational technology and student achievement in mathematics*. Princeton, NJ: Policy Information Center, Educational Testing Service.

Wiley, D. E., & Harnischfeger, A. (1974). Explosion of a myth: Quantity of schooling and exposure to instruction. *Educational Researcher, 3/4*, 7–11.

Cross-Cutting Themes in Research Designs for Technology

Barbara Means
Geneva D. Haertel

In recognition of the insufficiency of available data collections for answering questions about technology's effects on student learning, SRI commissioned papers from nationally recognized research methodology and technology experts, who were asked to provide guidance for a major research program addressing the problem. In this conclusion we attempt to synthesize some of the key arguments and convictions presented in the commissioned papers (which comprise the chapters in this volume) and at the February 2000 authors' design meeting, where early drafts of the papers were presented and discussed. Our synthesis is based on the ideas in the individual chapters and those discussed at the design meeting, but the interpretation and synthesis are our own. Individual chapter authors should be "held harmless" of responsibility for the implications we have drawn from their work.

POINTS OF CONVERGENCE

Chapter authors were in agreement that multiple and complementary research strategies are needed to measure the implementation and impacts of learning technologies. No single study, genre of studies, or methodology is adequate to the task. While formative studies provide information to refine particular technology innovations, the evaluation of technology's effects on student learning requires studies of mature innovations that have been implemented in diverse settings, including schools in high-poverty neighborhoods and schools that are *not* atypically rich in technology resources and support systems.

Across the range of chapters, no single research strategy was endorsed as most promising. As we reviewed the chapters, three promising general strategies for research designs emerged:

- *Contextualized evaluations,* which focus on studying the context within which an innovation is implemented and the way the innovation unfolds within a complex organizational system
- *Multilevel, longitudinal research,* which uses statistical models to estimate (1) the multiple contexts of students' learning environments, (2) the innovation's cumulative effects, and (3) the direct and indirect effects of contextual variables on outcomes and implementation
- *Random-assignment experiments,* in which students, classes, or schools are assigned at random to participate in a particular treatment or in a no-treatment control group

Each of these three designs was recommended, in one form or another, by multiple authors, although no single design was the method of choice for all the authors. Below we provide a description of the characteristics of each design and its application in studies of educational technology.

Despite these differences in preferred design approach, the chapter authors as a group, and for the most part individually, embrace:

- Collection of both qualitative and quantitative data
- Assessment of a range of student learning, attitude, and behavioral outcome measures, including measures of complex higher-order skills
- Assessment of both context and implementation, as well as the primary intervention
- Design of both small- and large-scale studies

Need for Clustered Studies

No single study, by itself, can eliminate the ambiguities in the relationship among the many influences that affect student and teacher outcomes in a myriad of relevant contexts. Thus, most of the chapter authors envision a program of interrelated studies to be linked not only to prior research but also to other studies that would be conducted in tandem or in sequence as part of a more comprehensive research agenda. Although we have almost as many variants of this idea and as many new terms ("partnership research," "firms," "testbeds," "embedded experimental studies within a larger sample," "heterogeneity of replication model," and "sentinel schools") as chapters, all exemplify the desire for integrating a series of studies.

Hedges and colleagues propose a network of "sentinel schools" (Chapter 7). This network is similar, in purpose and design, to Lesgold's "testbeds" (Chapter 2), Culp and colleagues' "partnership research" (Chapter 3), and Means and colleagues' "embedded studies" (Chapter 9). Each of these arrangements would provide an opportunity for researchers, practitioners, and policymakers to design, conduct, and collaborate on a family of studies and to share their results. Such arrangements could provide evidence of emerging trends and could make available to researchers a set of study sites willing to participate in sustained studies of technology effects.

A corollary of the proposed establishment of programs of interrelated studies is the need for "intermediary organizations." Such organizations would provide the infrastructure to support the interrelated program of studies. This type of organization was most fully described by Culp and colleagues. Intermediary organizations could provide a variety of research functions, such as reviewing existing research, identifying research questions, synthesizing results from other studies being conducted, creating templates or forms for data-collection instruments, and supporting local researchers in their efforts.

Intermediary organizations and networks of participating schools would bring together the resources of school systems, research organizations, universities, and government agencies. Such a consortium of collaborating institutions would provide the multiple capacities needed to achieve the overall goal of conducting programmatic research to determine the impacts of technology on educational outcomes. Target populations of students and teachers would be present and readily accessible. Manpower would be available to gather, score, and code large amounts of data, if needed. Given agreement on core sets of context variables, the intermediary organization could make available data-collection instruments for use across multiple studies. The methodological expertise needed to conduct rigorous research on learning technologies could be made available to all participating research organizations. The nature of the arrangement would be conducive to disseminating new knowledge to diverse target audiences, including practitioners, researchers, and the policy communities. The primary purpose of the intermediary organizations, however, would be support of quality research in this area, as opposed to the professional development, research dissemination, and technical assistance functions of today's Regional Technology in Education Consortia.

Need for Common Measures of Contextual Variables

To advance what we understand about technology use and effects, the results of multiple, contextualized evaluations must be combined and accumulated. The intent in such an effort is not to find uniform results but rather to aggregate findings across studies to enable inferences relating features of contexts to successful or unsuccessful implementations and degrees of impact. An existing methodology, meta-analysis, is available for aggregating quantitative results across studies (Hedges & Olkin, 1985; Lipsey & Wilson, 1993). Other methodologies have been used to produce qualitative summaries of multiple studies. Cross-case analysis methodologies, used to synthesize case study data or ethnographies from multiple sites, can be used to aggregate qualitative data. Elements of both of these methodologies may be required to combine results of these multiple, contextualized evaluations.

Whatever approach is used to combine the multiple and cumulative results of the contextualized evaluations, it would be greatly facilitated by the use of common definitions, a common conceptual framework, and common instruments and data-collection procedures. It should also be noted that simply applying these techniques to the extant research base will not suffice. As Baker and Herman point out (Chapter 4), the studies that have been submitted to meta-analysis fall far short of a representative sample of current educational uses of technology. An array of contemporary, parallel studies focused on several current and emerging technology practices and their impacts is a prerequisite for this approach.

MATCHING METHODS TO PURPOSES

Some recent documents and policy pronouncements have implied that random-assignment experiments constitute the only defensible methodology for education research. Both the Office of Management and Budget (OMB) and members of Congress have made assertions to the effect that only experimental studies, employing random assignment to treatment and control groups, constitute scientifically defensible research methods. The original House bill to reauthorize the Office of Educational Research and Improvement (H.R. 4875), for example, contained language calling for "scientifically based quantitative research" to obtain "understanding of the truth of a particular educational theory, practice or condition." The legislation went on to define scientific research as studies "in which individuals, entities, programs, or activities are assigned to different conditions with appropriate controls to evaluate the effects of the conditions of interest through random assignment experiments, or other designs to the extent such designs contain within-condition or across-condition controls."

The rising call for true experiments in education research was also reflected in a forum ("Can We Make Education Policy on the Basis of Evidence? What Constitutes High Quality Education Research and How Can it Be Incorporated into Policymaking?") held at the Brookings Institution in December 1999. (The transcript is available at http://www.brook .edu/comm/transcripts/19991208.htm.) At the Brookings meeting, Thomas Cook and Robert Boruch documented the scarcity of random-assignment experiments in educational research and argued that such experiments are both necessary to obtain sound evidence of causal effects and far more likely than quasi-experiments or other designs to influence policymakers' decisions.

In striking contrast to the dominant tenor of the Brookings dialogue and H.R. 4875, the March 1999 advisory report submitted by the National Academy of Education (NAE) to the National Educational Research Policy and Priorities Board (the congressionally mandated oversight body for the Office of Educational Research and Improvement) asserted that "progress toward high achievement for all students has been impeded by the belief that research, students' learning, and teachers' learning can be studied in isolation from important matters of context" (1999, p. 8). The NAE report calls for what they term "collaborative problem-solving research and development," which is defined as efforts focused on "solving specific current problems of practice and at the same time . . . developing and testing general principles of education that can be expected to apply broadly beyond the particular places in which the research is done" (p. 9). These projects would be joint efforts between researchers and professional educators to combine improvements in practice and research—intense collaborations difficult to reconcile with the tenets of random-assignment experiments.

More recently, a National Research Council committee, undertaking the task of elucidating the nature of "scientific research" in education, explicitly embraced a range of designs (bridging the gamut from random-assignment experiments to in-depth case studies and recording of evoked brain potentials) that meet certain standards:

To be scientific, the design must allow direct, empirical investigation of an important question, account for the context in which the study is carried out, align with a conceptual framework, reflect careful and thorough reasoning, and disclose results to encourage debate in the scientific community (Shavelson & Towne, 2001).

The debate over methods reflected in these documents and proceedings may instill a healthy dose of reflection and questioning of assumptions in the educational research field. For federal agencies, we would recommend an eclectic perspective with respect to research methods rather than championing one approach or another as "the gold standard." Studies of technology-supported educational practices are performed in many different contexts for many different purposes. The degree of definition and control of the practices under study differ markedly from case to case. We simply do not believe that any one research approach will cover all cases. Rather, we recommend an effort to clarify the purposes, constraints, and resources for any given piece of research or research program as a basis for choosing among methods.

Although there are no cut-and-dried rules for when to choose which method, we will try to elucidate some general rules of thumb based on our own and others' experience. We have organized the discussion below in terms of broad categories of research goals and circumstances with implications for the choice of methods. Like any categorical scheme, ours is an oversimplification that sounds neater in theory than it is in practice. Nevertheless, we have found the distinctions useful in matching research methods to purposes.

The overarching distinction in our scheme is between investigations of the workings and effects of specific projects (what we have called "project-linked research") versus studies of a range of "naturally occurring practices." In the first case, a particular initiative, approach, or project has been defined and is the focus of the research. In the second case, the researcher is seeking to understand "what's out there," defined in terms of practices or access to technology, rather than examining a particular project or funding stream. We can relate our scheme to what may be a more familiar distinction between evaluation and research: Evaluations, and certainly the narrower classification of program evaluations, are "project-linked," but there are many project-linked studies that would not qualify as evaluations.

Project-Linked Research

For simplicity's sake, we refer to this category simply as "project-linked" research, but we intend the term to include any defined innovation, regardless of whether or not the implementers of the innovation share formal membership in or funding from a given project. Examples in the educational technology area would include the GLOBE program, in which students and teachers collect scientific data on their local environments and submit their data to a central program-run web-based data archive; the adventure learning resources offered by the Jason Foundation; and the Generation WHY Technology Innovation Challenge Grant that trains students to provide technical support and consulting for teachers who want to use technology in their instruction.

Early-Stage Projects

In the case of evaluation studies conducted in conjunction with an evolving technology-supported innovation, contextualized evaluation studies will usually be the method of choice. At this early stage of work, it is important to understand how the innovation plays out in real classrooms, and the evaluator needs to be alert to unintended interactions with features of the environment that program designers may not have taken into consideration. Providing useful feedback to program developers and developing an understanding of project implementation in context—that is, how the elements of the innovation influence teacher and student behavior—will be paramount concerns at this stage.

Our methodologists' papers would suggest, however, that where possible, these evaluations should be conducted using common instruments and outcome measures and within a consortium that shares and aggregates data from individual projects. Such a step would make it much easier to achieve a higher, more uniform level of quality across individual evaluations and to combine findings across studies. Thus, if a funding agency were to follow this recommendation when launching a new school technology initiative on the order of the Technology Innovation Challenge Grants or Preparing Tomorrow's Teachers to Use Technology program, they would solicit proposals addressing one or more preselected types of outcomes (e.g., early literacy or mathematics problem-solving skills) and require use of some agreed-upon instruments for documenting contextual variables and for measuring key classroom processes and outcomes.

The NAE made a similar recommendation for coordinating studies in its recent report to the National Educational Research Policy and Priorities Board: "The recommendations include supporting federations of problem-solving research and development projects, linked in a hub-and-spoke relationship. The goal would be simultaneously to develop improved educational success in specific settings (the spokes) and to identify issues of common concerns [*sic*] and to carry out theoretical analyses and construct tools that are supported by and facilitate the work of the several projects in integrative ways (the hub)" (National Academy of Education, 1999, p. 11).

Another point about these studies, made strongly by Lesgold in Chapter 2, is that it is important to study an innovation in a range of contexts, including those most critical from a national policy perspective, and to measure elements of the context within which each implementation occurs. From a policy perspective, critical contexts include classrooms serving students from non-English-speaking or economically impoverished backgrounds, students with disabilities, and schools low in technology resources. Almost any approach produces good results in some settings with some kinds of students

and supports. Before recommending particular approaches for broader implementation, we need a basis for understanding the range of contexts within
which desired results are and are not likely to be forthcoming.

Mature Projects

As individual projects become more mature and more widespread, there
will be cases where further research is warranted. By a mature project, we
mean one where the intervention has been fairly well specified, such that its
elements can be delineated and an observer can make judgments as to the
extent to which they are being implemented. Further, mature projects are
ones whose model for producing desired changes is understood, at least in
theory. That is, the innovation is not just a black box placed between inputs
and outputs. There is some understanding of what classroom elements or
processes the inputs are supposed to alter and of how those altered processes
(or interim outcomes) produce the targeted student outcomes that are the
project's ultimate goals.

The question raised by the recent debate among national policymakers
and discussed intensively at our authors' meeting is whether the random-
assignment experiment is the method of choice when the research question
involves a mature innovation's effects. Several of our authors (Cook and
Moses) strongly support the position that the experiment is the only unimpeachable source of information about causal relationships and that such
experiments are eminently feasible within the educational domain. While
there was general agreement among authors that random-assignment experiments are desirable under circumstances where the nature of the innovation
is well understood and the experiment's implementation is feasible, there were
concerns about feasibility.

When Random Assignment Is Preferred.   As we have grappled with the issue
of the value and feasibility of random-assignment experiments for studies
of technology's effects on students, we have found the points made by Judy
Gueron at the Brookings forum mentioned above extremely helpful. Gueron
addresses the issue of when random-assignment experiments are more and
less appropriate and feasible on the basis of her experience at the Manpower Research and Demonstration Center, an independent research organization known for its running of large-scale field trials, principally in
the employment and training arena. Based on MDRC's experience running
30 major random-assignment experiments over the last 25 years, Gueron
provides eight guidelines for determining when random assignment designs
are appropriate:

- The key question is one of program impact.
- The program under study is sufficiently different from standard practice and you can maintain the distinction over time.
- You are not denying anyone access to an entitlement.
- You are addressing an important unanswered question.
- You include adequate procedures to inform program participants in advance and to ensure data confidentiality.
- There is no easier way to get a good answer.
- Participants are willing to cooperate in implementing the assigned conditions.
- Resources and capacity for a quality study are available.

We believe that Gueron offers a useful set of guidelines, some of which will be easier and some harder to achieve in designing studies of the impacts of technology-supported educational innovations. *Questions of program impact* are likely to be less central in research on newly developed (or developing) technology-supported innovations. They are likely to be regarded as critical, however, in cases of well-established innovations, particularly those that are candidates for wide implementation and expensive to implement. Addressing an *unanswered question* concerning impact will be an easy criterion to fulfill in the case of educational uses of technology. Much harder to meet in some cases will be the criterion that the "experimental" program be *distinct from practice as usual* and that the practice be *maintained over time*. If the innovation under study is a circumscribed curriculum unit supported by a particular piece of software, such a distinction may not be hard to enforce. (For example, the science of water quality can be learned using Model-It simulations or a chapter in a conventional text.) If, on the other hand, the innovation is broad ranging in scope and long term in duration—something on the order of process writing supported by word processors or the use of Internet resources to support learning and research skills—these conditions will be more difficult to satisfy. First, the open-ended nature of the technology will make it less likely that technology-using teachers will all be using the technology in the same way. Many may not really be doing anything distinctive from conventional practice. Descriptive studies of the use of technology tools, such as word-processing and spreadsheet software, suggest that teachers initially tend to incorporate the technology into their existing pedagogical practices and only over time evolve new, more student-centered practices (Sandholtz, Ringstaff, & Dwyer, 1997). Over time, too, both the nature of the available technology and students' and teachers' use of it are likely to change. Finally, over time, it will be difficult to keep students, classes, or schools assigned to the control condition from having access to and making use of the same technology resources, both in and outside of school. Although technology is not an *entitlement* in a legal sense, members of the public and educational administrators increasingly think of it as an entitlement in an ethical sense. Given the fact that more affluent students already have access to technology resources in their homes, many argue that students from less wealthy backgrounds are entitled to have these resources available in their schools and public libraries. It would be difficult indeed for principals or superintendents to commit to an experiment that might deny their students access to technology resources for any extended period of time. Thus, we conclude that relatively small units of instruction, specific pieces of software, or new technologies regarded as less basic (e.g., hand-held computing devices) will be more readily examined in experimental designs.

Concerns About Random-Assignment Experiments. Further discussion of the place for random-assignment experiments in education research occurred at a July 2000 open session of the National Academies' Board on Testing and Assessment. Robert Boruch gave a presentation to the board in which he pointed out that national random-assignment experiments on the effects of interventions—of the sort done in health, juvenile justice, and employment and training fields—cost on the order of $10–12 million if individual students are assigned to treatments at random and $20–25 million if classes, schools, or districts are assigned at random. Laurie Bassi, an economist formerly at the Department of Labor (DOL), noted that in DOL's experience, random-assignment experiments often consume all available research resources and take so long to run that the public policy questions they have been designed to address get acted upon prior to the availability of the research results. Bassi also noted that the fidelity of implementation of an intervention over time has been a serious problem and that differential attrition from either the experimental or the control group can introduce bias into experimental results. (Statistical techniques can be introduced to counteract such bias, but in this case the researcher is relying on the same kinds of corrections used in quasi-experiments.) (Bassi's experience-based concerns are not new ones; Cronbach [1982] raised similar concerns two decades ago. As Cook and colleagues point out in Chapter 1, careful monitoring of an experiment's implementation will reveal the extent to which differential attrition and treatment contamination or degradation are occurring.) Richard Shavelson of Stanford University argued that the pendulum in educational research methods needs to swing not to the extreme of doing only random-assignment experiments but to a middle position of asking whether an experiment is appropriate and feasible before moving to other approaches. Shavelson suggested that experiments are more likely to be feasible in the case of small studies of shorter-term, more discrete innovations. Shavelson's argument echoes our own suggestion that random-assignment experiments will be more feasible in research on particular pieces of software and new devices than when answers are sought to more macro questions about core technology infrastructures or technology-supported whole-school reforms.

In summary, we conclude that experiments with random assignment are an underutilized design in educational research. In combination with other designs, random-assignment experiments would add information about cause–effect relationships in educational technology. This design, by itself, provides little information about the conditions of applicability that support any given technology innovation or intervention, however. Implementation and context data are needed to increase the interpretability of the experimental outcome data.

Research on Naturally Occurring Practices

In many cases the question researchers are asked to address does not concern a specific project or innovation but rather a broad range of practices found in various schools to a larger or smaller degree. Here we have in mind questions such as "Does putting Internet-connected computers into instructional classrooms make a difference?" or "Do students who use graphing calculators learn more in high school mathematics?" Because the practices or resources that are the focus of study are arising from within disparate parts of the education system and not out of a particular innovation with a particular theory of change, they will not meet the criteria for an innovation distinct from standard practice that can maintain its distinctive character over time. Thus, these questions are difficult to address with either random-assignment experiments or quasi-experiments.

Many studies of naturally occurring practices have a strictly descriptive purpose—that is, they seek to describe the frequency of various technology uses rather than the effects of those uses. The statistics on Internet connections and technology use gathered by the National Center for Education Statistics and Becker and Anderson's 1998 Teaching, Learning, and Computing Survey would fall into this category. Other studies go beyond reporting technology access and usage frequencies per se to correlate degree of access or use with student outcomes. Such correlations often feed into arguments about the changes caused by technology, an interpretation that is hazardous, given the many other factors that might account for observed relationships.

Several of the chapters in this volume offer designs that can be applied to studying naturally occurring practices. The designs share these features:

- Looking at student performance longitudinally rather than at a single point in time

- Carefully delineating and measuring variables that may be alternative causes of the outcomes to be measured
- Using analytic techniques that permit an estimation of effects at different levels of the education system (e.g., classroom, school, and district effects)

CONCLUSION

The Panel on Educational Technology of the President's Committee of Advisors on Science and Technology (PCAST, 1997) asserted that "a large-scale program of rigorous, systematic research on education in general and educational technology in particular will ultimately prove necessary to ensure both the efficiency and cost-effectiveness of technology use within our nation's schools" (p. 7). PCAST argued that the investment in research in this area should be comparable in scope to that in pharmaceutical research, specifically calling for an annual investment of $1.5 billion. Given the fact that the current funding level for research on the learning impacts of technology-supported innovations (as described above) is closer to $50 million, any approximation to the PCAST recommendation would require a major change in the way the federal government thinks about and sponsors educational technology research. This synthesis is intended as a next step in conceptualizing the research needs, promising new approaches, and innovative research sponsorship arrangements to respond to that challenge.

REFERENCES

Becker, H. J., & Anderson, R. E. (1998, April). *Validating self-report measures of the constructivism of teachers' beliefs and practices.* Paper presented at the 1998 meetings of the American Educational Research Association, San Diego, CA.

Cronbach, L. (1982). *Designing evaluations of educational and social programs.* San Francisco: Jossey-Bass.

Hedges, L. V., & Olkin, I. (1985). *Statistical methods for meta-analysis.* Orlando, FL: Academic Press.

Lipsey, M. W., & Wilson, D. B. (1993). The efficacy of psychological, educational, and behavioral treatment: Confirmation from meta-analysis. *American Psychologist, 48*(12), 1181–1209.

National Academy of Education. (1999, March). *Recommendations regarding research priorities.* Advisory report submitted by the National Academy of Education (NAE) to the National Educational Research Policy and Priorities Board. Washington, DC: National Academy of Education.

President's Committee of Advisors on Science and Technology (PCAST), Panel on Educational Technology. (1997). *Report to the president on the use of technology to strengthen K–12 education in the United States.* Washington, DC: Author.

Sandholtz, J., Ringstaff, C., & Dwyer, D. (1997). *Teaching with technology: Creating student-centered classrooms.* New York: Teachers College Press.

Shavelson, R. J., & Towne, L. (Eds.). (2001). *Scientific research in education.* Washington, DC: National Academy Press.

About the Contributors

Russell G. Almond is a senior research scientist in the Center for Statistical Theory and Practice at the Educational Testing Service in Princeton, New Jersey. Before coming to ETS, he was a research scientist at StatSci Division of MathSoft, Inc. and a visiting assistant professor at the University of Washington in the Department of Statistics. He received his undergraduate degree from the California Institute of Technology in 1983 and received his Ph.D. in statistics from Harvard University in 1990. Dr. Almond's research interests include representations of uncertainty in artificial intelligence (especially belief functions and graphical models), uses of artificial intelligence techniques in data analysis, human factor design for data analysis and education, and risk analysis. His most recent research has been centered on using graphical models (related to influence diagrams and Bayesian networks) to model risk using both probability and belief functions as the principal representation of uncertainty. He is the principal designer of the Graphical-Belief software for manipulating these models. His work with Robert Mislevy and Linda Steinberg on assessment design received the 2000 National Council on Measurement in Education's award for outstanding contribution to educational measurement.

Eva L. Baker is a professor at the UCLA Graduate School of Education & Information Studies, director of the Center for the Study of Evaluation (CSE), and co-director of the National Center for Research on Evaluation, Standards, and Student Testing (CRESST). She teaches classes in assessment policy and design and in technology. Her background was in curriculum development for young children, instructional technology, and teacher professional development before she became interested in evaluation and assessment. She serves as the chair of the Board on Testing and Assessment of the National Research Council. She was a co-chair of the Joint Committee on the Revision of the *Standards for Educational and Psychological Testing* (1999), sponsored by the American Educational Research Association, the American Psychological Association, and the National Council on Measurement in Education. Her current interests are the development of technology tools for assessing achievement and interpreting data, with work supported by the Institute of Education Sciences and the Office of Naval Research.

Henry Jay Becker is a professor of education at the University of California, Irvine. His research focuses on instructional and organizational reforms associated with the use of computer technologies. Dr. Becker is beginning work on a study of the impact of high levels of out-of-school information technology access on high school students' schoolwork and a corresponding study of high-tech influences on high school teachers' pedagogy. In addition, he is completing analysis from Teaching, Learning, and Computing: 1998, the fourth in a series of national surveys of teachers and schools and their instructional use of computers, a series that stretches back to 1983. The 1998 survey focused on teachers' pedagogical beliefs and practices and their relationship to teachers' use of technology. Besides these national surveys, he has conducted studies of the National School Network, a collaboration of curriculum reform projects at the leading edge of Internet use, and studies of integrated learning systems. In the 1980s, he conducted a national field experiment on the effectiveness of typical practices of technology use in 50 pairs of classrooms across 13 states. Professor Becker holds a Ph.D. in sociology from the Johns Hopkins University, where he also worked as a research scientist at the Center for Social Organization of Schools between 1977 and 1992.

Thomas D. Cook is professor of sociology, psychology, education and social policy at Northwestern University and a faculty associate at the Institute for Policy Research there. He writes on social science methods, evaluation, education, and adolescence. He has written or edited 9 books and more than 100 articles and chapters. He has won the Lazarsfeld Prize of the American Evaluation Association (1982), the Donald Campbell Prize of the Policy Studies Association (1988), and a Distinguished Scientist Award from the American Psychological Association (1997). He is a Trustee of the Russell Sage Foundation and of the Textile Museum in Washington, D.C.

Katherine McMillan Culp is the assistant director for research at the Education Development Center/Center for Children & Technology, a nonprofit research and development organization. She has directed a range of evaluations of innovative programs to improve the quality of technology use in K–12 classrooms and informal educational settings. She has also conducted a series of program evaluations studying strategies for using modeling and simulation tools in science classrooms, as well as qualitative studies of technology integration at both the classroom and district levels. She holds a Ph.D. in developmental psychology from Teachers College, Columbia University.

Geneva D. Haertel is a senior educational researcher at the Center for Technology in Learning at SRI International. Her research has focused on influences on student learning, assessment, and evaluation of K–12 education programs. She has published more than 40 articles on the conditions that promote student achievement. She has also contributed to the knowledge base on research designs and assessments used in studies of educational reform. In 1997, she co-edited *Psychology and Educational Practice*; in 1993, she co-authored the *Resource Handbook of Performance Assessment and Measurement*; and in 1991, she co-edited the *International Encyclopedia of Educational Evaluation*.

Larry V. Hedges is the Stella M. Rowley Professor of Education, Psychology, and Sociology in the Harris Graduate School of Public Policy Studies at the University of Chicago. His research interests include the development of statistical methods for social research, the use of statistical concepts in social and cognitive theory, the demography of talent and academic achievement, and educational policy analysis. Much of his methodological work has concerned the development of statistical methods for combining evidence from multiple empirical research studies (meta-analysis) in the social, medical, and biological sciences. His sociological work has largely concerned the social distribution of cognitive test scores, their changes over time, and their relation to schooling and other social processes. His work on educational policy concerns the relation of school resources to educational outcomes such as academic achievement and the development of evidence-based social policy. He is a member of the National Academy of Education and a fellow of the American Statistical Association and the American Psychological Association. He has served as editor of the *Journal of Educational and Behavioral Statistics* and quantitative methods editor of *Psychological Bulletin*; he currently serves on the editorial boards of the *American Journal of Sociology*, the *Review of Educational Research*, and the *Psychological Bulletin*. He is currently the chair of the technical advisory group of the U.S. Department of Education's What Works Clearinghouse.

Joan L. Herman is co-director of the National Center for Research on Evaluation, Standards, and Student Testing (CRESST). Her research has explored the effects of testing on schools and the design of information systems to support school planning and improvement. Her recent work has focused on the validity and utility of standards-based assessment, the measurement of educational practice, and the integration of large-scale and classroom assessment. She also has wide experience as an evaluator of school reform, with recent concentrations on the effects of technology and the evaluation of state-wide professional development initiatives. Among Dr. Herman's books are

Tracking Your School's Success: A Guide to Sensible School-Based Evaluation coauthored with Lynn Winters (1992) and *A Practical Guide to Alternative Assessment* (1992), both of which have been popular resources for schools across the country. A former teacher and school board member, Dr. Herman has also published extensively in research journals. She is a frequent advisor to federal, state, and local agencies and current editor of *Educational Assessment*.

Margaret Honey, vice president of the Education Development Center and Director of EDC's Center for Children and Technology (http://www.edc.org/CCT), has worked in the field of educational technology since 1981. Beyond overseeing CCT's extensive involvement with educational technology research and development nationwide, she regularly contributes to educational publications and presents at major technology and education conferences. She has served on the board of the Consortium for School Networking and serves on advisory boards of math, science, and technology projects nationwide. In 1999 she was appointed to the Department of Education's Expert Panel on Educational Technology. She holds a doctorate in developmental psychology from Columbia University.

Harold S. Javitz is a principal scientist in the Health Sciences Center at SRI International. His research has focused on applications of statistics in the fields of education, computer science, toxicology, health, psychographics, chemical processes, environmental pollution, and industrial quality control. In his 25 years at SRI International, Dr. Javitz has been responsible for experimental design, survey design and implementation, and analysis of primary and secondary data in more than 100 projects for government, industry, and foundations.

Spyros Konstantopoulos is a doctoral candidate in education at the University of Chicago. His research interests include the extension and application of statistical methods to issues in education, social science, and policy studies. His methodological work involves statistical methods for quantitative research synthesis (meta-analysis) and mixed-effects models with nested structure. His substantive work encompasses research on class-size effects, technology effects, teacher and school effects, program evaluation, and the social distribution of academic achievement.

Alan Lesgold received his Ph.D. in psychology from Stanford University in 1971 and joined the University of Pittsburgh that same year. Until he became dean of the School of Education at Pitt in July 2000, he served as executive associate director of the Learning Research and Development Center

(LRDC). Dr. Lesgold founded and initially directed Pitt's interdisciplinary doctoral program in cognitive science and artificial intelligence. Over the period from 1986 to the 1999, Dr. Lesgold and colleagues developed a technology of intelligently coached learning by doing. More recently, he and colleagues also developed a technology for supporting rich collaborative engagement of students and professionals with complex issues and complex bodies of knowledge. Dr. Lesgold holds an honorary doctorate from the Open University of the Netherlands and is a fellow of the Divisions of Experimental, Applied, and Educational Psychology of the American Psychological Association, a fellow of the American Psychological Society, and a past president of the Society for Computers in Psychology. He was Secretary/Treasurer of the Cognitive Science Society from 1988 to 1997 and continues to serve on its Board of Governors. In 1995, he was awarded the Educom Medal by Educom and the American Psychological Association for contributions to educational technology. He received the 2001 Award for Distinguished Contributions of Applications of Psychology to Education and Training from the American Psychological Association.

Barbara E. Lovitts has been senior research analyst at the American Institutes for Research (AIR), program officer of the Research in Teaching and Learning program at the National Science Foundation, and program associate in the Directorate for Education and Human Resources at the American Association for the Advancement of Science. At AIR, she served as project director of the High Intensity Technology Sites Study and was a major contributor to the evaluation of the Technology Innovation Challenge Grants program. She is co-author of two chapters in the *Handbook of Research Design in Mathematics and Science Education* (2000). She is also the author of *Leaving the Ivory Tower: The Causes and Consequences of Departure from Doctoral Study* (2001). She currently works as an independent researcher and is conducting additional research on graduate education.

Barbara Means directs the Center for Technology in Learning at SRI International, an independent nonprofit research organization based in Menlo Park, California. Her research focuses on ways to foster students' learning of advanced skills and the changes in practice at the school and classroom levels associated with the introduction of technology-supported innovations. She has directed numerous research projects concerned with the design, implementation, and evaluation of technology-enhanced approaches to education reform. Her recent work includes case studies of technology use in urban high schools, published as *The Connected School* (2001). Her earlier published works include the edited volumes *Technology and Education Reform* (1994) and *Teaching Advanced Skills to At-Risk Students* (1991).

Vera Michalchik is a research social scientist at the Center for Technology in Learning at SRI International. Her research has focused on the comparative evaluation of formal and informal learning environments as well as the role of technology within these environments. She is currently editing a volume on research methods for studying technology learning across educational contexts.

Robert J. Mislevy is a professor of measurement, statistics, and evaluation at the University of Maryland, College Park. Before coming to Maryland in 2001, he was a distinguished research scientist at the Educational Testing Service. Dr. Mislevy's research interests center on applying developments in statistics, technology, and cognitive psychology to educational and psychological assessment. His contributions have included multiple-imputations methods for analyzing data from the National Assessment of Educational Progress (NAEP); with Darrell Bock, the BILOG computer program for item response theory; and with Linda Steinberg and Russell Almond, a framework for evidence-centered assessment design. Dr. Mislevy is the author of more than a hundred publications on measurement and assessment, a past president of the Psychometric Society, and the three-time recipient of the National Council on Measurement in Education's award for distinguished contributions to educational measurement (1988, 1990, 2000) and the 1988 Raymond B. Cattell Early Career Award for Programmatic Research (AERA).

Lincoln Moses is professor emeritus of statistics and biostatistics at Stanford University. He is interested in both statistical theory and its use in applications, specifically in the assessment of medical technologies. He has authored, edited, or co-edited several books and many papers over a period of 50 years.

William R. Penuel is a senior educational researcher at the Center for Technology in Learning at SRI International. His research has focused on assessment and evaluation of technology-supported reforms in science, mathematics, and social studies. His recent work has focused on the development of handheld computer–supported assessment activities for use in middle school science classrooms. He is author of a number of published studies of technology use in education and is co-author, with Barbara Means and Chris Padilla, of *The Connected School* (2001), a set of case studies of technology use in urban high schools.

Linda G. Roberts directed the U.S. Department of Education's Office of Educational Technology from its inception in September 1993 to January 2001 and served as the secretary of education's senior adviser on technology. Previously at the U.S. Congress, Office of Technology Assessment,

Roberts headed up that office's assessments of educational technology and authored three national reports: *Power On! New Tools for Teaching and Learning* (1988); *Linking for Learning: A New Course for Education* (1989); and *Adult Literacy and Technology: Tools for a Lifetime* (1993). She is a former elementary school teacher and reading specialist, K–12 reading coordinator, university professor, and academic dean. Roberts now serves as senior adviser to several companies, foundations, and government agencies; is a member of the board of trustees of the Sesame Workshop and the Education Development Center; and is a member of the boards of directors of Wireless Generation and Carnegie Learning.

Russell W. Rumberger is professor of education and director of the University of California Linguistic Minority Research Institute at the University of California, Santa Barbara. His research focuses on three areas: education and work, schooling of disadvantaged students, and research methods. His recent work has examined the causes and consequences of dropping out of school, student mobility, the schooling of English-language learners, the impact of school segregation on student achievement, and school effectiveness research. His research has appeared in journals in the fields of economics, sociology, and education, including *Economics of Education Review, Sociology of Education, American Journal of Education, American Education Research Journal*, and *Educational Evaluation and Policy Analysis*.

Robert Spielvogel directs technology planning and implementation for the Education Development Center as EDC's chief technology officer. Prior to this appointment, he was based at EDC's Center for Children and Technology in New York City as a senior scientist. A primary component of his research work at EDC has involved designing and conducting a wide range of evaluations and case studies for educational systems that utilize technology to improve teaching and learning. He has worked as the principal investigator for a series of studies that span 8 years on IBM's Reinventing Education initiative. Other evaluation and development work clients include NASA, Intel, the U.S. Department of Energy, the MIT Media Lab, the U.S. Agency for International Development, and the National Science Foundation. He has been the principal investigator leading EDC's support efforts for the last three National Education Summits in which innovative examples of technology were showcased for the nation's governors, business leaders, and education association heads.

Linda S. Steinberg is a student teacher in the Philadelphia public school system. Before entering the M.S.Ed. program at the University of Pennsylvania in July 2002, where she is an urban teacher education scholar, she was a senior development scientist at the Educational Testing Service. Ms. Steinberg's contributions have included design and development of computer simulation–based assessments and, with Robert Mislevy and Russell Almond, a framework for evidence-centered assessment design. Her current research interests center on applying an evidence-centered approach to the design of instruction as well as assessment. Ms. Steinberg is the author of several publications on assessment design and a recipient of the National Council on Measurement in Education's award for distinguished contributions to educational measurement (2000).

Amy Thoreson is a doctoral candidate in the measurement, evaluation, and statistical analysis program in the Department of Education at the University of Chicago. Her research interests include applying quantitative methods to assess the effects of educational policy on disparities in the access to high-quality educational experiences for students from traditionally disadvantaged backgrounds. Her current work focuses on the influences of race/ethnicity, gender, and socioeconomic status on student academic achievement and attainment.

Mary Wagner directs SRI's Center for Education and Human Services, whose mission is to use research and evaluation to improve policies and programs for children, youth, and families. She has specialized in the longitudinal study of educational, social, and other outcomes of children and youth across the age range, particularly those with disabilities. Her work also includes a program of randomized trials to evaluate interventions for at-risk young children and their families. She and her team have also evaluated complex statewide interventions in California, including the Healthy Start school-linked initiative and the First Five initiative to improve the health and developmental outcomes of young children and their families.

Index